Merleau-Ponty Vivant

SUNY Series in Contemporary Continental Philosophy
Dennis J. Schmidt, Editor

Merleau-Ponty Vivant

Edited by
M. C. Dillon

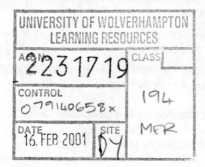
State University of New York Press

Published by
State University of New York Press, Albany

Production by Christine Lynch
Marketing by Theresa A. Swierzowski

For information, address the State University of New York Press,
State University Plaza, Albany, NY 12246

Library of Congress Cataloging-in-Publication Data

Merleau-Ponty vivant / edited by Martin C. Dillon.
       p.   cm. — (SUNY series in contemporary continental
philosophy)
    Includes bibliographical references and index.
    ISBN 0–7914–0658–X (alk. paper). — ISBN 0–7914–0659–8 (pbk.   :
alk. paper)
    1. Merleau-Ponty, Maurice, 1908–1961.   I. Dillon, Martin C.,
1938–   . II. Series.
B2430.M3764M48   1991
194—dc20   90-42946
                                                              CIP

10   9   8   7   6   5   4   3   2

Contents

Acknowledgments

As those whose eyes have reached these words know well, interest in Merleau-Ponty reached a peak in Europe and North America during the 1960s and 1970s, but subsided thereafter as the new wave of poststructuralism and postmodernism began to crest. Just as this new wave was gathering strength, a group of scholars formed an informal group devoted to the study of Merleau-Ponty's philosophy. The Merleau-Ponty Circle met for the first time in 1976, has met annually since then, and has been the matrix of sustained exploration and development of a philosophical style that is now resurgent. This book, like several others now appearing, emanates from the consciousness collectively incarnated in the Merleau-Ponty Circle, and those whose names appear in these pages have been nurtured by those whose absent presence is palpable to the sense of the invisible. It would be unjust not to evoke a few.

Galen Johnson, Hugh Silverman, and Stephen Watson made a grand gesture that launched the *Merleau-Ponty Vivant* project. As the project neared completion, Tom Busch and Shaun Gallagher acted in the same spirit of generosity to ensure the success of the book. Dennis Schmidt provided encouragement, inspiration, and editorial guidance from start to finish.

Jeanne Constable and Melanie Hazenstab adroitly managed a host of administrative tasks. Carolin Woolson assisted in preparing the manuscript for submission. Deborah Mullen compiled the index. Gnomi Schrift Gouldin saved us all from shame with her meticulous copy editing. And Christine Lynch, our production editor, supervised the whole process.

The State University of New York at Binghamton, through the good offices of Stephen David Ross, chair of the Department of Philosophy, supported the endeavor with generous allocations of necessary resources, both material and immaterial.

My own efforts are dedicated to my daughters, Kathleen, Elizabeth, and Sarah.

M. C. Dillon
March 1990

Preface:
Merleau-Ponty and Postmodernity

Almost three decades have passed since Maurice Merleau-Ponty's untimely death at age 53 on 3 May 1961. One wonders where he would have taken the line of thought that was beginning to emerge when his death interrupted the project of *The Visible and the Invisible*, how he would have responded to the chaotic geopolitics of the decade that had just begun, and what posture he would have assumed *vis-à-vis* his colleagues, Jacques Lacan, Michel Foucault, Jacques Derrida, et al. as they led continental thought into the era of postmodernity. To some extent, this wonder can satisfy itself only with speculation; nonetheless, some things are known. The demise of the transcendental subject as the guiding premise of the phenomenological tradition had already been heralded in several ways, among them Merleau-Ponty's own doctrines of the lived body and the incarnation of monadological consciousness in the generality of Flesh. The critique of Husserlian phenomenology was well underway in 1961, and Merleau-Ponty was among the intellectual leaders working at the task of shaping its sequel.

At the time Merleau-Ponty died, the focus of continental thought had shifted toward language. The influence of such seminal thinkers as Saussure, Wittgenstein, and Heidegger is as apparent in Merleau-Ponty's later works as it was in the writings of others of his generation to whom fortune granted longer lives. As the transcendental subject receded, language flooded in to take its place. And, as it is with tides, the shape of the hollows left by the ebbing thought shaped the ideas that surged in to fill them.

From Kant through Hegel to Husserl, the meaning to be found in the world was held to be deposited there by the transcendental activities of consciousness. The material given to consciousness from sources residing forever beyond its ken was held to be plastic and accommodating rather than structured and demanding. This thought was modified in the early writings of Heidegger and Sartre as transcendental consciousness was existentialized, reconfigured in the shapes of *Dasein* and Being-for-itself, and transformed from reflective spectation to engaged free agency. But the function, the hollow to be filled, remained relatively constant: the world given to us lacked meaning — significance, order, structure, organization — and the function of providing that meaning, of accounting for the superficial patterns of ordinary lives, was assigned to the second generation of transcendental subjectivity.

Lurking in the dark recesses beneath the foundations of churches, states, and other mundane edifices was the suspicion of absence, void, abyss implanted by Nietzsche's prophecies of the death throes of a divinity whose own authority of truth marked the expiration of its warrant. This suspicion, aggravated by the Great War and all the lesser ones, hot and cold, overt and covert, seemed to be confirmed by the inability of mundane authority to find a source of guidance, a ground on the basis of which to formulate and defend the decisions and policies that would shape the course of human events. Lacking the absolute ground of divine revelation, finite minds could not be bound to consensus. Heidegger left us with a lonely poet listening at the brink of madness to a silence not yet broken by the directing word of the gods to come. And his politically oriented followers groped in the sacristy of humanism for values to guide us through times when the superabundance of human bodies threatens the welfare of each one of them.

Now, as we enter the last decade of the twentieth century and survey the field of continental thought for ideas that might augur the destiny of the twenty-first, we find the familiar figure of philosophical Narcissus still absorbed in his own reflection, but the reflecting surface has changed. The surface is now the signifying text, and beneath it is abyssal darkness. Narcissus has always sought his reflection outside himself. He has always sought what he lacks to be himself in the Other that is beyond himself: Narcissus has always been decentered. The innate a priori of pure transcendental subjectivity grounds me because it eludes me; it contains the truth I lack: the structures that constitute my being and the being of the world in which I live. So it was, also, with the fundamental ontological structures of *Dasein*: the structures of my ownmost being, the structures of temporality constitutive of Being-in-the-world, necessarily elude my grasp in their intrinsic self-concealment.

The elusive structures are grounding structures by virtue of the function of transcendental constitution they fulfill, but beyond that they ground by virtue of being elusive: insofar as it is a nonarbitrary project to understand what and where I am, then my being is grounded in this necessary quest that is exactly as endless as the ground is elusive. *Dasein* is a being-in-question exactly to the extent that Narcissus cannot see his reflection clearly.

It is the same — and different — when the surface becomes the signifying text. It is the same because the signifying text performs the modern function of transcendental constitution of meaning. We read ourselves, as we read world and others, thus all we know and what we know is what we read. Because *il n'y a pas de hors-texte*. Or if there is, our only access to it is through the mediation of signifiers: the only meaning we can find in self-world-other is significance imparted — or mediated — by signifiers. Because I must read self-world-other, these things themselves elude me: effectively, they are transformed into texts.

It is different because, contrary to Bacon, there is no Book of Nature, any more than there is a definitive psychology, any more than there is a Book of the Self. There is no Book of Nature exactly because there is a *Physics*, a *De Rerum Natura*, a *Novum Organon*, and so on. There is no Book, no Bible; there are only texts. There is no Call of Conscience because there are many appealing voices.

This is a time in which many voices are heard speaking in a cacophony of tongues. If modernity was a time in which the disguise of secularity was torn from the body of the Transcendental Subject to reveal the self-dissembling phallic author, still intoning his own name even as he expired, his truth being crossed out by understanding, then the time after modernity is a time when authority establishes itself as such by the tearing of vestments. All devestated by this devastating divestiture, we are leveled out on a plane above those still adorning themselves with the Emperor's clothes. Freed to pick our own metaphors, we are comforted by the reassurance that our signifiers are secure from attack by an epistemological superior. We deploy our discourses in marginal spaces strategically crafted to keep the space of the main text blank: we know what is not true.

We know, for example, that science itself is metaphor only

dimly aware of itself as such — except of course when it vindicates its truth with technological prowess that hastens the death of *physis*, ourselves included.

We know, also, that metaphysics is a terminal case that has reached its proper fulfillment. We know this because we know that the question of the meaning of Being is finally answered by the nonbeing of the godhead. His theo-logical incarnation was crossed out in the recognition that his birth sign was *ressentiment*. His onto-logical inscription was deconstructed in the dismemberment of the transcendental phallus. We know this exactly because we know that that was all that Being ever meant: resentment of the phallus, the eternal absence.

And, ultimately, we, like Socrates, know that we do not know, but, unlike Socrates, we are aware, too, of the ultimate futility of trying to find our way out of this ignorance. How comforting it is to have the sanction of the enigmatic figure at the dawn of meta-physics, here at dusk, in the clearer light of the darkening of Being. We know that no progress has taken place — or can — because the metaphysical groundwork for the concept has been carefully dismantled.

Philosophical Narcissus is our metaphor, one among many possible metaphors, therefore insisting on no special privilege. We find him, as ever, bent over, gazing downward, but now seeking his reflection in a text. What does this signify?

Herman Hesse inscribes himself as Harry Haller in *Steppenwolf*. In the novel, Harry Haller finds himself inscribed in another text, "The Treatise on the Steppenwolf." Philosophical Narcissus reads the text, *Steppenwolf*, in search of himself, in search of a self Herman Hesse could never have known. And finds this self revealed, at least in part. What does this signify? How does this signify? How did Narcissus find himself in Hesse's fictional self-inscription in this Treatise?

In attempting to answer these questions, we must not cheat, but remain within the precept: *il n'y a pas de hors-texte*.

There must be another text. Given the precept, there can be no other answer. Actually, there must be three texts. There is one text, "Treatise on the Steppenwolf," constructed around the metonymy: Harry Haller = Steppenwolf. There is a second text, *Steppenwolf*, constructed around the metonymy: Herman Hesse = Harry Haller = Steppenwolf. Then there is the third text constructed around the metonymy: Philosophical Narcissus = Herman Hesse = Harry Haller = Steppenwolf. Who is the author of these texts?

It would be naive to say that Hesse wrote the first two. Who, after all, is Herman Hesse? What does that signifier signify? We may know Hesse as the author of *Steppenwolf*, but, under our hypothesis, Hesse knew himself only after he wrote *Steppenwolf* to find himself. And then, even after he wrote *Steppenwolf* — which ends in the aporia of Harry Haller's failure to find himself — Hesse knew himself only in the failure to find himself. Herman Hesse wrote the first two texts, but 'Herman Hesse' signifies to us an aporia at the end of the quest of self-knowledge. And that aporia is inscribed in a text.

Still, what of the third text, the one constructed around the metonymy: Philosophical Narcissus = Herman Hesse = Harry Haller = Steppenwolf? Perhaps the author of that text is M. C. Dillon, the author of this text, the one in which the metonymy is made explicit. But I, that shiftless shifter, did not construct that metonymy, I found it. If I had constructed that metonymy, if I were its author, then the relevance of fiction to life would have come into being twenty minutes ago. That not being the case, there must be a third text that is not this text.

The third text is the one in which the relevance of fiction to life is inscribed. Where is that text and who is its author? Several answers are possible. But one of them is not: every work of fiction that is relevant to life. Because there is no text that is every text of a given genus. Perhaps the author of that text is one of the authors who wrote about the relevance of fiction to life. Sartre, perhaps, in *What is Literature?* Or Plato, in the *Republic*. Or one of the myriad left unnamed. But none of them wrote about the metonymy that now concerns us.

Of course — as has been apparent for some time now to the philosophical reader bent over this text (for whose patience I am grateful) — I, that shifter, am being characteristically shiftless. The answer to the question about the third text is the world or, perhaps, the world of culture. It is in this world that the general relevance of fiction to life is inscribed, as well as the particular displacement that allows the reader of *Steppenwolf* to identify with its author and his alter egos.

Now, where is this text and who is its author?

Granting, for the sake of argument (and only for that sake and with that proviso), (1) that there is no authority behind any text, and (2) that most texts are dispersed in different worldly locations, there is still a peculiar difficulty with these questions about the text of the world, even the text of the cultural world. This text is everywhere and nowhere. And its shifting authority comes to pause in no name or discrete set of names. The text of the world is an unusual text. What language would one need to know in order to read it?

In what language is the text of the world written? Or the text of the self and its others? How do signifiers work or play in these texts?

There is another metonymy operating here. It is constructed around the equation: world = text. But this is a metonymic equation and not the assertion of a literal identity. The questions assume, in a contrary fashion, that the metonymic equation is a literal identity. And that assumption is inappropriate.

And, because that was the point, this marks the end of this phase of questioning. In this text, the one in your hands.

Unless, of course, one wants to challenge the distinction between metonymic equations and assertions of literal identity. If one wants to do that, one must go back to the paragraph that begins "Philosophical Narcissus is our metaphor," substitute the signifiers 'world,' and 'text' for their correlates in the equations offered and run through the loop again. One can do this as many times as needed to prove that *il n'a pas de hors-texte*. This can be done. That is the point.

That is the point at which we find ourselves. The next series of questions is the first series of questions: how did Merleau-Ponty respond to the founding ideas of postmodern thought? And how might his thoughts be brought to bear on contemporary debate?

It is a half-truth, become commonplace, that Merleau-Ponty replaced the transcendental subject with the lived body. The half that is true is that Merleau-Ponty did stress the embodiment of the subject and attribute to the body-subject a transcendental function: in the *Phenomenology of Perception*, the structure of the human body —

its upright posture, its opposed thumb, its modes of perception, its motility, its sexuality, and so forth — was described as a ground of the constitution of the human world. The colors of the visible world, for example, are revealed and obscured by the physiology of our vision: if we could see beyond the limits of infrared and ultraviolet, the world would look different to us. The half that is not true is that the body-subject functioned for Merleau-Ponty as the transcendental subject functioned for Kant and Husserl. The most important difference between the transcendental subject and the body-subject is that the former was conceived as sheer immanence and the latter was acknowledged as transcendent as well as immanent: the body is also an object, a worldly object, and its thingly character was seen by Merleau-Ponty as a condition for its subjectivity.[1] To touch the world we have to be touched by the world; We have to be the sort of thing that can be touched. To be living flesh is a condition for being conscious, but that living flesh transcends consciousness: it comes into being and passes away without the consent of conscious intent being necessary. It misses the ball, stumbles, falls, and scrapes its knees; it cannot read the fine print without glasses; it acquires secondary sexual characteristics that are burdensome and embarrassing; it trembles and breaks out in sweat when it is appropriate to be cool; it wants a cigarette; and, alas, it ages, loses its grasp, and dies. The body contributes to the constitution of the world we live in, but the reverse is also true: the world contributes to the constitution of our body.

It is an extrapolation from Merleau-Ponty's thought — but not without textual support[2] — to suggest that our very physiology is a response to worldly demands, that the world demanded that we learn to walk on our back legs, that we develop portions of our body to be sensitive to light and attune them to a certain range of frequencies in the continuum of electromagnetic radiation, that our hands and arms evolve an ability to articulate in the plane of the body facing front; that is, in the direction our eyes have learned to look and our toes have learned to point. "Everything in man is a necessity.... It is no mere coincidence that the rational being is also the one who holds himself upright or has a thumb which can be brought opposite to the fingers; the same manner of existence manifests itself in the one instance as in the other" [PP 170]. If the world conforms to our perceptual abilities, it is equally true that our perceptual abilities conform to the world. And if evolution does not work fast enough, we make up the difference with prostheses: microscopes and telescopes, parabolic dishes, radar, sonar, and all the instruments designed to tune in the world.

There is, as Merleau-Ponty says, a "circular process" by which "the organism itself measures the action of things upon it and itself delimits its milieu" [SB 148].[3] In *The Structure of Behavior*, this circular process is conceived under the heading of "dialectical relations"; later, in the *Phenomenology of Perception*, this is refined and generalized as the asymmetrical *"Fundierung"* relation,[4] and, finally, in *The Visible and the Invisible*, it becomes the thesis of the reversibility of the Flesh. In all three works, there is the central idea of an interested, questioning attunement to the world by which the body learns to come to terms with its environment — and then returns to the world through its acquisition, now a sedimented form that structures the world with a *habitus* derived from it.

Kant and Husserl generated an apodictic grounding for knowledge at the price of reducing the phenomenal world to the correlate of an understanding that had no capacity for growth, modification, learning, accommodation. It had no such capacity because its categories were conceived as a priori, as universal, timeless, and necessary. But, for Merleau-Ponty, "there is in human existence no unconditioned possession, and yet no fortuitous attribute." He goes on to say that "human existence will force us to revise our usual notion of necessity and contingency, because it is the transformation of contingency into necessity by the act of renewed grasp."[5] The point of the passage is that the contingency of worldly emergence motivates us to transform the categories of transcendental projection: Merleau-Ponty's a priori is not timeless and oblivious to the transcendence of our situation; its necessity is provisional, its pro-vision is open to modification in the light of what shows itself.[6]

In Merleau-Ponty's critique of the transcendental subject, both the subject and its transcendental function are preserved, but transfigured to be responsive to worldly conditions. Inasmuch as only I dwell on the hither side of my skin, my body individualizes me to a unique and concrete existence. But inasmuch as I lose myself in the generality of prereflective communality from which I emerged as ego, I participate in a world without center. And my reflection on this ambiguous mode of existence deprives me of any stronger privilege than that which I have earned through the effort of a cognition I know ahead of time is destined to be surpassed. There is no possibility of confusing this finite embodied subject with the Transcendental Subject that finally divulged itself as God.

The transcendence of the phenomenal world as it is described by Merleau-Ponty might well be summarized in the transcendence of worldly time. For Hegel, the incarnation of the Absolute subject becomes finally unthinkable because its descent into time is both necessary and impossible: the final synthesis has to be the identification of self-sufficient Being and the essential incompleteness of becoming. Becoming simply cannot reach self-coincidence without ceasing to be becoming, without reducing time to an illusion generated by self-consciousness alienating and deceiving itself into thinking that it is, for the present, finite. For Merleau-Ponty, the incarnation of the body-subject is also finally unthinkable, but for different reasons. That is, I can certainly think my embodiment, my physical presence in the world I have inhabited since birth and in which I will linger till I die; I can think this thought hyper-reflectively[7] by neutralizing the reflective alienation that would posit itself above and beyond the foreclosure of death. But I cannot think my totality concretely, as Hegel's Absolute must, simply because I cannot be present at my birth and my death. I can think of my birth and death through the abstract medium of language, and through that medium attempt to assimilate the events to which others have been and will be unproblematically present, but, for me, my concrete absence from these situations makes the fulfillment of the witnessing intention an absolute impossibility. That is part of what it means to be a finite embodied subject subject finally to the inexorable process of becoming: all eternal being is a fantasy that cannot exist for me. That — exactly that — is the meaning of eternity for me. I am finally transcended by time.

The problem of time is that it, like all worldly phenomena, must be both immanent and transcendent: it must be revealed, but transcend its revelation.

> Time must *constitute itself* — be always seen from the point of view of someone who *is of it*.

But this seems to be contradictory, and would lead back to one of the two terms of the preceding alternative.

The contradiction is lifted only if the new present is itself a transcendent: one knows it is not there, that it was just there, one never coincides with it — (VI 184)

The key to understanding the transcendence of time for Merleau-Ponty is in the last phrase quoted: one never coincides with the present. For Hegel, time is for-itself, self-constituting: the alienation from itself (or self-externalization)[8] that is finally overcome in eternal self-presence or self-coincidence.[9] For Merleau-Ponty, the self-coincidence is a reduction to immanence, a denial of temporality, a denial that one is of time. If the self-conscious subject is fully for-itself in Hegel's sense, it cannot be temporal in the manner of a living body destined to die from the moment of its conception.

Merleau-Ponty unself-consciously appropriates much of Husserl's teaching on the subject of time, even reproduces Husserl's diagram in his chapter on temporality in the *Phenomenology of Perception*. But he definitively distances himself from Husserl's reduction of time to an immanent form of synthesis. "[Husserl] is right to say that it is not I who constitute time, that it constitutes itself, that it is a *Selbsterscheinung* — . . . . A *Selbsterscheinung*, an autoapparition, an apparition that is pure apparition. . . . But all this presupposes the idea of the for itself and in the end cannot explain transcendence — " (VI 190–91). What, then, can explain transcendence?

The crucial term for Merleau-Ponty is *écart*: separation, dehiscence, fission. Taking up the issue of the "primal impression" that Husserl held to be the "source point" of an enduring temporal object (such as a melody),[10] Merleau-Ponty asks an ontological question: "what is the impressional consciousness, the *Urerlebnis*?" His answer to this question constitutes a clear break from Husserl's conception of time consciousness as immanent, as internal: Merleau-Ponty says that the *Urerlebnis* is a "transcendent," "an *etwas*," and that "the 'to be conscious' of this *Urerlebnis* is not coincidence, fusion with . . . it is separation (*écart*) . . . which is the foundation of space and time" (VI 191). To think the temporality of the for-itself (consciousness or subjectivity) with Merleau-Ponty, one must think of a separation from itself that is not *aufgehoben*, but remains always at a distance from itself, always present to a transcendent other. The transcendence, the otherness, is expressed as *écart*, as separation.

The transcendence of which Merleau-Ponty speaks can be explicated through the triad: world, subjectivity, time. Through the doctrine of reversibility, we learn that phenomenal self-manifestation is the flesh of the world folding over upon itself and becoming aware of itself. The conscious subject is itself flesh, that part of the flesh of the world that is sentient-reflective, that senses the world in sensing itself: I touch things by feeling myself being touched by things. Reversibility is, thus, the flesh of the world as it is present to itself.[11] But this presence to itself is not coincidence with itself — that would be the culmination of the Hegelian Absolute finally returned to itself, a culmination ruled out by Merleau-Ponty because it would be a denial of otherness, a denial of transcendence. In Merleau-Ponty's doctrine, the folding over upon itself of flesh is a separation from itself, *écart*; likewise, the reflective subject, unique and individualized, and the prereflective subject, decentered and generalized, both function through a reflexivity essentially characterized by a lack of self-coincidence: the I thought in the cogito is not coincidental with the I that thinks, and the finger that touches the table is not coincidental with the finger that is touched by the table. There is reversibility between the two, the possibility of a shift — a change of aspect, a reconfiguration of the gestalt — but this reversibility of subject-role and object-role is possible only because the roles are not coincidental. The signifier 'I' can be a shifter only because the body is ambiguously subject and object, and because whenever it intones its own name, the I is not absolute self-coincidence, but ek-static, displaced from itself in space-time and community.

Perhaps this will be clearer if we take up the third term in the world-subjectivity-time triad, and the meaning that presence or the present has for Merleau-Ponty. "The for-itself itself [is] an incontestable, but derived characteristic: it is the culmination of separation (*écart*) in *differentiation* — Self-presence *is* presence to a differentiated world — (VI 191).[12] The identity asserted in the last sentence makes the point misconstrued by Derrida and all those who piously incant his mantras abominating the metaphysics of presence: presence to itself is ek-stasis, *écart*; it is not self-coincidence. It is true that Husserl was mistaken on this point, but, as demonstrated here, Derrida was not the first to point this out.

Nor does it follow by any other logic than Hegel's that the phenomenon of presence must necessarily culminate in the self-coincidence of transcendental subjectivity. Heidegger entertained that thought as a hypothesis; Derrida espouses it as a foundational truth. I am willing to grant that antecedents for the Hegelian culmination can be traced to Aristotle.[13] But it is equally the case that presence as the moment of noncoincidence, as ek-static opening to transcendence — in a word, as perception — had roots that pass through Aristotle[14] as they extend into prehistory. And nowhere has that thought been stated more clearly than in the words Merleau-Ponty wrote on 20 May 1959: "the present itself is not an absolute coincidence without transcendence" (VI 195).[15]

When Husserl, as Derrida is fond of reminding us, took the self-coincidence of transcendental subjectivity as the principle of principles for phenomenology, he spoke for himself and of phenomenology as he conceived it.[16] He did not, could not, speak for the others who transformed phenomenology into a philosophy of existence. Nor should Husserl's pronouncement be read as an iteration which betrays the repetition of metaphysics that, having reached its end, can only say the same thing over and over again. Husserl's principle does betray the longing of a long-standing philosophical dream: if the world can be successfully bracketed and perception neutralized into fantasy, then nothing can contest the validity of the philosopher's dream. That is the meaning of the retreat to immanence: whether it is a retreat to the immanence of consciousness or a retreat to the immanence of language, it is a retreat, that is, a negative response to the transcendence of the world. As such, it is betrayed by the fact that it is a *response*.

This betrayal betrays *différance*. As Derrida presents the term to us, *différance* differentiates in space and time:[17] *différer* is "to be not identical, to be other, discernible," and it is also temporization, to delay or defer in a self-dissembling way.[18]

The functions assigned to *différance* betray a close resemblance to the dialectical process through which Hegel's absolute *Begriff* differentiates itself and all finite things in the descent into becoming that generates space and time.[19] Derrida may be read as betraying an awareness of this similarity. "In a conceptuality adhering to classical strictures *différance* would be said to designate a constitutive, productive, and originary causality, the process of scission and division which would produce or constitute different things or differences."[20] Derrida purports to displace this conceptuality and thereby erase responsibility for this remarkable similarity, but — we may ask — what differentiates *différance* from the agencies of transcendental constitution that classically function to generate space and time?

Derrida's answer is recorded under the heading of "the problematic of the sign." Signs defer presence.[21] And they do so indefinitely. One never reaches the referent, the transcendental signified, be it meaning or thing, because signification *is* the deferral of presence. One never gets beyond the signifiers because signifiers refer always and only to other signifiers in the chain of substitutions.

> The signified concept is never present in and of itself, in a sufficient presence that would refer only to itself. Essentially and lawfully, every concept is inscribed in a chain or in a system within which it refers to the other, to other concepts, by means of the systematic play of differences. Such a play, *différance*, is thus no longer simply a concept, but rather the possibility of conceptuality, of a conceptual process and system in general.[22]

Furthermore, *différance* is that which accounts for the differentiation of the signs themselves (which, in turn, account for the differentiation of everything else). "What is written as *différance*...will be the playing movement that 'produces' — by means of something that is not an activity — these differences, these effects of difference."[23] It would seem, then, that *différance* differs from the classical agencies of transcendental constitution because

    1. Being the 'producer' of differences, it cannot be differentiated;

    2. It cannot appear in the system of signs it makes possible;

    3. Being the sheer possibility of "differences *without positive terms*,"[24] *différance* is not a possible presence or absent presence; and,

    4. Finally, the *différance* that allows us to distinguish things

disallows those things from ever presenting themselves to us except by way of re-presentation.

"There never was any 'perception'; and 'presentation' is a representation of the representation that yearns for itself therein as for its own birth or its death."[25]

In sum, the theoretical posture constructed around the notion of *différance* effectively amounts to a retreat to linguistic immanence. *Effectively* amounts to such a retreat, the qualification is necessary because it is not necessary for Derrida to assert the non-existence of worldly things. The transcendent thing retains the same ontological status for Derrida as it had for Kant: the thing may *be* in itself, but it cannot manifest itself except by way of representation. Worldly things are inaccessible. "There never was any 'perception.'"[26]

Insofar as all use of language is ultimately a response to the world, so must the prose of Derrida's reduction to linguistic immanence be such a response — but it responds to a world to which it cannot allow itself to refer. Thus Derrida fulfills the philosopher's dream of being free from contestation — as it was in the Husserlian reduction, so it is in the Derridean reduction: if one makes no reference to a transcendent world, one cannot be wrong. But one cannot be right, either.

The debate I have reconstructed between Merleau-Ponty and Derrida may be seen to turn on the difference between *différance* and *écart*. Both notions undermine the self-coincidence definitive of the classical transcendental subject: Derrida and Merleau-Ponty concur in rejecting Husserl's "principle of principles." That is, they agree that presence to _____ cannot coincide with presence to itself. And the reasoning in both cases centers on the issue of time and the temporal ek-stasis. If the now moment of presence to _____ must embody an intrinsic relation to both past and future, and if that presence to _____ coincides fully with itself, then time collapses to the present eternal and we are left with Hegel's Absolute as the final name of the transcendental subject. Derrida is entirely right on this point: if phenomenology rests on the principle of self-coincidence, then it is onto-theo-logical. In light of this, both

Merleau-Ponty and Derrida stress differentiation, separation, difference, fission; that is, *écart* and *différance*.

At this point, however, their paths diverge. Derrida makes all presence to _____ dependent upon self-coincidence and rejects the concept of presence for that reason. Merleau-Ponty incorporates the ek-stasis within the field of presence with the doctrine of reversibility: presence to _____ is presence to itself mediated through its contact with transcendence. Here, again, there is a similarity. Derrida has a doctrine of mediated self-contact, too. For him, the mediator is the signifier. But the signifier, as conceived by Derrida, cannot mediate in the strong sense of providing contact with the transcendent world. The signifier, for Derrida, can mediate only by indefinitely deferring that contact: it refers always and only to other signifiers. The system of signifiers is transcendent, to be sure: nobody is the master of language as the sedimented vehicle of culture and history. But the transcendence of language is not the transcendence of the world.

The difference is this: contact with the transcendent world gives us knowledge about the world and ourselves as worldly beings, whereas contact with language gives us knowledge about language and ourselves as texts inscribed within language. For Derrida, a heart attack is a signifier; for Merleau-Ponty it was a death sentence. In technical terms, the difference is this: Derrida has reduced transcendence to a relation between signifiers, transcendence is a meaning constituted within language that may refer to the impossibility of perception as a direct relation to things; but, for Merleau-Ponty, 'transcendence' is a signifier that refers to our relationship to the world, each other, and ourselves as worldly beings, and perception is privileged as the mode of relatedness that separates us from ourselves and thereby brings us into contact with the things that teach us about themselves and ourselves.

This difference, as suggested earlier, may be brought to its crux by focusing on the issue of time. Time, for Derrida, is generated by *différance*: as temporization, *différance* "is also temporalization." How does *différance* temporalize, how can it function as the "'originary constitution' of time and space" (bearing in mind that "the name 'origin' no longer suits it")? For both Derrida and

Merleau-Ponty, the temporalizing of time is conceived in terms of the ek-stasis of self-differentiation: time temporalizes by dehiscence, fission, *écart* — by not coinciding with itself. But, for Derrida, this differing-from-itself is conceived grammatologically, as writing.

> It is because of *différance* that the movement of signification is possible only if each so-called 'present' element, each element appearing on the scene of presence, is related to something other than itself, thereby keeping within itself the mark of the past element, and already letting itself be vitiated by the mark of its relation to the future element. ...An interval must separate the present from what it is not in order for the present to be itself. ... This interval is what might be called *spacing*, the becoming-space of time or the becoming-time of space (*temporization*). And it is this constitution of the present...that I propose to call archi-writing, archi-trace, or *différance*. Which (is) (simultaneously) spacing (and) temporization.[27]

This thought is developed two pages later in Derrida's text.

> The practice of a language or of a code supposing a play of forms without a determined and invariable substance, and also supposing in the practice of this play a retention and protention of differences, a spacing and a temporization, a play of traces — all this must be a kind of writing before the letter, an archi-writing without a present origin, without archi-. Whence the regular erasure of the archi-, and the transformation of general semiology into grammatology.[28]

Note that more than differentiation is required for temporalization; there has also to be connection. The interval that separates the present from what is not itself must also join or relate the present to "something other than itself." This is the play of traces that constitutes the text as text, as something that can be deciphered. Without the joining or relating, the traces would be disconnected, could not stand in relation to each other. Derrida describes this relating play as "a retention and protention of differences."

Note, also, that this "movement of signification" which temporizes is conceived as a writing. Time is written in traces that differ from each other but relate to each other in the play of deferring presence. This is a semiological model of time.

The question upon which I have been insisting is this: how literally are we to understand the underlying metonymy, world = text? Where is this text written?

Three answers suggest themselves:

1. Grammatology literally replaces ontology: there is literally nothing outside the text. What exists is the play of signifiers, and beyond that, nothing.

2. The trace is not restricted to the signifier, narrowly conceived. The trace is whatever signifies: stones and birds, temples and priests, earth and world. What exists is what always has existed: things whose significance is revealed-concealed by language.

3. The trace as conceived in 2 erases itself in the text.

> Presence, then, far from being, as is commonly thought, what the sign signifies, what a trace refers to, presence, then, is the trace of the trace, the trace of the erasure of the trace.[29]

> The trace is not a presence but the simulacrum of a presence that dislocates itself, displaces itself, refers itself, it properly has no site — erasure belongs to its structure.[30]

This interpretation (3) contends that every presentation is already a representation, that the trace as present thing erases itself in the production of the trace as signifier. The erasure of the trace refers to the impossibility of a present origin, the impossibility of perception as original presentation.

These suggestions may be labeled: (1) idealism, (2) realism,[31] (3) semiological reductionism.

Where is Derrida to be situated on the question of the world = text metonymy? Insofar as idealism and realism are inscribed within the text of metaphysics, 1 and 2 must be discounted in the economy of Derridean thought. The world = text metonymy, for Derrida, must be read in a way that exceeds metaphysics. "In order to exceed metaphysics it is necessary that a trace be inscribed within the text of metaphysics, a trace that continues to signal not in the direction of another presence, or another form of presence, but in the direction of an entirely other *text.*"[32] Looking beyond metaphysics, all that Derrida can see is another text.

The crux is time, and the crucial question asks about the relation between time and writing. Is time inscribed? Or does inscription take time? Does writing effect the 'production' of time? Or
does time surpass all signifying production? Is time finally inscribed
in the *gramme*?[33] Or does time transcend delineation?

Here Derrida encounters his own aporia. If temporal differentiation is accomplished by (archi-)writing, then there is no time
before inscription and time is confined to history. If the trace of
time extends beyond history, then the trace is more than is written.

Homonymy is at work or play in Derrida's trace. There is the
$trace_1$ that signifies by re-presenting the $trace_2$ that effaces itself in
the signification. Derrida trades on the metonymy: $trace_1 = trace_2$:
"what a $trace_1$ refers to, presence, then, is the $trace_1$ of the $trace_2$,
the $trace_1$ of the erasure of the $trace_2$."[34] $Trace_1$ is a signifier, referring here to 'presence'. $Trace_2$ is the thing, conceived in classical
metaphysics as a presence or absent presence.

If the metonymy is taken as a literal identity, then the difference between $trace_1$ and $trace_2$ is erased. That would leave us in
one or the other of the two standpoints labeled (1) idealism and
(2) realism earlier.

If the metonymy is taken metaphorically, we are left with
another variant of Derrida's aporia. Either [I] $trace_2$ is fully erased
in $trace_1$ (thus leaving no trace of itself that anyone could trace), or
[II] it is not (thus leaving some traceable residue). But [I] is
equivalent to (1) and [II] is equivalent to (2).

The question is how seriously to take the metonymy text =
world. When the issue is time, the question is forced. Either time is
delimited by writing or writing is delimited by time. If it is indeed
the case that time is "but the name of the limits within which the
gramme is...comprehended," if these limits also delimit "the possibility of the trace in general," and if "nothing other has ever been
thought by the name of time"[35] by anyone including Derrida, then
writing is delimited by time and not 'produced' by it.

If this is the case, then Derrida joins the company of Kant and
Husserl as one forced to advert to a tacit temporal realism to assert
an overt thesis of the immanence of time.

To defer is not to produce time. To defer presupposes that there
is time to take. I can defer on the analyst's couch as long as I live:

that is true. It is equally true that I can defer on the surgeon's table for the same length of time, and that this is not a matter of the production of signifiers.

Time is differentiation: *différance* or *écart*. Time is also connection: protention, retention, and the intrinsic reference of the differentia to each other. So far, there is agreement between Derrida and Merleau-Ponty. The disagreement between them lies in their accounts of the differentiation and the interconnectedness.

In the *Phenomenology of Perception*, Merleau-Ponty had not yet fully worked through the dialectic of ek-stasis and self-coincidence. Like Heidegger in *Being and Time*, Merleau-Ponty is still working with the equation of temporality and subjectivity.[36] The guiding hypothesis, taken from Husserl in both cases, was that the ek-stasis of temporality could provide a transcendence-within-immanence for subjectivity: time is still preeminently the form of inner sensibility, but, as ek-static, it could accommodate the distance from itself needed to account for the transcendence of outer experience.

The movement beyond this position was, however, already prefigured within it. The present had to be essentially linked to past and future to avoid the atomization of time and the aporias of the isolated now point, but this link could not be so strong as to amount to coincidence because that would collapse duration into eternal presence. These two requirements cannot be met as long as time is conceived as immanent, as the form of subjective experience — because past and future cannot be experienced in the present and still be past and future. The ek-stasis has to be real: past and future have to transcend consciousness, but still be linked to the present. This means that the present has to transcend consciousness as well. The conclusion to which this line of thought is bound to lead is that of the *écart* articulated in *The Visible and the Invisible*. But this does not amount to a reversal in Merleau-Ponty's thinking; it is rather a surfacing of the thought of the transcendence of the phenomenal world already implicit in his doctrine of the primacy of perception: perception is the transcendence of the present to consciousness, the openness to what is genuinely other that takes place in the enduring moment of presence. In this understanding of presence, the relation of the present moment to past and future becomes comprehensible: it is the unfolding of the phe-

nomenon, the appearance of movement and change (with its privative moment of stasis), the style of worldly disclosure.

Time is not constituted by synthesis: *time* is an abstract noun
that refers to the manner in which the phenomenal world becomes.
It would be more appropriate to think of time as adverbial: it is the
manner, the style, the how. Given the open-ended unity of worldly
style, the question of synthesis is preempted. The question is not,
how do moments get connected with one another? The question is,
how did we come to reify the notes in the melody? And the answer
here is well-known: by notation. By inscribing the passage of time
in signifiers that give the false impression of timelessness — and the
equally false impression of the need for an agency of synthesis.

If time is the product of synthesis, then it is composed of parts.
But time has no parts: past, present, and future are not discrete
units. One way to conceive the present is as a theme emerging
from the background of global time. In this model, the *écart* is the
foregrounding of the present as this phase of the world's unfolding,
this manner of the flesh of the world folding back on itself. *Now*,
this moment of the unfolding, is how the world senses itself across
the multitudes of its individual sensors in the present phase of
its becoming.

The present distinguishes itself from the horizon of global time
as a moment of *its* unfolding. No synthesis is required to bring
about the connection: the figure-ground relation is "the simplest
'*Etwas*'" (VI 192), "one cannot go back any further" (VI 191). This
is both a transcendent fact and a ground of reason: it is a structure
of what Merleau-Ponty calls "autochthonous organization."[37] It is
revealed in perception, not constituted by it: if "to be conscious =
to have a figure on a ground" (VI 191), this is because consciousness has evolved a *habitus*[38] demanded by the needs of worldly
self-disclosure.

It is not writing that produces time because time is not produced. It is not the play of signifiers that synthesizes time because
time is not synthesized. The thesis of the transcendence of time:

- Solves the problem of interpersonal coordination. If it is language that coordinates the running-off of phenomena in the
  world = text in which you are inscribed with the unfolding
  going on in mine, then we have to be reading the same text.
- Solves the problem of time before human sensors. Is it

language that coordinates sedimented layers of the earth's crust with the decay rate of carbon 14?
• Defines perception in a decentered way. Do I escape from myself only through signifiers, or am I drawn elsewhere by an *éclat* that motivates philosophical Narcissus to lift his gaze from pond or text?

And it does all this simply by saying that the world is transcendent, has a history of which we are a moment, and that this moment is but a moment in a process of becoming that depends on us only to the extent that we affect it.

NOTES

1. "One would...have to describe in terms of facticity, and not in terms of essences, a subjectivity situated in space and time." *The Visible and the Invisible*, trans. Alphonso Lingis (Evanston: Northwestern University Press, 1968), p. 46; henceforth cited as VI. *Le Visible et l'Invisible* (Paris: Gallimard, 1964); henceforth cited as VI-F.

2. In addition to the passages that follow, there is the discussion of habit that describes the body's ability to reconfigure its typicality to adjust to new worldly demands and, in doing so, to establish a new typicality. Merleau-Ponty concludes this discussion as follows: "At all levels, [the body] performs the same function which is to endow the instantaneous expressions of spontaneity with 'a little renewable action and independent existence.' [The quote is from Valéry.] Habit is merely a form of this fundamental power. We say that the body has understood, and habit has been cultivated when it has aborted a new meaning, and assimilated a fresh core of significance [lors qu'il s'est assimilé un nouveau noyau significatif]." *Phenomenology of Perception*, trans. Colin Smith (London: Routledge & Kegan Paul, 1962), p. 146; henceforth cited as PP. *Phénoménologie de la perception* (Paris: Éditions Gallimard, 1945), p. 171; henceforth cited as PP-F.

"The analysis of motor habit as an extension of existence leads on, then, to an analysis of perceptual habit as the coming into possession of a world. ...For the child to be able to perceive blue and red under the category of color, the category must be rooted in the data, otherwise no subsumption could recognize it in them. ...To learn to see colors is to acquire a certain style of seeing, a new use of one's body" [PP 153]. In quoting passages from English translations, I have taken the liberty of making modifications where to do so seems appropriate.

3. *The Structure of Behavior*, trans. Alden L. Fisher (Boston: Beacon Press, 1963), p. 148; henceforth cited as SB. *La Structure du Comportement* (Paris: Presses Universitaires de France, 1942), p. 161; henceforth cited as SB-F.

4. See PP 127, 394; PP-F 147–48, 451.

5. "L'existence humaine... est le changement de la contingence en nécessité par l'acte de reprise" (PP 170, PP-F 199).

6. See M. C. Dillon, "Apriority in Kant and Merleau-Ponty," *Kant-Studien* 17, no. 3 (1987).

7. Hyperreflection (*sur-réflexion*) is a term Merleau-Ponty introduces in *The Visible and the Invisible* to denote a form of reflection that takes into account its own proclivity to distort its subject matter: "We are catching sight of the necessity of another operation besides the conversion to reflection, more fundamental than it, of a sort of hyperreflection that would also take itself and the changes it introduces into the spectacle into account" (VI 38).

8. "Difference has stepped out of space; this means that it has ceased to be this indifference [i.e., the indifference of mere self-externality, of mere undifferentiated spatiality], it is for itself in all its unrest, is no longer paralysed. This pure Quantity, as self-existent difference, is what is negative in itself, Time; it is the negation of the negation, the self-relating negation." *Hegel's Philosophy of Nature: Being Part Two of The Encyclopedia of the Philosophical Sciences* (1830), translated from Nicolin and Pöggeler's edition (1959) and from the Zusätze in Michelet's text (1847) by A. V. Miller, (Oxford: Oxford University Press, 1970), Zusatz to § 257, p. 34.

9. "Absolute timelessness is distinct from duration; the former is eternity, from which natural time is absent. But in its Notion, time itself is eternal; for time as such — not any particular time, nor Now — is its Notion, and this, like every Notion generally, is eternal, and therefore also absolute Presence. Eternity will not come to be, nor was it, but it *is*. The difference therefore between eternity and duration is that the latter is only a relative sublating of time, whereas eternity is infinite, i.e., not relative duration, but duration reflected into self." Ibid., Zusatz to § 258, p. 36.

10. Edmund Husserl, *The Phenomenology of Internal Time-Consciousness*, ed. Martin Heidegger, trans. James S. Churchill (Bloomington: Indiana University Press, 1964), p. 50: "The 'source-point' with which the 'generation' of the enduring Object begins is a primal impression."

11. Note the decentering of subjectivity implied in the generality of this statement. See M. C. Dillon, "Merleau-Ponty and the Reversibility Thesis," *Man and World*, 16 (1983).

12. A critical reader will turn to the text to find the context for these remarks. In so doing, he or she will find that the passage quoted continues as follows: " — The perceptual separation (*écart*) as making up the 'view' such as it is implicated in the reflex, for example — and enclosing being for itself by means of language as differentiation" (VI 191). If inclined to think within the confines of the semiological reduction, the reader will point out that Merleau-Ponty says that it is the differentiating function of language that encloses being for itself. To this I reply that that it is, indeed, a function of language to enclose being for itself, but that this enclosure is necessarily a reduction of the savage or brute being that language always ultimately refers to, that language always seeks to capture, but that always eludes complete enclosure. Here, again, there is never coincidence, always *écart*.

13. After defining time as "number of motion in respect of 'before' and 'after'," Aristotle asks whether it is dependent upon mind. "Whether if soul did not exist time would exist or not, is a question that may fairly be asked; for if there cannot be someone to count there cannot be anything that can be counted, so that evidently there cannot be number; for number is either what has been, or what can be, counted. But if nothing but soul, or in soul reason, is qualified to count, there would not be time unless there were soul, but only that of which time is an attribute, i.e., if *movement* can exist without soul, and the before and after are attributes of movement, and time is these *qua* numerable" (Aristotle, *Physics*, IV, 14, 223a. *Physica*, trans. R. P. Hardie and R. K. Gaye, in *The Basic Works of Aristotle*, ed. Richard McKeon [New York: Random House, 1941], p. 299).

Insofar as time is the enumeration of movement, then to the extent that enumeration depends on mind, so does time. But, to the extent that movement is independent of mind, then the substance-subject of which time is an attribute is independent of mind.

This is an odd conjunction: a subject or substance-substratum (movement, change) independent of mind has an essential attribute that is dependent on mind. The question arises as to whether, absent mind, there could be movement without time.

One solution to this conundrum is provided by the Absolute under the heading of prime mover. Aristotle does not believe in inertia: what is moved has to be moved by a mover. Ultimately, then, the prime mover is responsible, not only for setting things in motion, but for keeping things moving. And the prime mover must be thought as self-conscious. So there is always awareness of movement. To the extent that such awareness is constitutive of time, there are grounds for seeing in Aristotle's doctrine a precursor to the Hegelian standpoint.

14. Aristotle admits that "it is hard to say" whether the 'now' that is essentially bound to past and future always remains "one and the same" or is "always other and other," but it is clear that he rules out the self-coincidence that would render the 'now' equivalent to the eternal present. "If coincidence in time...means to be 'in one and the same "now",' then, if both what is before and what is after are in this same 'now,' things which happened ten thousand years ago would be simultaneous with what has happened today, and nothing would be before or after anything else" (*Physics*, IV, 10, 218a. *Physica*, pp. 289–90).

15. "Le présent même n'est pas coïncidence absolue sans transcendance" (VI-F 249).

16. For Derrida, however, phenomenology is circumscribed within the Husserlian conception. In *Speech and Phenomena* he writes the following: "In phenomenology, the idea of primordial presence and in general of 'beginning,' 'absolute beginning' or *principium*,* always refers back to...the self-identity of the now as point, as a 'source-point.'" At * Derrida quotes Husserl's statement of the "principle of principles" from *Ideas I*, § 24. (Derrida, *Speech and Phenomena and Other Essays on Husserl's Theory of Signs*, trans. David B. Allison [Evanston: Northwestern University Press, 1973], pp. 61–62; hereafter cited as SP.)

17. "*Différance* is the...structured and differentiating origin of differences. [However,] the name 'origin' no longer suits it" — because, I surmise, 'origin' denotes a possible presence. (Jacques Derrida, "Différance," in *Margins of Philosophy*, trans. Alan Bass [Chicago: University of Chicago Press, 1982], p. 11. And later, "Differences...are 'produced' — deferred — by *différance*" [Différance,", p. 14].)

18. "*Différer* in this sense to is temporize, to take recourse, consciously or unconsciously, in the temporal and temporizing mediation of a detour

that suspends the accomplishment or fulfillment of 'desire' or 'will,' and equally effects this suspension in a mode that annuls or tempers its own effect" ("Différance," p. 8).

19. "This temporization is also temporization and spacing, the becoming-time of space; and the becoming-space of time, the 'originary constitution' of time and space, as metaphysics or transcendental phenomenology would say" ("Différance," p. 8). Derrida criticizes and purports to "displace" the language of this saying.

20. "Différance," pp. 8–9.

21. "The sign is usually said to be put in the place of the thing itself, the present thing, 'thing' here standing equally for meaning or referent. The sign represents the present in its absence. It takes the place of the present. When we cannot grasp or show the thing, state the present, the being-present, when the present cannot be presented, we signify, we go through the detour of the sign. We take or give signs. We signal. The sign, in this sense, is deferred presence" ("Différance," p. 9).

22. "Différance," p. 11.

23. Ibid., p. 11.

24. The phrase is quoted [ibid., p. 11] from Ferdinand de Saussure, *Course in General Linguistics*, trans. Wade Baskin (New York: Philosophical Library, 1959), p. 120.

25. SP, p. 103. As Derrida is himself wont to show, there are antecedents for all four points in classical conceptions of transcendental subjectivity.

26. Thus one possible interpretation of "*il n'y a pas de hors-texte*" reads it as denying, not the existence of anything outside texts, but the appearance or self-manifestation of any extratextual presence.

27. "Différance," p. 13.

28. Ibid., p. 15.

29. Derrida, "*Ousia* and *Gramme*: Note on a Note from *Being and Time*," in *Margins of Philosophy*, trans. Alan Bass (Chicago: University of Chicago Press, 1982), p. 66; hereafter cited as OG.

30. "Différance," p. 24.

31. That is, (2) lends itself to the realist construction intended here.

There is another reading of (2) that would qualify it to be placed under the heading of a genuinely phenomenological ontology.

32. OG, p. 65, emphasis added.

33. "The *gramme* is *comprehended* by metaphysics between the point and the circle, between potentiality and the act (presence), etc.; and all the critiques of the spatialization of time, from Aristotle to Bergson, remain within the limits of this comprehension. *Time*, then, would be but the name of the limits within which the *gramme* is thus comprehended, and, along with the *gramme*, the possibility of the trace in general. *Nothing* other *has ever been* thought by the name of time" (OG, p. 60).

34. See note 29.

35. See note 33.

36. "Our analysis of time has confirmed, initially, [a] new notion of significance and understanding. Considering [time] in the same light as any other object, we shall be obliged to say of it what we have said of other objects: that it has meaning for us only because we 'are it.' We can designate something by this word only because we belong to past, present, and future. It is literally the sense [*sens*] of our life, and, like the world, is accessible only to the person who has his place within it, and who follows its direction. But the analysis of time has not merely provided an opportunity of reiterating what had been said about the world. It throws light on the preceding analysis because it discloses subject and object as two abstract 'moments' of a unique structure which is *presence*. It is through time that being is conceived, because it is through the relations of time-subject and time-object that we are able to understand those obtaining between subject and world. Let us apply to those problems with which we began the idea of subjectivity as temporality. We wondered, for example, how to conceive the relations between the soul and the body, rejecting as hopeless any attempt to tie up the for-itself with a certain object in-itself, to which it is supposed to stand in a relationship of causal dependence. But if the for-itself, the revelation of self to self, is merely the hollow in which time is formed, and if the world 'in-itself' is simply the horizon of my present, then the problem is reduced to the form: How is it that a being which is still to come, and has passed by, also has a present — which means that the problem is eliminated, since the future, the past, and the present are linked together in the movement of temporalization" (PP 430–31; PP-F 492–93).

37. "There is an autochthonous significance of the world [*un sens autochtone du monde*] which constitutes itself in the dealings which our incarnate existence has with the world, and which provides the ground of every deliberate *Sinngebung*" (PP 441, PP-F 503).

38. Thus Hume and Mill were not entirely wrong, but only half right. The other half of the story was told by Kant. The persistence of this autonomy may be attributed to the allegiance of ideological thinking. See note 2.

1

"The Element of Voluminousness": Depth and Place Re-examined

Edward S. Casey

> Four centuries after the 'solu-
> tions' of the Renaissance and
> three centuries after Descartes,
> depth is still new, and it insists
> on being sought, not 'once in a
> lifetime', but all through life.
> — Merleau-Ponty,
> "Eye and Mind"

> Space has depth which reaches
> beyond the seen into the unseen.
> — Erwin Straus,
> *The Primary World of Senses*

> Where abstract space consists of
> points, ecological space consists
> of places — locations or positions.
> — J. J. Gibson, *The Ecological
> Approach to Visual Perception*

I

William James, writing a hundred years ago, observed that every
form of sensation brings with it an "element of voluminousness," a
"feeling of crude extensity."[1] Unlike Bergson, who, two years earlier
in *Les données immédiates de la conscience*, had argued for the prac-
tically inevitable tendency to regard space as homogeneous (a
tendency that renders it eminently unsuitable for the representa-

1

tion of durational time), James emphasized from the very start the multiplicity of forms in which we experience space. The voluminous, which is the primary quality of immediately experienced spatiality, comes with "varying vastness"[2] in keeping with differences in kinds of sensation. As James stated with phenomenological precision:

> We call the reverberations of a thunderstorm more voluminous than the squeaking of a slate-pencil; the entrance into a warm bath gives our skin a more massive feeling than the prick of a pin; a little neuralgic pain, fine as a cobweb, in the face, seems less extensive than the heavy soreness of a boil or the vast discomfort of a colic or a lumbago; and a solitary star looks smaller than the noonday sky.[3]

Part of James's agenda in the chapter of *The Principles of Psychology* from which this passage comes — a chapter entitled "The Perception of Space" — is to refute the Berkeleyian notion that we grasp depth or distance (terms not distinguished by Berkeley himself) by means of tactile experience alone. James argued that vision is also a source, and perhaps the leading source, of our experience of what he preferred to call "volume." "The field of view," he remarked laconically, "is always a *volume*-unit."[4] By "volume" James meant the kind of unstructured vastness "so vague that in it there is no question as yet of surface as opposed to depth."[5] Depth and distance are thus tributary from volume — its further specifications, as it were.

Moreover, depth and distance do not exist on a par, as Berkeley had supposed. If distance represents an objectification of volume and thus involves an element of estimation or judgment, depth lies concealed within volume as its own proper dimension. James admits as much by asserting that "all objects of sensation are voluminous *in three dimensions*."[6] And one of his most delicious descriptions of "the third dimension" itself makes it clear that this dimension is nothing other than depth: "It is impossible to lie on one's back on a hill, to let the empty abyss of blue fill one's whole visual field, and to sink deeper and deeper into the merely sensational mode of consciousness regarding it, without feeling that an indeterminate, palpitating, circling depth is as indefeasibly one of its attributes as its breadth."[7] From volume, then, we are led immediately to depth, and depth in turn shows itself to be, despite its classical designation as "third," the leading dimension, indeed "the first dimension" as Merleau-Ponty will ultimately call it. James is already acutely aware of this paradoxical aspect of depth, according to which the last will be first: "it happens perhaps most often that the breadth- and height-feeling take their absolute measure from the depth-feeling."[8]

James' otherwise perspicacious account of the perception of space at its most elementary level runs into difficulty only when he posits a specific "sensation of depth," overlooking his own animadversions against the constancy hypothesis (for which there is a constant correlation between sensations and judgments of depth).[9] Although James's effort to locate the experience of depth — and of spatiality in general — at a primordial level is commendable (especially when compared with Helmholtz's claim that "all spatial attributes are results of habit and experience"[10]), his recourse to sensation, even in his own expansive sense of the term, is fraught with difficulty: above all, the difficulty that it is not clear how depth affects "the stimulation of the sense-tract."[11] If depth is the primary dimension of the voluminous and if the voluminous is as "crude" and "vague" as James himself says it is (and justifiably so, as we shall see), how will it manage to become sufficiently determinate to stimulate the nervous system in a way that transmits precise information about its extent? It is not surprising that in this impasse James falls back on Lotze's dubious doctrine of "local signs" as the basis of spatial discriminations.[12]

What James needs is a systematic distinction between "sensation" as strictly physiological and "perception" as a higher order modality of awareness that is capable of monitoring such a complex variable as depth. It is this very distinction on which J. J. Gibson, arguably the most subtle perceptual psychologist since James, insists. Gibson says strikingly that "sense perception need not be founded on sensation."[13] Sensation on the Gibsonian paradigm is a sensitivity to physical energy directly dependent on physiological organs, whereas perception is a sensitivity to information from the environment that is only indirectly dependent on physiology. Gibson cites instances of perceptions that are not founded on sensation; for example, the perception of orientation vis-à-vis the vestibular organ, or kinaesthetic experiences in which information concerning body motion may be discerned without the registration of any corresponding sensory quality.[14]

Most significant of all is Gibson's critique of depth cues. Although foreshadowed by certain remarks of James,[15] this critique is much more thoroughly set forth by Gibson. The traditional idea that there are certain cues of depth was predicated on the assumption, prevalent since at least Descartes, that retinal sensations offered only a two-dimensional representation of the surrounding world. Because that world (the world of *res extensa*) exists in three dimensions, there must *ex hypothesi* exist specific cues for projecting three dimensional realities from their two-dimensional replicas in sensation. The cues in question are such things as perspective, overlap, and decreasing size. In Gibson's judgment, these cues derive mainly from devices of landscape painting — that is, from a two-dimensional (but now external) representation of physical reality — which have been illicitly imported, sub rosa, into the physiological interiority of the perceiving subject. Whatever their value in landscape painting (where the creation of the illusion of the real is so often at stake), they are distinctly misleading as imputed to perception. In a classical experiment, Gibson showed that an ingenious placement of spurious depth cues in the perceiver's visual environment led the perceiver to suppose that a playing card which was actually at a considerable distance was very close — and vice versa with a second card.[16] Thus depth cues were shown to be insufficient for the veridical perception of depth. Nor are they even necessary for such perception. The correct perception of depth may occur in their absence.

This is not to say, however, that depth perception lacks determinate grounds. Gibson singled out various gradients of depth that in effect replace the classical depth cues: increasing density of texture, differential "reflectance" of light from the surfaces of seen objects, and motion parallax. Density and reflectance belong to the perceived world and are grasped directly as "affordances" offered by this world. They are not creatures of sensation but features of perception. When they are combined with an active, mobile body on the part of the perceiver, one has all the ingredients one needs in order to apprehend depth.[17]

Given this new *armamentarium* of depth determinants, Gibson is acerbic in his rejection of the assumption that we project a separate, third dimension on the basis of the depth cues supposedly furnished in the two dimensions of a retinal image:

> No one ever saw the world as a flat patchwork of colors — no infant, no cataract patient, and not even Bishop Berkeley or Baron von Helmholtz, who believed firmly that the cues for depth were learned. The notion of a patchwork of colors comes from the art of painting, not from any unbiased description of visual experience. What one becomes aware of by holding still, closing one eye, and observing a frozen scene are not visual sensations but only *the surfaces of the world that are viewed from here*. They are not flat or depthless but simply unhidden. One's attention is called to the fact of occlusion, not to the pseudofact of the third dimension.[18]

"The pseudofact of the third dimension": this says it all in one phrase. What had been taken as axiomatically true of depth since at least Descartes — that it is the third of the three Euclidean dimensions as represented by the three axes of height, breadth, and depth in solid geometry — may not be true of depth as actually experienced by human perceivers. Indeed, it may even be distinctly false to such depth, a depth Merleau-Ponty considers to be *primordial*.[19] And yet a preoccupation with depth as a third dimension of space has been a leitmotif of philosophers and psychologists alike from Descartes to James. How can this have happened?

II

The extraordinary concern — indeed, the obsession — with depth as a third dimension can be traced to two sets of beliefs, the combination of which occasions the preoccupation in question. On the one hand, there is the conviction, ultimately inherited from Euclid and already evident in the *Timaeus*, that depth as the third dimension is what makes solid bodies in space *solid*. Depth (*bathos*) is what gives to material bodies not just their form but their protrudingness, their well-roundedness, their resistance, and their very voluminosity. In fact, to the exact extent that depth is identified with the third dimension and both together with the voluminous, it becomes ipso facto indispensable to everything that is a proper denizen of space:

that is to say, all material bodies (in contrast, notably, with depic-
tions of these bodies on a two-dimensional plane in paintings or in
photographs). On the other hand, as we have just seen, there is an
equally entrenched conviction that such solid bodies in space are
represented — that is, projected and condensed — on the surface of
the retina (and perhaps also on its replica in the brain) in a strictly
bidimensional format. That this belief, which can be traced back at
least to Leonardo da Vinci,[20] dies hard is evident in the following
unselfquestioning claim from a recent book tantalizingly entitled
Visual Information Processing: "Our perceptions of patterns [i.e., as
arising from material things in the visual world] are three-
dimensional, but only two of these dimensions, the horizontal and
vertical axes, have a geometrical basis in the flat image of the world
formed on the retina. *The depth dimension is not geometrically represented
on the retina*."[21] If this claim were to be true, then we would indeed
have a vexatious problem on our hands. For we would be saddled
with a problem of translation — or more exactly, of transformation,
of two-dimensional data into three-dimensional objects. Short of
some neurological or physiological tour de force, how are we to
effect such a translation or transformation?

It is at this very point that the notion of visual depth cues is
invoked as the mediating term that brings together the flat retinal
field with the solid physical world. The authors of *Visual Information
Processing* do so with dutiful predictability:

> Nonetheless [i.e., despite the discrepancy between two-dimensional
> data and a three-dimensional world], the flat retinal image provides
> some cues concerning depth. ... These include the cue of interposi-
> tion (a near object partially covers a far object), the cue of shadows
> or shading (the direction of shadows registers the relative positions in
> depth), the cue of aerial perspective (far objects contain less detail),
> the cue of linear perspective... [22]

Plausible as such cues may seem — as if to clinch the case, the
authors list four others as well — they are in the end post hoc inventions created to save an embarrassing situation. As just one example, take the putative cue of "interposition" (i.e., of "superposition"
or "overlap" as it is also sometimes called). Here we must ask, do
we use the overlapping of objects *in order to* derive a sense of depth,

or does not the obscuring of one object by another *already* express (and thus presuppose) depth — a depth *in which* they can stand in overlapping relations? If the latter is the case, then it is question begging to invoke interposition as the source of the very thing which it itself presupposes. As Gibson puts it: "The phenomenon of the superposition of objects is actually not a clue to the depth of objects but a perception which requires explanation. A man knows that a near object can partially obscure a far object but his retina does not, and the retinal explanation should be sought first."[23]

In other words, the "retinal explanation" requires recourse to what "a man knows" — and what a man knows is already present in the world of *perception*, quite apart from whatever basis it may have in sensation. For in the world of perception, depth has always already insinuated itself. Indeed, it has *presented itself* — and it has done so on its *own* terms, terms that do not call for contrived intermediaries to tie together the second and third dimensions. Once we recognize that depth is already given with perceived objects as their very medium, their interpenetrating ambience, then the presumed mystery of the link between the plane and the solid in perception — and thus the preoccupation with the nature of this link — dissipates in thin air. As Gibson remarks pertinently, "the problem of the restoration of the lost third dimension in perception is a false one."[24] It is false to the exact extent that the third dimension was never lost in the first place in the two-dimensional display of the retina. If the third dimension is present at all, it is present in the world being perceived *from the beginning*. It is not a conclusion from the observation of depth cues — for example, from the fact of interposed objects — but itself a given. The experience and knowledge of depth is immediate, or it does not exist at all. The constructivist view that depth and other features of space are somehow projected *on the basis of* cues given in sensations (above all, but not exclusively, retinal sensations) is here contested and, with it, the mentalism on which it is founded.[25]

Once we reject the false problem of how to connect the second with the third dimension in space, the burden falls on us to propose a viable alternative model. All who have attempted to do so, including James, Gibson, and Merleau-Ponty, are agreed on the very first step. This is to dissociate "depth" from the "third dimension." The latter is ineluctably tied to the third axis, the Z axis, of solid geometry as represented on a Cartesian grid of coordinates (a grid in which the X, Y, and Z axes coincide at the same zero point). Space in general, and depth in particular, do not present themselves in any such well-ordered tridimensional way. The proof of this is that on the Euclidean-Cartesian model depth itself is at most just one of the three dimensions — hence *indifferently any of them* because, by a mere rotation of the model, depth can come to substitute equally well for height or for width. As Descartes wrote, "there is a merely nominal difference between the three dimensions of body — length, breadth, and depth; for in any given solid it is quite immaterial which aspects of its extension we take as its length, which as its breadth, etc."[26] Hegel expressed the matter best when he said that

> the three dimensions [of Euclidean space] are merely different, and quite devoid of determinations. ... Consequently one cannot say how height, length, and breadth [i.e., depth] differ from one another...it is a matter of indifference whether we call a certain direction height or depth; it is the same with length or breadth, which is also often called depth, for nothing is determined in this way.[27]

In this astute comment, which is at once a summation of the problematic traditional view and a critique of it, it becomes evident from Hegel's own wording just how "indifferent" depth indeed becomes in this view. When Hegel substitutes *breadth* for *depth* and adds, as if in apology, the revealing clause "breadth, which is also often called depth," he illustrates that for him depth is merely one of the three Cartesian dimensions and has no privileged role to play in the structuration of space. As Gibson observes wryly, "If depth means the dimension of an object that goes with height and width, there is nothing special about it. Height becomes depth when the object is seen from the top, and width becomes depth when the object is seen from the side."[28] In short, the indifference to which Hegel points is rooted in the facile interchangeability of depth with the other two congeneric dimensions of space. Such mutual exchangeability signifies that no single dimension, not even depth, has any intrinsic determination of its own — and thus that any difference between the dimensions is (in Hegel's revealing words) "a merely superficial and completely empty difference."[29]

III

And yet is it not evident to everyone, sophisticated psychophysicist of perception as well as ordinary perceiver, that depth is *not* a matter of indifference? Depth matters greatly in human (and indeed in all animal) experience, and this is so whether we consider such experience in its origin (e.g., at the primal moment of the visual cliff as described by Eleanor Gibson)[30] or at its end point (that is, when it has been made subject to philosophical or psychological reflection). When Hegel himself says straightforwardly that "the things of nature are in space,"[31] we can be certain that he means that natural things exist *in depth* in a sense of 'depth' that exceeds any mere third dimension. Even J. J. Gibson, who says shockingly that "we do not live in 'space'"[32] and who is so concerned with replacing the language of "depth" with the idiom of the "layout of surfaces," cannot resist saying in an unselfconscious moment that "one sees two surfaces, *separated in depth*."[33] Here depth exceeds surface, the basic unit of the visual world in Gibson's cosmic model.

The fact is that we are everywhere caught up in depth, that experience rarely if ever reveals itself as depthless, and that we are continually entering new depths (even when we think we are staying on the surface of things). Whitehead remarks that "contrast elicits depth."[34] If this is so, depth must be everywhere, given that we continually experience contrasts. The three dimensions of space are themselves forms of contrast; their supposedly indifferent differences nevertheless give a certain valency to the abstract and formal depth of solid geometry, however inadequate such depth may be as a model of perceived depth.

But if depth is indeed an integral part of our ongoing experience — of our perception of "the things of nature" (not to mention the things of the mind, which has its own depths as well) — and if depth is not just an indifferent axial dimension of this experience of perception, how are we to conceive it, or even to describe it? Granting the shortcomings of a Cartesian or a Berkeleyian account, what is depth as a positive phenomenon? James took one decisive step toward answering this question by designating it as felt volume; but his insistence on the vagueness of the voluminous discourages examination of its intimate infrastructure. Gibson took another step by thinking of depth as a layout of surfaces, as a complex function of low-level gradients given in the environment. But, as I have just hinted, the very idea of surface layout may presuppose rather than underlie depth; and in any case it calls for further specification than Gibson was willing to give it.

Merleau-Ponty offers promise at this particular point. His concern is with depth as a manifest, indeed a literally visible, phenomenon rather than something privative or merely inferred. In the *Phenomenology of Perception* he designates such depth as "primordial." By "primordial" is meant at least three things. First, depth of this order is not constructed but concretely *given*: "depth cannot be understood as belonging to the thought of an acosmic subject, but [is] a possibility of a subject involved in the world."[35]

Second, depth is less a dimension than a *medium* in which the perceiving subject and the perceived world are both immersed. As such, it "immediately reveals the link between the subject and space."[36] But as a medium it is more than a mere mediator. Where a sheer mediating factor may be diaphanous or invisible in the manner of aether, primordial depth is "the thickness of a medium devoid of any thing."[37] As dense, such depth is something we actually see and touch and move through. Its thickness harbors a polyvalence of qualities that is the equivalent within the perceived world of the subject's inherently possessed synaesthesias.

Primordial depth is primordial in a third way as well: by virtue of subtending "objectified depth." *Objectified depth* is "a relation between things or even between planes...[which is] detached from experience and transformed into breadth."[38] Berkeley (whom Merleau-Ponty, like Gibson, takes as a prime target) had declared depth to be nothing other than distance as measured in "paces or miles."[39] But primordial depth cannot be so measured — in paces, miles, or any other unit of mensuration. Instead of being the kind of thing that yields to measurement, it is like an aura or atmosphere that resists precise specification. Yet it is not simply vaporous; it has sufficient structure to underlie and make possible objectified depth itself. This structure allows it to be "a pre-objective standard of distances and sizes."[40] In this capacity, primordial depth reminds us more of Platonic *chōra* — that matrix of cosmic spatiality — than of *bathos*, which is a characteristic of already formed material things. Like *chōra*, primordial depth "does not yet operate between [determinate] objects."[41] Neither a substance nor a relation, it is what makes both spatial substances and relations in space possible; it is "the means whereby the positing of things becomes possible."[42] The forced choice between a Newtonian and a Leibnizian model of space — a choice Kant believed he had to make — is in fact a choice between two modes of objectified space, one substantial ("absolute space" in Newton's term) and the other relational ("the order of co-existence" in Leibniz's lingo). Subtending both is primordial depth, which precedes all modes of objective space, including the Euclidean mode. Summing up this line of thought, Merleau-Ponty writes,

> This being simultaneously present in experiences which are never-theless mutually exclusive, this implication of one in the other, this contraction into one perceptual act of a whole perceptual process, constitutes the originality of [primordial] depth. It is the dimension in which things or elements of things envelope each other, whereas breadth and height are the dimensions in which they are juxtaposed.[43]

In this passage from the *Phenomenology of Perception* Merleau-Ponty names the main character of the positive structure of depth: *envelopment*. And he hints at its modalities: simultaneous presence (in effect a rewriting of "the order of co-existence"), mutual implication (literally, a 'folding into'), and contraction (suggesting the economy of depth instead of its infinite extent). Where juxtaposition (seemingly a re-expression of "the order of succession") acts to exclude — to set objects at separate points on a planiform grid of homogeneous space, an action of which interposition is a paradigm case — envelopment acts to conjoin. It is, we might say, the actively structuring factor of depth taken as a dense and encompassing medium, as "a thickness...devoid of any thing."

In this early treatment of depth — the most complete treatment he gives of the subject anywhere — Merleau-Ponty makes an auspicious start. He begins to get a grip on what had remained "crude extensity" for James, and he anticipates Gibson in a number of important respects. Were we to compare the three thinkers in detail, we would find explicit agreement on the following crucial points, all of which contest a Berkeleyian-Cartesian model of depth: the primacy (though not the exclusivity) of the visual world in depth experience, along with the claim that depth is itself visible; the centrality of the body in this same experience; the circumambient status of depth and its direct perceivability; a rejection of depth as mere distance or interval; a scathing critique of traditional depth cues (and for many of the same reasons); and a resolute renunciation of depth as a barren third dimension.[44] We would also find a common groping toward a positive paradigm of depth perception. Merleau-Ponty's idea of envelopment is strikingly similar to Gibson's notion of the layout of surfaces, especially insofar as this layout involves "an array of adjoining surfaces."[45]

At the same time, however, we must recognize that Merleau-Ponty shares with Gibson two critical shortcomings. First, we are left wondering as to what is the exact character of the relationship between primordial and objective depth (in Gibson's language, between layout and dimension). It is certainly meritorious to distinguish the two levels of depth — this is just what previous accounts had failed to do — but it is quite another thing to bring them back into concert with each other: to show their mode of "interinvolvement" (in a favorite word of Merleau-Ponty's). Neither Gibson nor Merleau-Ponty undertakes this reparative work, or even hints at how it could be done. Should we think of the relationship between the two forms of depth as a mere matter of determination or specification, whereby "depth" qua third dimension is a miniaturized or particularized version of "Depth" as primordial? But then there would be only one kind of depth after all. Or should we say that it is not a matter of determination at all — in which case we are left with two different *kinds* of depth whose relation to each other is left unclarified? Here we encounter a difficulty that is the converse of that which we meet in Descartes, Berkeley, and Hegel — for all of whom depth is an utterly indifferent dimension, with no determination of its own. For Merleau-Ponty and Gibson, depth is so burning a consideration in its two basic modes (each of which is definite in its different way) that they fail to provide an explanation of the continuity, the ongoing coherence, of our ordinary spatial experience, in which we do not customarily distinguish between primordial and objective levels.

A second shortcoming concerns the relationship between depth and other basic parameters of spatial experience. How, for example, is depth related to "movement" and especially to "level," both of which Merleau-Ponty explicitly discusses in the same chapter on "Space" in which depth figures? At one point in this chapter Merleau-Ponty declares primordial depth to be a function of "a level of distances and sizes."[46] Does this mean that depth is subordinate to level, or merely that the two are continuous with each other? I find the same ambiguity in Gibson's conception of depth as the layout of surfaces. "Layout" suggests level, and in particular the horizontal level of things arranged on a plane that recedes from the perceiver; and Gibson himself underlines the role of "ground" in the determination of depth *qua* layout: layout signifies "the relations of surfaces to the ground and to one another, their arrangement."[47] As in the case of Merleau-Ponty, this begins to sound as if depth is resolvable into level — that is, as if depth is not primordial after all. But to give up the idea of the primordiality of depth is to accede to the very view that both authors so effectively and mordantly contest, namely, the view that it is determinate, and secondary, a matter of measurable dimensionality and thus a matter of indifference.

IV

What are we to do in this impasse? Is there a way of saving depth as an irrecusable feature of perceptual experience while not having to posit it either as merely dimensional or indeed even as "primordial"? The notion of primordiality, after all, engages us in a perceptual foundationalism, which is debatable on its own grounds; and it also implicates us in futile battles as to primacy (in asking whether "level" or "depth" was more fundamental, I was myself engaging in one such skirmish).

There is a way out of the impasse, and it consists in the insight
that *place grants depth*. It is place that provides the critical
parameters of depth. Place, plain old place, is depth-dealing — far
more so than the retinal image, the classical depth cues, or even the
layout of surfaces postulated so ingeniously by Gibson. Notice that
I am not saying merely that *places have depth*. This they surely do,
especially when depth is construed (as it is all too often construed)
as interval or distance. But beyond this fundamental fact about
places we need to recognize that places themselves furnish depth to
the entities and events which they serve to locate and circumscribe.

The situation can be put thus. If the preceding parts of this
essay have argued that depth matters in human experience — that it
is not a factor of indifference in the manner expressed so poignantly
in Hegel's *Philosophy of Nature* — the task is now to show that *place
matters to depth*. It must be shown that the link between depth and
place is profound, that these two "elements" (to use James's word,
which he reserved for the voluminous) of our ongoing perceptual
experience are, at the very least, codetermining, being coeval and
covalent. In addition, it must be indicated how place contributes
specific features to depth, helping depth to become, if not primordial, then indispensable to such experience.

That there is an intimate tie between depth and place is suggested by both Merleau-Ponty and Gibson. Merleau-Ponty asserts
that because of level (which we have seen to be closely, if ambiguously, related to depth) "there is a determining of up and down,
and *in general of place*, which precedes 'perception'.[48] This promising
idea is not further developed, however; and the exact role of place
in the *Phenomenology of Perception*, as well as in later writings of
Merleau-Ponty, is not taken up with the kind of sustained attention
devoted to the lived body, speech, or the phenomenal field (a
notion itself permeated with place properties). Similarly, in Gibson's case the importance of place for depth is suspected but not
pursued. He avers that the layout of surfaces which is so determinative of depth includes "both places and objects, together with
other features."[49] This is certainly to give place more prominence
than it receives in Berkeley, who reduced place to the mere *position*
of objects at a definite distance.[50] But in the end (and with the
exception of certain claims on which I shall draw in a moment),

Gibson envisages place as only one of a list of eight environmental factors that bear on depth, and it is not even included in the "short list" of the four most critical such factors.[51]

Despite Gibson's ambivalent treatment of place, we may take from this treatment one highly suggestive clue. "Places," he writes, "are ecological layouts."[52] An ecological layout contrasts with a mere position, which is always conceived on the basis of the location of a point in homogeneously constituted and isotropically oriented space. Where a position has the intrinsic isolatedness of any point — of a position, as of a point, we can say that it is located "just here" — a place as an ecological layout cannot be pinpointed to the same degree. Its spatiality need be neither homogeneous nor isotropic, and it often exhibits indeterminateness of location. Hence the paradigm of place as ecologically conceived is a habitat or a region — ultimately, an eco- or bioregion. Gibson sets forth this interpretation of place in a key passage in *The Ecological Approach to Visual Perception*:

> A *place* is a location in the environment as contrasted with a point in space,[it is] a more or less extended surface, or layout. Whereas a point must be located with reference to a co-ordinate system, a place can be located by its inclusion in a larger place (for example, the fireplace in the cabin by the bend of the river in the Great Plains). Places can be named, but they need not have sharp boundaries. The habitat of an animal is made up of places.[53]

Another way of putting the contrast is to say that whereas a mere position in space has a definite terminus — whether a *terminus ab quo* or a *terminus ad quem* — a place as an ecological layout is not terminal in any such sense. Not only "need [it] not have sharp boundaries," but we may even say that a place *cannot* have precisely delineated boundaries. (That spatial extent which has such boundaries, or more exactly *limits*, I prefer to call a *site*.)

The most convincing instances of such indeterminate boundaries of place are also of major import for the issue of depth. I refer to the outer visual horizon on the one hand and to one's self-apprehended body on the other. Gibson himself claims that these very factors "anchor" our perception of distance (which he does not here distinguish from depth):

[Distance] is projected as a gradient of the decreasing optical size and increasing optical density of the features of the ground. ... But this gradient of forms getting smaller and finer and more closely packed together has a limit at the horizon of the earth where, according to the laws of natural perspective, all visual solid angles shrink to zero. The gradient is also anchored at another limit, by the forms projected from the nose, body, and limbs. The nose projects at the maximum of nearness just as the horizon projects at the maximum of farness.[54]

The horizon, as the appropriate outermost circumambient edge of any given place, *gives depth* — in Gibsonian nomenclature, it "affords" depth. Here then is a quite concrete manner in which place (or, more exactly, an aspect of place) provides depth: as we experience each time we gaze at the horizon of a landscape. Although we do speak of a "horizon line," we rarely perceive the actual horizon of a given landscape as a simple fixed line (it is on such a line that positions, not places, can be located). Instead, we are aware of the horizon as something akin to an indeterminate region in which definite shapes and colors tend to fade out — and where the texture of the landscape (its "optical density") becomes increasingly fine-grained. In this respect, the horizon is a special case of what I would prefer to call *zonal place*. It is special just inasmuch as in it and through it — or, more precisely, *out of it* — we grasp recession in depth. Thanks to the immanent perceptual action of "horizoning," we see various things (material objects, events, people) existing in depth, that is to say, *occupying various places* in relation to the ultimate outer boundary region which we term "the horizon."

V

Our own lived body is coperceived along with the horizon — *mitgemeint*, "cointended," as Husserl might say — as another zonal place that serves as a boundary of the visual world at any given moment. It, too, is indeterminate in its exact outline. It is felt and perceived as an indefinite, encompassing presence that, just as much as the visual horizon, resists reduction to a linear representation: it is glimpsed, literally 'out of the corner of our eye,' as a silent and steady mass constantly subtending our perceptual activity, whether we are stationary or moving. Of the body as the nearest boundary, we would say the same thing as Heidegger said of boundary in general: here "something begins its presencing."[55] And the presencing once more has to do with depth, albeit differently this time. Now depth is determined by a backward reference of perceived things to ourselves as perceivers: these things, "the stars of our life" in Merleau-Ponty's phrase,[56] are situated (wherever they may be in the visual field) in relation to the perceiving body whose vague contours we coperceive as a margin of the immediate perceptual environment. Although the body thus coperceived does not contain perceived things in the strict manner of an Aristotelian *topos* — it is less a container than a shadowy outline, as we notice in the case of our own nose, to which Gibson draws our attention — it is no less a *place for* these things. And it is a place that provides depth to them: a depth-in-relation-to-body that complements the depth-out-from-the-horizon. The two forms of depth go together hand in hand — or more exactly, eye to eye, as the eyes of the perceiver sweep out a visual swath through the perceptual field bounded in the end only by the horizon and by the body.[57]

Between body and horizon we perceive many things, all of them in depth and in place — and *in one because in the other*. James Mill enumerates some of these "things": "When I lift my eyes from the paper on which I am writing, I see from my window trees and meadows, and horses and oxen, and distant hills. I see each of its proper size, of its proper form, and at its proper distance; and these particulars appear as immediate informations of the eye as the colors which I see by means of it."[58] "Trees and meadows, and horses and oxen" — these are the kinds of things that populate our visual field, appearing at their "proper distance." The same is true of such existentially engaging items as other people — and even of such ethereal entities as clouds.[59]

Whatever its degree or type of materiality, each of the things just mentioned, from clouds to oxen, presents itself to us as possessing its own characteristic depth. This is so thanks to the fact that each such entity at once: (1) constitutes a place, and (2) belongs in its own place-being to a more inclusive local place. This dual character confronts us everywhere within the perceptual world.

1. On the one hand, anything that we can discriminate at all — by any of the senses, not just by sight alone — has its own place of occupancy. It is this kind of place (a "seat," we might also call it; *hedra* in Plato's word) that has been so frequently confused with "position," which is the geometrically determined, pointillistically conceived residuum (or the indicative representation) of place of occupancy.[60] Being mere points in space, positions have no depth; they are constituents of that flat optical array which Gibson and Merleau-Ponty alike take such pains to question. But a place of occupancy — which is to say, the 'spot' that is taken up by a particular entity or event — has its own depth: it is already "three-dimensional": it has volume. Indeed, it is just this special (and quite limited) kind of depth that so easily submits to a reduction to "the pseudofact of the third dimension." Which is to say, to the kind of indifferent dimension that is in principle interchangeable with height or breadth. But its integrity is not compromised in the end by any such reduction, as we witness each time we "take the measure" of any given object in our environment. Measure-taking is not mensuration, to which depth in the Cartesian acceptation is rigorously submitted. Where *"dimension* means for Descartes "a mode or aspect in respect of which some subject is considered to be measurable,"[61] the dimension inherent in a place of occupancy is less to be measured than itself *measuring*; it is a leading instance of what Merleau-Ponty designates as a *"measurant."*[62] When we take the measure of an object, we find its measuring power, its capacity for being or becoming the measure of depth, beginning with its own perceived depth of place. This depth of occupancy is thus depth *qua* voluminous — even if it is not literally volumetric.

2. On the other hand, there is a second sense of depth, that of the inclusion of the place of occupancy in a more capacious place. Let us call this second sense of place *region*.[63] In this case the depth accrues not to the object or event *per se* — to its intrinsic voluminosity — but to the insertion of the object or event into a more encompassing space. This more encompassing space is itself a place; or more exactly, it is a region *for* various places of occupancy that fit within it thanks to their respective voluminosities. The fitting itself need not be neat or tight: once more, we are not confined to an Aristotelian containership model of place. In fact, it is usually quite

loose-ended, since a region is itself constituted by indeterminate, bleeding boundaries. Think, for example, of a forest regarded as a bioregion. Within its own somewhat indefinite borders (just where does a forest begin or end?), it harbors a plurality of "ecological layouts" — glades, clearings, myriad microenvironments — each of which can be considered a place of occupancy and each of which also has less than fully precise boundaries of its own. Just as to be in an occupying place is to be given depth, to be included in any such bioregion is to gain new depth: *depth in depth*, the depth of volume inscribed in the depth of region. The double implacement afforded by a regional location brings with it depth to the second power.

VI

Depth and place, then, are not only connected. They are indissociable. These two vital parameters of our experience — and not just of perceptual experience but of memory, thought, and even language — are mutually coinherent and coconstitutive. To be in place is to be in depth (and often, as we have just seen, in more than one kind of depth) and to experience depth is to be presented with places (and just as often by several kinds of place). Gibson and Merleau-Ponty gesture in this direction with their notions of the layout of surfaces and envelopment, their own preferred models of depth, respectively. Neither model is fully successful, however, in explaining the power and ubiquity of depth within human experience. In particular, both layout and envelopment focus too exclusively on the factor of overlap — *occlusion* in Gibson's term — and in this respect represent a rewriting of the classical variable of interposition. This rewriting is important, but it cannot offer us a sufficient account of depth in all of its complexity.[64] Gibson himself is therefore led to add the variables of increasing optical density and of differential reflectance. And he is led, in his last book, to speculate as to the role of a specifically ecological layout in the determination of depth. I have attempted, in the last section, to carry forward what remains merely adumbrated in Gibson — even though I have come to my own point of view by a distinctly separate route.[65]

But I do not want to leave the last word to Gibson, much less reserve it for myself. It turns out that Merleau-Ponty in his last published essay, "Eye and Mind," returns suddenly to the issue of depth as part of his meditation on painting. In one remarkable passage, he manages to pick up just where he had left off fifteen years before in the *Phenomenology of Perception*:

> Depth cannot be the unmysterious interval between nearby and distant trees which I would see from an airplane. Nor can it be the reciprocal concealment of things which a perspectival drawing represents for me. Both these approaches to depth are very explicit and do not raise any question whatsoever, The riddle of depth lies in the connection between these two views, in what is between them: the fact that *it is precisely because things disappear behind each other that I see them each in its place, [and] the fact that it is precisely because each is in its place that they are rivals for my gaze*. The riddle of depth lies in the fact that the externality of things is known through their reciprocal concealment, and their mutual dependence through their autonomy.[66]

Merleau-Ponty here deftly reinscribes his earlier notion of envelopment (itself a response to the classical idea of overlap, here designated as "the reciprocal concealment of things") in an expanded context provided by *place* — of all things! Moreover, he envisages the mutual relationship between depth and place by the cryptic but suggestive "riddle" contained in the dual fact that because of the disappearance of one thing behind another we grasp each thing securely in its place and that each thing's being in place makes it a competitor for my vision. The depth that had been conceived exclusively in terms of interposition is shown to depend not on occlusion as such but on the implacement that occlusion itself paradoxically occasions. And place in turn is given perceptual reinforcement equally paradoxically by the factor of disappearance — "eclipse" as it could also be called — whereby things come to occlude each other from full view.

Merleau-Ponty also adds one further remark that merits citing:

> We cannot say of depth in this sense that it is a 'third dimension'. To begin with, if it were any dimension at all it would be the first: there are forms and definite planes only if the distance of their different parts from me is stipulated. But a first dimension which contains all the others is not a dimension, at least not in the ordinary sense of a

certain relationship in terms of which one measures [this is Descartes' sense of dimension]. Depth in the sense in which we are now discussing it is more our experiencing of *the reversibility of dimensions, of an overall 'locality' in which everything exists at once and from which height and width and distance are abstractions, of a voluminousness which we express in a single word by saying that a thing is 'there'.*[67]

By invoking the "reversibility of dimensions," Merleau-Ponty does not wish to reinstate the Cartesian-Hegelian notion of the indifferent interchangeability of dimensions.[68] Instead, as we know from his treatment of the reversibility of the flesh in *The Visible and the Invisible*, such reversibility is distinctly directional and even asymmetrical (when my right hand touches my left hand that touches a physical object, I cannot maintain symmetry of sensation throughout).[69] It is also powerfully ontogenetic — which helps to explain why depth as a reversibility of dimensions is now claimed to be the first dimension. As first, depth gains a new sense of primordiality, that of a global "locality" in which all things exist together and in relation to which the three determinate dimensions of height, width, and distance (i.e., depth in its most restricted guise) are mere abstractions. If such a locality is a dimensional ground, it is not a foundation in any classical-metaphysical respect. As itself a place (and thus as ultimately contingent despite its massiveness), it does not justify or legitimate, nor can anything be deduced from it. Rather, things are situated in it, not as points or positions but as themselves located in those discrete places that I have called "places of occupancy." The grouping of such places into regions and eventually into a global (but not necessarily a total) collection constitutes depth on the new — or more exactly, the renewed — conception that Merleau-Ponty here sets forth so eloquently.

But I am not sure we should leave the last word to Merleau-Ponty either. His own last word on the topic of depth explicitly mentions "voluminousness": "a voluminousness which we express in a single word by saying that a thing is 'there.'" A strange and telling return to our starting point in William James occurs just here. There is something about volume that, despite its manifest crudeness and vagueness, foreshadows the detailed discussions of depth into which we have been drawn. Or rather, it is the very crudeness and vagueness that offers the key — as Merleau-Ponty himself indicates in his linking of the voluminous with that which is overtly "there." To be *there* — before us, back of us, around us — is to be in depth. It is to be in the "element" of depth (in James's term),[70] even if it is not yet to be fully engaged in its detailed structure. Depth is something we first of all *feel* (and "feeling" is precisely how we connect with "crude extensity" according to James). Lived depth is felt as voluminous, and we experience depth this way before we sense its finer structuration as occlusion or envelopment or its more encompassing presence in entire regions. The voluminous as felt signifies more than mere "volume" (itself a concomitant of three-dimensional models of space) and more even than place of occupancy (in which it plays a valid but delimited role). I would suggest that it is the "primordial depth" which Merleau-Ponty otherwise sought in vain.[71]

We may conclude that "the element of voluminousness" to which James first pointed is the beginning of the matter of depth, even if it is not the end of the matter: an end to be found in place. For in the end it is place that affords depth. It does so to begin with as place of occupancy — place as bound to the specific voluminosities of the things that occupy it — and then as place *qua* region (finally, as "world," construed as a whole of regions). Along the way of this topogenesis, place also makes possible the classical depth cues of interposition, perspective, and decreasing size. Where else, how else, than *in place* can we experience things as occluding each other, as seen from certain points of view (in particular, from *my* point of view as provided by the body), and as diminishing in apparent size in the distance (a distance that is itself a function of the depth which place effects)? Everywhere we turn, then, we turn in the depth and in the voluminousness granted by places — those places in which we live and move and know our being-in-the-world as creatures of continuing implacement.

NOTES

1. William James, *The Principles of Psychology* (New York: Dover, 1950), II, 134. The chapter on "The Perception of Space" is itself a revised version of an essay on the same topic which appeared in *Mind* in 1887.

2. Ibid.

3. Ibid.

4. Ibid., p. 213. His italics. At ibid., p. 135, he observes that "skin and retina are...the organs in which the space-element plays the most active part." The treatment of Berkeley occurs at ibid., pp. 211–15.

5. Ibid., p. 136.

6. Ibid., p. 212; my italics.

7. Ibid., pp. 212–13.

8. Ibid., p. 213. James cites these examples: "if we plunge our head into a wash-basin, the felt nearness of the bottom makes us feel the lateral expanse to be small. If, on the contrary, we are on a mountain-top, the distance of the horizon carries with it in our judgment a proportionate height and length in the mountain-chains that bound it to our view" (ibid., pp. 213–14).

9. Sensations of depth are designated at ibid., p. 215; in italics in text. Note that the voluminous itself is said to be an "element" in the various bodily sensations (ibid., p. 134). On the constancy hypothesis (this is Gurwitsch's later term for what James is here discussing), cf. ibid., pp. 211–12: "If we study the facts closely we soon find no such constant connection between either judgment and retinal modification, or judgment and muscular modification, to exist."

10. Cited from Wilhelm Helmholtz's *Physiological Optics* by James at ibid., p. 218.

11. I draw here upon James' own definition of sensation: "the mental affection that follows most immediately upon the stimulation of the sense-tract" (ibid., p. 216). James emphasizes that sensation is "directly physical" and involves "no psychic links, no acts of memory, interference, or association" (ibid.). It is striking that James admits, shortly after positing a sensation of depth, that the full experience of space (including presumably its depth dimension) calls for "association" or "suggestion" — and thus that it requires something more than sensation, by his own definition, can deliver.

12. Ibid., pp. 157–58 and 167 ff. For James, such a sign is "a quality of feeling" (p. 158) — a puzzling assertion at best.

13. J. J. Gibson, *The Senses Considered as Perceptual Systems* (Boston: Houghton Mifflin, 1966), p. 71.

14. For these examples, see ibid., p. 71 and p. 111, respectively. On the general distinction between sensation and perception, see ibid., p. 58. Gibson traces the distinction itself to Thomas Reid at ibid., p. 1 (but for James's much more skeptical treatment of Reid, see *Principles of Psychology*, II, 218). I should make it clear that I find the distinction in question to be untenable; but I shall respect it in the following discussion *faute de mieux* and in deference to the fact that both Gibson and James rely on it.

15. See *The Principles of Psychology*, II, 217, where such traditional cues as convergence, accommodation, parallax, etc. are said to have "*something to do* with the perception of 'far' and of 'near'" (his italics) but to be so easily reversible as to be unreliable guides.

16. See the account of Gibson's experiment in R. L. Gregory, *Eye and Brain: The Psychology of Seeing* (New York: World University Library, 1976), pp. 182–83.

17. On the three gradients in question, see J. J. Gibson, *The Perception of the Visual World* (Cambridge, Mass: Houghton-Mifflin, 1950), pp. 137–44. For Gibson's later restatement, see *The Ecological Approach to Visual Perception* (Ithaca, N.Y.: Cornell University Press, 1976), p. 117; on the same page, Gibson cites the role of the perceiver's own body.

18. Gibson, *Ecological Approach*, p. 286. His italics.

19. M. Merleau-Ponty, *Phenomenology of Perception*, trans. Colin Smith (New York: Humanities Press, 1962), p. 266.

20. Cf. Leonardo's drawings as reproduced in Gregory, *Eye and Brain*, p. 168.

21. Kathryn Spoehr and Stephen Lehmkuhle, *Visual Information Processing* (San Francisco: Freeman, 1982), p. 87; my italics.

22. Ibid.

23. Gibson, *The Perception of the Visual World*, p. 142.

24. Ibid., p. 9.

25. On perception as an "immediate process" requiring no "mental construction," see Gibson, ibid., pp. 11, 69, 116. Here Gibson and James part company, because James, as we have seen, insists on importing the mentalistic factors of association and suggestion into the full-fledged grasping of depth.

26. René Descartes, *Rules for the Direction of the Mind*, in *The*

Philosophical Writings of Descartes, eds. J. Cottingham, R. Stoothoff, & D. Murdoch (Cambridge: Cambridge University Press, 1985), II, 63. Gibson remarks that "the notion of space of three dimensions with three axes for Cartesian coordinates was a great convenience for mathematics...but an abstraction that had very little to do with actual perception" (*The Ecological Approach to Visual Perception*, p. 148).

27. G. W. F. Hegel, *Philosophy of Nature*, sections 255–56 in M. J. Petrey's translation, *Hegel's Philosophy of Nature* (London: Allen & Unwin, 1970), I, pp. 255–56. Much of this passage is in italics in the original.

28. Gibson, *Ecological Approach*, p. 148. Gibson italicizes *depth*.

29. Hegel, *Philosophy of Nature*, p. 226. Another form of indifference is also to be noted: if "dimension" means (in Descartes' definition) "simply a mode or aspect in respect of which some subject is considered to be measurable" (*Rules for the Direction of the Mind* p. 62), then there can be in principle an indefinite plurality of dimensions, not just three.

30. See E. J. Gibson and R. D. Walk, "The Visual Cliff," *Scientific American* 202 (1960), pp. d64–71. For J. J. Gibson's discussion of this celebrated experiment — in which infants will refuse to climb onto a perfectly safe piece of plate glass through which a view into a depth of several feet is showing — see *Ecological Approach*, pp. 156–58.

31. *Hegel's Philosophy of Nature*, p. 225.

32. *Ecological Approach*, p. 148.

33. Ibid., p. 152; my italics. Cf. also ibid., p. 148: "there is no special kind of perception called depth perception"; and p. 37: "the perception of layout takes the place of the perception of depth or space in traditional terminology."

34. A. N. Whitehead, *Process and Reality*, ed. D. R. Griffin and D. W. Sherburne (New York: Free Press, 1978), p. 114.

35. *Phenomenology of Perception*, p. 267. By *acosmic subject* Merleau-Ponty is presumably thinking of the Kantian epistemological subject, who constructs depth as a dimension of space.

36. Ibid.

37. Ibid., p. 266.

38. Ibid.

39. *Essay Toward a New Theory of Vision* (1709) in *The Works of George*

Berkeley, ed. A. A. Luce and T. E. Jessop (London: Nelson, 1948), I. p. 171. On the same page Berkeley says that depth as distance "being a line directed end-wise to the eye, it projects only one point in the fund of the eye, which point remains invariably the same, whether the distance be longer or shorter." Depth is thus rendered literally invisible, and only by moving through it — pacing it off and feeling the paces kinaesthetically and tactually — can one determine its extent. Berkeley is drawing on Molyneux in this classical formulation of objectified depth; and he is doing so in such a way as to set up the problem — or rather, as Gibson would have it, the pseudo-problem — of deriving a third dimension (depth or "distance") from two dimensions.

40. *Phenomenology of Perception*, p. 267.

41. Ibid., p. 266: "There is, then, a depth which does not yet operate between objects [and] which, *a fortiori*, does not yet assess the distance between them."

42. Ibid., p. 243.

43. Ibid., pp. 264–65.

44. On the primacy of the visual world, see *Phenomenology of Perception*, p. 262, and *Ecological Approach*, p. 147; about the visibility of depth, *Phenomenology of Perception*, p. 266, and *Ecological Approach*, p. 117; on the role of the body in depth perception, *Phenomenology of Perception*, p. 283, and *Senses as Perceptual Systems*, p. 72; concerning the circumambience of depth, Merleau-Ponty, *The Visible and the Invisible*, trans. A. Lingis (Evanston: Northwestern University Press, 1968), p. 220, and *Ecological Approach*, p. 147; on the direct perceivability of depth, *Phenomenology of Perception*, p. 267 and, in Gibson, the repeated use of the phrase "direct perception" (e.g., in *Ecological Approach*, p. 147); on the critique of depth as distance or interval, *Phenomenology of Perception*, pp. 255–56, and *Ecological Approach*, p. 148; on depth cues, *Phenomenology of Perception*, pp. 256–57, 265, and *Ecological Approach*, pp. 148–49; and concerning the third dimension, "Eye and Mind," p. 180, and *The Perception of the Visual World*, p. 9, *Ecological Approach*, pp. 148, 286. This is not to mention a convergent critique of Berkeley, e.g., at *Phenomenology of Perception*, pp. 254–55 and *Ecological Approach*, p. 117.

45. *The Perception of the Visual World*, p. 6. Layout also involves what Gibson calls technically the "occlusion" of the edges of one surface by those of another. But occlusion in turn entails a complementary inclusion

not unlike envelopment. (On occlusion, see *Ecological Approach*, pp. 286 and 308.)

46. *Phenomenology of Perception*, p. 266.

47. *Ecological Approach*, p. 148.

48. *Phenomenology of Perception*, p. 285; my italics.

49. *Ecological Approach*, p. 148.

50. One of the rare references to place in Berkeley's writings occurs in his *Essay Toward a New Theory of Vision*, p. 176: "the mind makes use of the greater or lesser confusedness of the [visual] appearance, thereby to determine the apparent place of an object." The phrase *apparent place* is revealing: it shows that Berkeley has in mind only place in its phenomenality and not in its actuality. Phenomenal place is positioned but not situated — thus is appropriate to geometric locus but not to experiential placement.

51. See *Ecological Approach*, p. 36, where the factors in question are considered to be substances, surfaces and their layout, enclosures, objects, places, events, and other animals. The reduced list of four is given as surfaces, layouts, objects, and events; where, we may ask, has place gone?

52. Ibid., p. 200.

53. Ibid., p. 34; his italics.

54. Ibid., p. 117; Gibson italicizes *gradient*.

55. "A boundary (*Grenze*) is not that at which something stops but, as the Greeks recognized, the boundary is that from which something *begins its presencing*" ("Building Dwelling Thinking" in *Poetry Language Thought*, trans. A. Hofstadter [New York: Harper, 1971], p. 154; his italics).

56. Merleau-Ponty, *The Visible and the Invisible*, p. 220.

57. For Gibson's not altogether successful effort to sketch the form of the boundary furnished by the perceiver's own body, see Figures 7.1 and 7.2 in *Ecological Approach*, pp. 113, 118–19. On the nose in particular, see ibid., p. 104. I should add that the kind of boundary formed by my own body is not the same kind of boundary as that provided by the visual horizon. Pending a more complete treatment of the two kinds of boundary — or *peras* in the Greek sense — all that we can say now is that they realize a close cooperation despite their differences.

58. James Mill, *Analysis of the Phenomena of the Human Mind* (1829); cited by Gibson at ibid., p. 60.

59. The latter are especially revealing in the circumstance, for they emerge in depth and yet at no determinate distance. On Gibson's theory, however, they are highly problematic beings, given that their surfaces are so ephemeral and immaterial. He observes the following about clouds: "in the upper hemisphere of the ambient array, cloud surfaces dissipate, and we say they vanish. The optical texture is supplanted by the absence of texture. Cloud surfaces also form in the sky, and we say that they have materialized." But here we must ask, even when clouds do materialize, do they present edges that are determinate enough to convey depth? Still, as every meteorologist knows, despite this blurredness of boundaries, clouds (and, on a larger scale, entire weather masses) are fully forceful entities, with powers and properties of their own. They certainly possess directionality and depth, even we cannot easily determine their exact shape or precise distance from our point of observation. Indeed, depth is quite compatible with a radical indeterminateness of distance — a point that Erwin Straus has developed in detail. (See E. Straus, *The Primary World of Senses*, trans. J. Needleman [New York: Free Press, 1963], pp. 164–65, 379–85.

60. On positions versus places, see *Phenomenology of Perception*, pp. 100, 144–46, 244; and *The Visible and the Invisible*, p. 222: "locality not by inherence in a spatio-temporal point — but locality by elastic tie."

61. Descartes, *Direction of the Mind*, p. 62. As Descartes points out himself in ibid., in this definition of *dimension*, weight is as much a dimension of a physical thing as are height, length, and width (i.e., breadth).

62. *The Visible and the Invisible*, p. 103. A "measurant" in Merleau-Ponty's conception is the equivalent of "dimension" in his expanded sense of the term.

63. Compare Gibson's usage of *region*: "the habitat of a given animal contains places. A place is not an object with definite boundaries but a region" (*Ecological Approach*, p. 136).

64. Furthermore, it overlooks the way in which place of occupancy is responsible for occlusion because of the limited voluminosity it provides. Overlapping of volumes occurs even when one volume is considerably more capacious than another. A mere desk, with its limited place of occupancy, overlaps the room in which it is situated, and in this way *its* place helps to determine our sense of the room's depth.

65. This route is traced out in my forthcoming book, *Getting back into Place* (Bloomington: Indiana University Press, 1991).

66. "Eye and Mind," in Richard McCleary's new translation (manuscript version), p. 180 in C. Dallery's earlier translation in Merleau-Ponty, *The Primacy of Perception*, ed. J. Edie (Evanston, Ill.: Northwestern University Press, 1964); my italics.

67. McCleary's translation; p. 180 in *The Primacy of Perception*; my italics, except for the first phrase.

68. For James's version of this interchangeability, see *Principles of Psychology*, II, pp. 213, 215–16.

69. On this aspect of reversibility, see *The Visible and the Invisible*, pp. 9, 147–48. It is already remarked upon in *Phenomenology of Perception*, p. 93.

70. See *The Principles of Psychology*, II, pp. 134–35. For Merleau-Ponty's use of *element* in a suggestively similar way, see *The Visible and the Invisible*, p. 139, where "flesh" is said to be an element that is located.

71. It will be noticed that Merleau-Ponty says that painting allows use to "possess the voluminosity of the world," in "Eye and Mind" (p. 166, Dallery translation). Merleau-Ponty's only specific discussion of the voluminous in the *Phenomenology of Perception* refuses to recognize it as primordial; it is only an aspect of pathologically perceived space that occurs as mediated by color; cf. *Phenomenology of Perception*, p. 266.

2

Reversible Subjectivity:
The Problem of Transcendence and Language

Duane H. Davis

How is it that I am able to make myself understood by others and that they are intelligible for me? There is a sense in which speech, written discourse, and gesture all permit some sort of transcendence whereby I can be said to 'get outside of myself.' If this is so, an examination of language ought to reveal a great deal about this transcendence, and thereby make room for a discussion of such ethical implications of transcendence as might be disclosed within this examination.

But to attempt to give such an account of discourse is to make the epistemological error of beginning with a privileged notion of subjectivity, we are told. The proponents of more fashionable accounts are quick to demand that any felicitous account of discourse will include a notion of subjectivity that is displaced from its epistemological throne. Unfortunately, in many of these accounts subjectivity is not merely displaced, but misplaced altogether.[1] There is speech, writing, and gesture, but to understand these texts we need not posit the nimiety of subjectivity 'behind' them. If any talk of subjectivity need be tolerated at all, it is at most as a site where language is, we are told, and nothing more. The problem of transcendence is thus obviated with respect to language.

One unhappy consequence of such a solution is that any meaningful notion of responsibility becomes jejune to philosophical inquiry. It ought to be expected that the dissolution of subjectivity often results in subjectivity which is dissolute. A propitious solution to this problem will be obtained only by taking into account the individual whose collaborative project is discourse, while nevertheless heeding the critique of radically privileged subjectivity.

The thesis of this paper is that such an account can best be given by appropriating Merleau-Ponty's rich notion of 'reversibility,' which he began to explore in his unfinished final work, *The Visible and the Invisible.* A notion of subjectivity that is reversible avoids the errors associated with an epistemological privilege while allowing the discussion of a focus of responsibility within the context of the transcendence of language. Transcendence is accomplished by reversible subjectivity through the eventfulness of language, and leads us to an enriched notion of responsibility.[2] Focusing on transcendence, perhaps the central theme in Merleau-Ponty's ontology,[3] allows for a very different understanding of language than has been provided heretofore.

* * * * *

The notion of reversibility is the very heart of Merleau-Ponty's "endo-ontology."[4] He saw this as an advance over the results of his earlier interrogations of embodied subjectivity, since heretofore he had maintained a philosophy based on consciousness. This perspective had to be abandoned in favor of an ontological interrogation conducted from within the very texture of the life-world. Reversibility is "a lateral, pre-analytic participation" of embodied subjectivity within its world.[5] Because reversibility is an ontological notion, it describes a reciprocity of Being and accounts for transcendence in the following exemplary relationships.

First, let us witness tactile reversibility, the relation of the thing touched and the touching thing. Merleau-Ponty describes their interrelation of one to the other as the obverse and the reverse. One is the relief of the other. Reversibility is that kinship, that latency of Being which tactile reversibility shares with its counterpart and which allows palpation to occur. It is precisely by virtue of the nature of my body as something touchable that I may touch another. We must share participation in a real tactile world where such stimulation may occur. "The thickness of the body, far from rivaling that of the world, is on the contrary the sole means I have to go into the heart of things, by making myself a world and by making them flesh."[6] Surely this caress is neither mine nor my partner's alone; it is shared. To use one of Merleau-Ponty's favorite examples, if my own two hands touch, my left hand and my right hand are not "little subjectivities" that objectify one another upon contact. Rather, they are of a "prereflective and preobjective unity of my body."[7] So, just as a synergy exists within my own unitary body, it may be said to exist between my hand and my partner so long as one understands the caress as the return of the tactile to itself, as a torsion, as a turning back of the flesh upon itself. Just as the contact was shared between my two hands, likewise the unitary caress is shared with my partner. But although we are fundamentally together, we are not identical. Reversibility is never complete, but always latent.[8] The tactile experience we share is as much evidence of our lack of identity as of our lack of difference. It is a movement of *divergence*, a novel kind of transcendence in an interstitial play of reversibility.

> If one wants metaphors, it would be better to say that the body sensed and the body sentient are as the obverse and reverse, or again, as two segments of one sole circular course which goes above from left to right and below from right to left, but which is but one sole movement in its two phases. ... Where are we to put the limit between the body and the world, since the world is flesh?[9]

The ontological insight of reversibility allows us to think of our shared experience of the caress as a latent transcendence between me and my partner, so that to say I touch her is to be with her in a tactile world, to be touchable in that same tactile world. Reversibility allows for the discussion of the transcendence that determines that our bodies are predisposed to such caresses and yet allows for the recognition that they are just as predisposed to violations. For the same ontological guarantor of accessibility that allows my cupped hand to conform with the supple skin of my partner in our home allows for my vulnerability late at night in a place where I thought I was alone.

Likewise, there is reversibility and transcendence in the domain of visual perception. To be a seer is to share visibility, to be of the visible. "Through other eyes we are for ourselves fully visible."[10] Here, transcendence is the ontological venture of perception whereby I present things with my body "in order that they inscribe upon it and give me their resemblance."[11] For example, as light strikes something visible, the light that it reflects forms my image of the thing. This remainder of reflection — this inscription — is composed only of the light the object has not taken for itself. The light the object takes for itself is exactly the remainder of the spectrum, not what we see in its presentation. In this way, my embodied image is like a relief of the thing. It is quite literally the impression

the visible thing makes on me as a visible *peer*. The transcendence
of vision takes place thanks to the reversibility of the seer and the
seen that defines the visible texture of the life-world.

And there are reversible relationships in the domain of language. One such dimension is the reversible relationship between
thought and 'language.'[12] The explication of this reversibility
discloses an ideality of human existence and renders the responsibility shared between interlocutors intelligible in a new way, as we
shall see shortly.

In his essay, "Cezanne's Doubt,"[13] Merleau-Ponty shows that
representation is an inadequate way to account for creative artistic
expression, although it is clear from the context that he intended
his critique to extend to the domain of speech as well. "What [the
speaker or creative artist] expresses cannot...be the translation of
a clearly defined thought, since such clear thoughts are those which
have already been uttered by ourselves or by others. 'Conception'
cannot precede 'execution.'"[14]

As I have argued elsewhere,[15] a hierarchy between thought,
speech, and written language has been tacitly assented to by most
Western philosophers since the time of Aristotle. According to this
traditional account, speech is strictly a representation of thought,
whereas written language is similarly a representation of speech. I
think it is imperative to call into question this ancient hierarchy. A
richer notion of language is available if one understands all
language as an *event*, the coming to presence (and abiding) of the
absent, shared by interlocutors.

Ideas are known to us by virtue of our corporeality, not in spite
of it. There is an ideality to experience which is not alien to the
flesh, but which resonates there for its richness, its depth. Language,
be it spoken, written, or gestured, is of this same flesh. It is inspired
with ideas, with the ideal Word. Thus, the event of language is an
incarnation, the Word made flesh.[16] It is the inosculation of
'language,' a moment of language (i.e., the physical phenomenon of
a system of signifiers), 'within' ideas, and vice versa, that affords
intelligible meaning. Language is not merely a flawed copy, a
representation that pales before its standard idea. Nor is language
entire of itself, a standard somehow distanciated from humankind.
It is a human event, made animate by this divergence between the

ideal and the corporeal, the lack of coincidence within their inter-
penetration and intertwining. Reversibility defines the unique texture
of language by virtue of this endowment — its latency to become
ideal, and the idealization of what comes to pass. Language comes
to presence and abides in the world as a human creation, alongside
its creators and changes their understanding of the world. Insofar
as language is incarnate human meaning, it is all *about* us.

Another dimension of the reversibility of language pertains to
the interrelationship of interlocutors. In speech, writing, and
gesture my relationship with the other is an integral part of my
world. Ostensibly, I ascribe an 'objective' existence to myself
analogous to the way I experience the other, and I ascribe a 'subjective' existence to the other analogous to the way I experience
myself. But such simplistic analogical explanations are vestiges of
the epistemological philosophy of consciousness Merleau-Ponty has
abandoned.

One might be tempted to regard this dismissal of an analogical
understanding of the other as hasty and unfortunate in light of
Merleau-Ponty's important discussion of the 'transfer of the body-
schema' in "The Child's Relations with Others."[17] Perhaps the
preceding formulation does belie the complexity of the matter. For
now, let me simply state that throughout his philosophical works
Merleau-Ponty rejects any analogical account that fails to
acknowledge that *it is by virtue of, and not by the establishment of, my
similarity with the other that I can understand the other.*[18] Our similarity is
the dialectical encroachment of identity and difference, the transcendence of subject and object. In each case we are both, and yet
never quite either one.

Such sites are just the projected poles of an interstice.[19] In fact,
the expression I share with the other in language can best be seen
as "two sides of the same Being."[20] My experience *of* the other is
always an experience *with* the other for better or for worse. I am
not simply throwing out words from which the other may somehow
independently extract a meaning. As I speak, write, or gesture, I
do not choose my words or movements in isolation of the other, for
we are of the same flesh. The other leads me toward an utterance
and partially determines its propriety. My words are always
already interaction; my expression is never mine alone.

Keeping in mind both aspects of the reversibility of language just discussed — the reversibility of thought and 'language,' and the reversibility of interlocutors — allows us to see that the ideality of language is determined only by virtue of our mutual physical accessibility and vulnerability, and not in spite of it. It is telling that in everyday discourse there are a variety of ways we associate physiological metaphors with effectiveness or propriety. For example, we might say that the jilted lover was "hurt by those words"; that "it pained him to hear that"; and so on. Such metaphors trade on the shared corporeality of reversible subjectivity.

So far, I have stressed speech in this account of language. But likewise, there is reversibility in written discourse and gesture. Even though my interlocutor may not be "literally" copresent with me as I read or write, the other *is* present for me by virtue of the unique style of the text. It is in this sense that I recognize the other in the text. And it is in this sense that we say an author lives in his or her works. As the text of another opens before me, I am called to interpret it. And note that my calling does not issue from a universal abstraction, but from the individual flesh and blood author to me via the event of language that we share.

Merleau-Ponty provides an example that will illustrate that the same holds true for gesture.

> When I motion my friend to come nearer, my intention is not a thought prepared within me and I do not perceive the signal in my body. I beckon across the world, I beckon over there, where my friend is; the distance between us, his consent or refusal are immediately read in my gesture; there is not a perception followed by a movement, for both form a system which varies as a whole. If, for example, realizing that I am not going to be obeyed, I vary my gesture, we have here, not two distinct acts of consciousness. What happens is that I see my partner's unwillingness, and my gesture of impatience emerges from this situation without any intervening thought.[21]

There is a unitary movement of gesture shared by the "interlocutors" in the entreaty just described, and it is clear that the ideality of the gesture is nothing if not embodied.

Thus, the reversible nature of subjectivity in speech, written discourse, and gesture becomes manifest via the eventful nature of language. "Language is a life, is our life and the life of things."[22] Language, as flesh, folds back upon itself recognizable as the interstitial play of reversible subjectivity. The tension of implosion and explosion are transcendence. Just as reversibility was the key to understanding the transcendence of perceiving subjectivity, so it defines the texture of the unitary event of language I share with the other in our similarity. This transcendence of reversible subjectivity in language is the phenomenon which, when understood in this new context, will enhance our understanding of responsibility.

And just as reversible subjectivity does not fuse with the world in the transcendence of perception, it remains at least a virtual focus of experience in communicative praxis. This is because reversibility is never complete, as noted earlier. It is a divergence, a *non*identity of subjectivity as it opens upon the other. Like *transcendence*, 'subjectivity' is also the proper term here because it accounts for the endowed movement of reversibility without failing to acknowledge the propriety determined by the mutual appropriation endemic to this event. It allows for the shaping of world through language without failing to acknowledge that this shaping is itself an enworlded existential project. There is no problem of epistemological privilege insofar as the ontological import of reversibility is considered. Language is not mine alone, as something that is somehow magically hurled toward the other. Language is not a projectile, but a collaborative project of reversible subjectivity.

*   *   *   *   *

The realm of ethics is *prima facie* the realm of the tension between the universal and the particular. It just makes good sense to claim that any talk of ethical standards and responsibility would obtain in a world shared with others. After all, without all those *others* whose behavior requires recourse to such standards, what need would there be for ethics?

However, to claim that ethics, and in particular its implicit notion of responsibility, have some universal aspect is a far cry from grounding them in universality. The acknowledgement of alterity — the *need* for ethics — and of similarity — the *possibility* of ethics — does not in and of itself warrant the conclusion that ethics must privilege the universal as that by which the individual is understood to be responsible. Yet universality has been the pre-occupation of Kant, and of most post-Kantian Western thinkers, whose vocation has involved giving an account of a ground for morality.

For Kant, one is moral only if one acts in such a way that one can also will that the maxim of one's action should become a universal law.[23] Of course, according to Kant it is true that although this universal law is to be necessary *a priori*, it must also be self-imposed by the autonomous individual.[24] "The will is therefore not merely subject to the law, but is so subject that it must be considered as also *making the law* for itself and precisely on this account as first of all subject to the law (of which it can regard itself as the author)."[25] Particularity is also an aspect of morality for Kant insofar as my actions are mine, and even insofar as the maxim of my actions is determined "in accordance with the conditions of the subject (often his ignorance or again his inclinations)."[26] Never-theless, Kant makes it clear that he sets forth "to investigate the Idea and principles of a possible *pure* will, and not the activities and conditions of willing as such, which are drawn for the most part from psychology."[27] The supreme principle of morality, for Kant, must be a necessary command of reason, an imperative that is universal and categorical, not hypothetical. Kant rests the *force* of the categorical imperative entirely on the formal universality of the law. He states that "there remains nothing over to which the maxim has to conform except the universality of a law as such; and it is this conformity alone that the imperative properly asserts to be necessary."[28] Thus, the 'ought' must obtain without regard to the human situation in which it becomes an issue. My particular act is moral *only if* the maxim of my actions is universalizable.

In addition to being universal, Kant says the law must also be purely rational. For if one heeds the demand of irrational inclina-tions, one has failed to act out of duty, and thereby abnegated one's freedom.[29] The establishment of good will, the highest practical function of reason, is a kind of contentment "in fulfilling a purpose which in turn is determined by reason alone."[30]

This traditional approach to moral responsibility — inherited from Kant, regardless of whether or not it is but a synecdochical caricature of Kant's moral thought — results in the denigration of the particular in favor of the universal and an overemphasis of rationality at the expense of the corporeal.[31] According to this approach, our responsibility toward others is of a derivative status with respect to duty toward the universal, rational law. It simply seems counterintuitive to claim, as Kant does, that "all reverence for a person is properly only reverence for the law."[32] It is my opinion that by examining Merleau-Ponty's reversible subjectivity, and its transcendence in language, a new notion of responsibility can now be unfolded that overemphasizes neither universality nor rationality.

This ought not be taken as tantamount to advocating the commission of the inverse error of foregoing any talk of reason or universality in the moral domain. Indeed, it is to Kant's credit that he was sensitive to the tension between the role of the universal and the particular, as well as to that tension between reason and 'inclinations,' in morality. Unfortunately, he found it necessary to ground ethics in the universal and the rational as a safeguard against the threat of moral skepticism. The point is not to opt now for a denigration of universality and rationality in favor of radical particularity and irrationality, but rather to recognize the tension between them as what creates the need for, and at the same time the possibility of, the lived human ethical situation. What is indicated is a rethinking of intersubjective reciprocity, and one way to explore it is through the transcendence in language of reversible subjectivity. This will require the projection of Merleau-Ponty's thought into the ethical realm insofar as reversible subjectivity can be extended to be a *virtual focus of responsibility* as well as a focus of experience.

We do *not* find justification for beginning with the types of reversibility and transcendence germane to language in order to construct some sort of linguistic idealism. Surely it has become clear in the preceding discussion that language does not speak only of itself for Merleau-Ponty,[33] nor in the account offered here. Since "it is only through the world that I can leave myself," I cannot conduct such a solipsistic withdrawal to the depths of nothingness.[34] My environment is the life-world, and even in the transcendence in language I may never quit it. We must not misunderstand, then, when Merleau-Ponty states: "It is by considering language that we would best see how we are and are not to return to the things themselves."[35] This notion of transcendence — always non-coincidental — is the crucial one for our discussion, whether the 'things themselves' be human or non-human.[36]

Now, keep in mind that the reversibility of language and ideas allows for the fact that discourse is steeped in ideality by virtue of the eventfulness of language. Propriety is not something I determine alone. Instead, it is codetermined in an event of mutual appropriation. Both I and the other share this project insofar as we share a "primordial property that belongs to the flesh, being here and now, of radiating everywhere and forever, being an individual, of being also a dimension and a universal."[37] To participate in this ideality of language is to participate in the "invisible society" of humanity.[38] Whenever I share language with another, we are both intimately involved with this ideality generated therein. I am intimately involved with my interlocutor, as we share the same discourse, and as propriety is determined. But this intimacy need not be defined as harmonious. To state that the sharing of language invokes a mutual participation in a certain kind of ideality ought not to be confused with the hopeful but naive claim that such participation is idyllic. As the discussion of tactile reversibility revealed earlier, accessibility is exploitable for a disturbing variety of purposes. By writing, speaking, or gesturing, we 'get outside of ourselves.' Our divergence is this same shared event whereby we become accountable to and for one another. This is where values are determined, and where the need for such values arises. Our opening onto each other and our divergence, "overlapping and fission, identity and difference...bring to birth a ray of natural light that illuminates all flesh and not only my own."[39] Sometimes it is a light that sears, causing indescribable pain. We do not always agree.

Considering the phenomenon of transcendence in language directs us to a new understanding of responsibility. We are no longer relying on a notion of an exclusively rational and universal ground for responsibility since we need not rely on an impoverished transcendence grounded in an epistemologically privileged subjectivity. Instead, the transcendence of reversible subjectivity allows room for a responsibility that is *pre*rational as well as *pre*universal.

This might be termed a *responsibility of ideality*. By appealing to an ideality that is intersubjectively shared in the transcendence of reversible subjectivity, reverence for the other, and not the law, may be seen to assume its rightful paramount position in moral philosophy. I am with the other in such a strong sense via this transcendence that the sharing of our Being renders us commensurately responsible to and for one another.

This in no way precludes the array of heinous acts of which our species is capable. These are the need for ethics. The force of the 'ought,' which obtains in any human ethical situation, issues *not* from our potential as rational beings ;to conform with "the universality of a law as such," but from our potential to conform with another. The propriety of an act is visible in an action that is spoken of as befitting the situation. And the manner in which we 'fit in' with one another is not to be grounded on anything more, nor on anything less, than the realm of human existence and praxis. The force of the ought obtains because I can both bleed and draw blood; because the shedding of blood is a singular event that I share with the other; because whether I hold the blade or the handle of the knife, I know what it is to be on the "other side." Indeed, I am that moment of shared divergence that I recognize as me only insofar as I am also a determination of, and am likewise determined by, what it is to be on the other side. Our "landscapes interweave," our "actions and...passions fit together exactly."[40] Ethical obligation is no longer merely a rational determination which, as Hume correctly observed, could never motivate me to action.[41] Indeed, freedom and responsibility are not purely rational; nor are they purely universal. Likewise, they cannot be purely irrational, nor can they be radically particular. As a vestige of the transcendence of reversible subjectivity, responsibility takes on a carnal dimension.[42]

NOTES

1. It is certainly unusual to maintain the apparently traditional language of 'subjectivity' in the wake of the sharp attacks levied against it by Heidegger, Derrida, and others. Indeed, Merleau-Ponty has seemingly abandoned the language of subjectivity by his final writings. The prob-

lem can be posed in this manner: if one begins in the Cartesian tradition that was Husserl's bane — trying to understand the world from an isolated subject pole distanciated from it — one is condemned to the same insurmountable difficulties that Husserl only began to work through in his last writings. Knowledge of the subject is immediate and knowledge of the world becomes impossible. But once such a gulf between the knower and what is to be known is no longer assumed, understanding the world is no longer problematic in the same way. Why, then, advocate the use of the unfashionable language of subjectivity here?

Without taking the discussion too far afield, I will attempt a brief answer. Heidegger and Derrida have embarked on their projects by fundamentally rejecting the notion that the subject is epistemologically privileged in the aforementioned manner. To avoid propagating the same errors, they have found it necessary to reject the language of subjectivity completely and redirect the focus of their inquiries accordingly to the understanding of language. Unfortunately, this also has resulted in the recognition of human experience only as linguistic mediation. The same thing cannot be said of Merleau-Ponty. In this sense, he can best be seen as offering a different sort of response to Husserl than the kind(s) offered by Heidegger and Derrida. The question of whether Merleau-Ponty would have condoned this language of subjectivity is extraneous to the discussion here. How he diverges from these other thinkers is not. From the first sentence of *The Structure of Behavior* to the last incomplete notes of *The Visible and the Invisible*, the main focus of Merleau-Ponty's inquiry is best seen to be the relation between the self and the world. Thus he is *rethinking* Husserl's project rather than abandoning it. Certainly his immediate project develops over time from an attempt to rethink 'consciousness' to an attempt to rethink 'nature' or 'world,' but nowhere does he take the unfortunate route that tends toward linguistic idealism, and perhaps ultimately toward nihilism. So, I maintain the use of the language of subjectivity to set my understanding of the self apart from the Heideggerian/ Derridian projects and their progeny. One can alleviate the epistemological difficulties traditionally associated with subjectivity, and consequently with transcendence, by allowing Merleau-Ponty's ontological insight of reversibility to inform a new understanding of transcendence and subjectivity. I will use the term *subjectivity* to connote a focus of experience and of responsibility — a moment of divergence in the shared existence it partially determines.

For a full account of another notion of subjectivity in the wake of the postmodern proclamation of the death of the subject, and one to which I am certainly indebted, cf. Calvin O. Schrag, *Communicative Praxis and the Space of Subjectivity* (Bloomington: Indiana University Press, 1986).

2. It ought to be noted from the beginning that language is not the only human activity appropriate as subject matter for the interrogation of transcendence. I am not advocating any sort of linguistic idealism. Nonetheless, owing to the malignant, if not pervasive, nature of language within human existence, a phenomenological examination of language provides an excellent starting point — not the only one — for a philosophical inquiry into transcendence. As Martin Dillon notes correctly in his provocative study that stresses the importance of transcendence in understanding the whole of Merleau-Ponty's written corpus, "it is a mistake to put language in the place of the world as the ultimate theme of philosophical interrogation" (Martin C. Dillon, *Merleau-Ponty's Ontology* (Bloomington: Indiana University Press, p. 177).

3. Ibid., p. 35.

4. Maurice Merleau-Ponty, *The Visible and the Invisible*, trans. Alphonso Lingis (Evanston, Ill.: Northwestern University Press, 1968), p. 229; hereafter cited as "*VI.*"

5. Ibid., p. 203.

6. Ibid., p. 135.

7. Ibid., pp. 141–42.

8. Ibid., p. 272.

9. Ibid., p. 138.

10. Ibid., p. 143.

11. Ibid., p. 146.

12. In this essay, to avoid an important ambiguity, I will use 'language' to mean the physical phenomenon of a system of signifiers, and language (without single quotes) to mean the full event of human experience.

13. This essay appears in Maurice Merleau-Ponty, *Sense and Non-Sense* (Evanston, Ill.: Northwestern University Press, 1964), pp. 9–25.

14. Ibid., p. 19.

15. For a more complete discussion of the relation between the

44 DUANE H. DAVIS

eventfulness of language and subjectivity, see my "Completing the Existential Recovery of Language," *Journal of the British Society for Phenomenology* 21, no. 2 (May, 1990), pp. 175–84.

16. *VI*, p. 229.

17. See Dillon, pp. 113–29 for a full discussion of this important theme and the many relevant passages in *Phenomenology of Perception*, with respect to the Husserlian provocation of the problem of intersubjectivity Merleau-Ponty is rethinking.

18. One does not establish the similarity by arguments to analogy. Rather, Merleau-Ponty rethinks the Husserlian notion of *Lebenswelt* to show that my similarity is pre-given. This does not preclude the influence of language upon this similarity. Nor is similarity a stasis.

19. Again, it is important to note that this is not merely the position of the Merleau-Ponty who penned *The Visible and the Invisible*. Martin Dillon (in *Merleau-Ponty's Ontology*) has effectively shown that the explicit ontology of this work is in fact implicit in Merleau-Ponty's earlier writings.

20. *VI*, p. 225.

21. Maurice Merleau-Ponty, *Phenomenology of Perception*, trans. Colin Smith (London: Routledge & Kegan Paul, 1962), p. 111.

22. *VI*, p. 125.

23. Immanuel Kant, *Groundwork of the Metaphysics of Morals*, trans. H. J. Paton (New York: Harper & Row, 1964), p. 70.

24. Ibid., p. 98: Kant understands "the Idea of the will of every rational being as a will which makes the universal law."

25. Ibid., pp. 98–99.

26. Ibid., p. 88, n. 1.

27. Ibid., p. 95.

28. Ibid., p. 88; also cf. p. 68: "Only something which is conjoined with my will solely as a ground and never as an effect — something which does not serve my inclination, but outweighs it or at least leaves it entirely out of account of my choice — and therefore only bare law for its own sake can be an object of reverence and therewith a command."

29. Ibid., pp. 68–69, 108.

30. Ibid., p. 64.

31. It sets the universal and the rational over against the particular and the corporeal, thus confining the ground for ethics to a realm disparate from the realm of human interaction.

32. Ibid., p. 69, n. 2.

33. *VI*, pp. 125–26: "It is the error of the semantic philosophics to close up language as if it spoke only of itself."

34. Ibid., p. 11. Also, p. 143: "They betray the solipsist illusion that consists in thinking that every going beyond is accomplished by oneself."

35. Ibid., p. 125.

36. The transcendence to which I refer here, and have alluded to earlier, is picturesquely described as *écart*, dehiscence, or non-coincidence. I have tried to offer a sort of depiction of this radicalized notion of transcendence through the above descriptions of a few types of human praxis where transcendence occurs — i.e., perception, language, etc. In short, transcendence is *lived* reversibility. Reversible subjectivity was described earlier as a moment of divergence in the shared existence it partially determines [cf. note 1]. The potential for this divergence is reversibility. The divergence itself, within the lived context of human praxis, is transcendence.

37. *VI*, p. 142.

38. Ibid., p. 235.

39. Ibid., p. 142.

40. Ibid.

41. David Hume, *A Treatise of Human Nature* (Oxford: Oxford University Press, 1983), p. 413.

42. I would like to thank Martin C. Dillon for his many helpful and instructive comments, which were instrumental in revising this essay. A shorter version of this essay was presented at the Thirteenth International Merleau-Ponty Circle in October 1988 at Villanova University.

3

Visions of Narcissism:
Intersubjectivity and the Reversals of Reflection

David Michael Levin

> [I]n Hegel's youthful writings,
> the option of explicating the eth-
> ical totality as a communicative
> reason embodied in intersubjec-
> tive life-contexts was still open.
> — Jürgen Habermas,
> *The Philosophical Discourse of
> Modernity* p. 40

INTRODUCTION

There is widespread agreement, now, that philosophical discourse
must finally recognize an *embodied* reason. But what, more concretely, does this mean? How should we understand the body, if the
body is to be such that it can carry and embody reason? There is also
widespread agreement that philosophical discourse must renounce
its commitment to a *subject-centered* reason. Does the embodiment of
reason contribute, then, to the overcoming of a subject-centered
reason? Does the body give any support to the conception of a genuinely communicative rationality? Habermas ventures no answers
to these questions.

   As a way of understanding the workings of power, Foucault
proposed that we study the body, observing it as the instrument
and object of power. Foucault opened up an entire new problematic
when he began to study what he called, in his Preface to volume
two of *The History of Sexuality*, "the formation of a certain mode of
relation to the self in the experience of the flesh." But the body as
he conceived it is without subjectivity, without any *experience* of

47

power. If the body is only an object, how can it be a source of resistance? How can it embody praxis? We need an understanding of the body that truly empowers it. What does the body of experience, the body-as-subject, contribute to our understanding of praxis, a politics of resistance? Drawing on the work of Merleau-Ponty, and more particularly, on his phenomenology of perception, I shall attempt to answer these difficult questions. I shall also attempt to show how Merleau-Ponty's phenomenology of the flesh opens up the possibility of an historically different relationship to the self.

In his book, *After Virtue*, Alasdair MacIntyre asserted that "We do not fully understand the claims of a moral philosophy until we have spelled out what its social embodiment would be." (p. 22) In a political reply, William Galston added this: "Neither have we fully understood it until we have seen the kind of social criticism to which it gives rise."[1] In this chapter, we shall be reflecting on Merleau-Ponty's contribution to our understanding of the sociality of our embodiment and the embodiment of our sociality. But we shall also be thinking about the significance of Merleau-Ponty's phenomenological illuminations for critical social theory. The body is our medium for the complex dialectic between individuation and socialization. It is the body's intersubjectivity that makes possible the paradoxical reflections that stimulate our narcissism, only to reverse it. And the body's inherently interactional nature deeply informs and inhabits our inaugural sense of justice.

According to Merleau-Ponty, "there is a fundamental narcissism in all vision." (See *The Visible and the Invisible*, p. 139) In the years that immediately preceded his death, it seems that Merleau-Ponty was attempting to work out a new, more radical phenomenology of perception. What he wanted to achieve by this was nothing less than an end to the philosophy of consciousness: an ontology and epistemology no longer under the spell of a narcissistic, subject-centered metaphysics. Thus he set out to articulate a new understanding of the philosopher's traditional subject, demonstrating his vision in a hermeneutical phenomenology of the flesh. (I use the word *hermeneutical* to characterize his phenomenology because I understand hermeneutics to be the articulation — always only partial and always belated or *nachträglich* — of a background richness of implicit experiential meanings that is always already constellated prior to the constitutive, meaning-bestowing activity of the enquiring subject.) As we shall see, Merleau-Ponty connected his ground-breaking account of perception — a postmetaphysical account that leads us into a decentering and communicative vision and lets us see the depth of its intertwinings, its intersubjective tangle of roots, the dimensionality of being he called "the flesh" — with the psychoanalytic theory of narcissism. "Make not an existential psychoanalysis," he wrote, "but an ontological psychoanalysis" (*The Visible and the Invisible*, p. 270). "Do a psychoanalysis of Nature: it is the flesh, the mother" (ibid., p. 267).

In his recent work on narcissism, Alford attempted to show that "the psychoanalytic theory of narcissism can help us better understand certain basic philosophical issues, by enabling us to distinguish fruitful from sterile modes of philosophical speculation" (*Narcissism*, p. 1). I disagree and shall explain why. However, I do think that Merleau-Ponty wanted his phenomenology of narcissism to accomplish something convergent: revisioning our understanding of identity-formation, clarifying the conflict between autonomy and interdependence, and recasting the dialectic between individuation and socialization. With the power of phenomenology, he distinguished different modes and dimensions of visual interaction — and not merely different modes of *philosophical* reflection and speculation. Resisting the power of metaphysical speculation, Merleau-Ponty examined the ambiguities of reflection and clarified our experience of the birth of the self in a continuing dialectic of reflection and alienation. Moreover, he disclosed the existence of a schematism of reciprocity always already in operation within the familiar narcissism of gazes and glances. There is a surprise for us in this demonstration, for what his phenomenology illuminates is the paradoxical truth that, in the dialectic of reflection, our moment of narcissism is subject to reversal: seduced into openness, we find ourselves in each other and are slowly appropriated, by and for a more mature intersubjective life. What Merleau-Ponty shows is the origin of our structures of mutual recognition in the very nature of the sensorimotor body, the body of perception. Thus, as we shall see, there are always, in the vision of this philosopher, images of justice for reflection.

I submit, however, that Merleau-Ponty's attempt to conceptualize his phenomenology with language borrowed from the psychoanalytic theory of narcissism is unfortunate. To explain my disagreement with Alford, I shall argue that the narcissism of our visionary flesh, the self-mirroring that Merleau-Ponty brings to light, is *essentially different* from the narcissism interpreted by Freud; that it differs significantly from the phenomenon described by Lacan; and that, if Descartes's *Meditations* may be read as a work of epistemological narcissism, then the experience disclosed by the hermeneutics of the flesh is certainly not narcissism, but rather its postmetaphysical deconstruction: a phenomenology of perception that shows the *impossibility* of Cartesian subjectivity. Considered in relation to the historical discourse of reflection, a discourse inaugurated by Descartes and continued, not only by Freud but also, despite all protestations, in the work of Lacan, the "narcissism" that appears in the reflections of the flesh can be seen only as ironic. Whereas some have seen a pathological narcissism of withdrawal and self-absorption that isolates the self from the social world, others have seen a narcissism of self-constitution and self-recognition that ultimately alienates the self from itself in a relentlessly hostile world, and others have seen a pathological narcissism of self-aggrandizement and will to power, Merleau-Ponty saw the potential for a positive and constructive moment. He saw a narcissism of ecstatic intertwinings, consonances, and reversibilities, transpositions in which the self can see itself being "completed" — unified, made whole, and to some extent perfected — through social relationships of communion and reciprocity.[2]

The first sustained analysis of narcissism appeared in 1914 with the publication of Freud's "Zur Einführung des Narzissmus." Freud distinguished two stages of narcissism, each of them capable of both normal and pathological formations. What he called *primary narcissism* refers to the condition of the infant prior to the emergence of a stable ego- structure; it was thought to be — and was seen as — an autoerotic state of symbiotic, relatively undifferentiated awareness in which the differences between self and world, self and other, subject and object were not yet stabilized in a dialectic of oppositions. Because of this alleged primal fusion, this ontological state of "confusion", the dimensions of the infant's being were thought to be virtually coextensive with the dimensions of the world. "Primary narcissism" described the infant whose experience is that of an eternal being, omnipotent and omniscient — very much, in fact, like a god. Freud regarded this condition as normal. But he showed that it can become pathological — indeed, a psychosis — should the child refuse the steps of separation and independence necessary for individuation.

Secondary narcissism is Freud's term for the later developmental stage in which the erotic libido of the id is withdrawn from "love-objects" in the world and takes the ego itself as the "object" of its love. To the extent that this takes place as part of a process in which an ego ideal is constituted within the ego, it may be seen, according to Freud's theory, as a normal transitional phase in the healthy maturation of the ego — as a phase culminating in the formation of a stable and civilized superego structure. However, insofar as there is a disengagement from the world that becomes fixated libidinally on the needs of the ego, the narcissism is seen as pathological.

Contemporary psychiatry has legitimated a distinctive way of looking at this pathology. Through its clinical and discursive practices, it has reduced the crisis *of* the isolated individual in late capitalism to a problem than can be isolated *in* the individual and treated with the standard remedies of medicine. This medicalization makes it difficult to see any constructive potential in narcissistic pathology — and absolutely precludes the perception of its larger social meaning: what critique of society and culture is implicit in its suffering.

The third edition of the *Diagnostic and Statistical Manual of Mental Disorders*, published in 1980 to report the official consensus of the American Psychiatric Association, describes the "narcissistic character" as a "Disorder in which there is a grandiose sense of self-importance or uniqueness; preoccupation with fantasies of unlimited success; exhibitionistic need for constant attention and admiration; characteristic responses to threats to self-esteem; and characteristic disturbances in interpersonal relationships that alternate between the extremes of over-idealization and devaluation, and lack of empathy" (see p. 315). It adds "The exaggerated sense of self-importance may be manifested as extreme self-centeredness and self-absorption. Abilities and achievements tend to be unrealistically overestimated. Frequently the sense of self-importance alternates with feelings of special unworthiness" (ibid.). Narcissistic disorders frequently involve extreme mood swings, states of depression, and profound disturbances, ruptures, or instabilities in the person's sense of identity — one's sense of being, for example, a firm, independent center of initiative. Self-esteem is often extremely fragile, and often entails, correspondingly, that there is a very weak sense of reciprocity: "Interpersonal exploitativeness, in which others are taken advantage of in order to indulge one's own desires or for self-aggrandizement, is common; and the personal integrity and rights of others are disregarded" (ibid., p. 316).

Sullivan, Lacan, and Kohut significantly enriched Freud's original interpretation of narcissism by contributing an analysis that (1) focused clinical attention on the disturbances and inadequacies in the kind of "mirroring" infants and children receive from their relationships with others during the early years of life, and (2) broke away from the Freudian commitment to ego psychology, interpreting the two-faced character of narcissism, letting it be seen in relation to the formation of a self and as a pathology in self-identity — some kind of block to its process of individuation and self-development. (What is the difference between the ego and the self? Stated very briefly, the ego is a relatively settled, permanent structure, a defensively organized identity, mostly consisting of socially established roles and routines, and representing the individual's adaptation to prevailing social reality. The self enjoys a more individuated, more differentiated identity, carrying the process of maturation beyond the roles and routines required by socialization. If the ego is defined in terms of structure, the self is defined in terms of process. The self is an ego open to processes of further self-development; it is an ego whose identity is always an open existential question.)

Alford emphasizes these points, observing that "the denial of genuine, realistic dependence and relatedness is as characteristic of [pathological] narcissism as is the quest for fusion" (p. 149). "Indeed," he argues, "it is the paradoxical coexistence of these two orientations that is one of the leading themes associated with the theory of narcissism" (ibid.). Such narcissism exemplifies what Habermas defines as psychopathology: a "deviation from the model of the language of communicative action, in which motives of action and linguistically expressed intentions coincide" (*Knowledge and Human Interests*, p. 226). But Alford also sees in narcissism the possibility of a more "positive" moment: "Narcissism, understood as the quest for unity, wholeness and perfection, can be viewed as the telos served by eros, as well as by the ego. In this way, narcissism gives meaning and direction...to human life, by connecting the mature quest for fusion with the ego ideal and with the primitive quest for fusion with the All" (*Narcissism*, p. 160).

The position for which I want to argue in this chapter is that Merleau-Ponty's hermeneutics of the flesh shows narcissism in the light of a phenomenology that articulates its normative and utopian dimension: there is a schematism of mutual recognition already inscribed in the flesh, and it implicates the achievement of an ideal communicative situation. According to my reading of Merleau-Ponty, his phenomenology helps us to see that what Alford calls "the quest for unity, wholeness and perfection" can be an individual and collective task directed toward the realization of the utopian potential always already implicate in the reversibilities of the flesh. If individuation and socialization are inseparable processes, then the individual's quest for unity, wholeness, and perfection raises analogous questions for society, questions that cannot be separated from the larger processes of enlightenment engaging our society — struggles for liberty, equality, new forms of solidarity, and the "perfection" of justice.

As Habermas points out, however, neither justice nor freedom, as the fundamental principles of modernity, can really be adequately conceptualized in the vocabulary of the philosophy of the subject:

> In all attempts to grasp self-determination and self-realization, that is, freedom [and justice]...with the tools of the philosophy of the subject, one immediately runs up against an ironic inversion of what is actually intended. Repression of the self is the converse side of an autonomy that is pressed into subject-object relationships; the loss of self — and the narcissistic fear of its loss — are the converse of an expressivity brought under these concepts. ...To be sure, as long as we only take into account subjects representing and dealing with objects, and subjects who externalize themselves in objects or can

relate to themselves as objects, it is not possible to conceive of
socialization as individuation. (*The Philosophical Discourse of Modernity*,
p. 292)

Considered in the light cast by this analysis, Merleau-Ponty's
hermeneutics of the flesh, and the phenomenology of narcissism he
examines within this field, make an extremely important contribution to the contemporary discourse on modernity. Contrary to widespread misprisions — the misreadings, for example, of Foucault,
Derrida, and Habermas, Merleau-Ponty's phenomenology of the
flesh is a chapter in the story of the postmodern revolt against the
metaphysics of consciousness and subjectivity: a revolt that
Merleau-Ponty helped set in motion.

In Part 1, I shall attempt to show that the narrative moments
in Descartes's *Meditations* mirror the symptomology Freud interpreted as "narcissistic psychopathology". Because it was in the
Meditations that Descartes began the philosophical discourse of
modernity, writing from the position of a self-grounding subjectivity,
this correspondence suggests that our late modern culture of narcissism is very deeply rooted, its elements already at work in the
subjectivism proclaimed by philosophical reason at the beginning
of the modern age. In Part 2, I shall outline the critical points in
Jacques Lacan's theory of ego formation as a narcissistic process.
In Part 3, I shall examine texts by Merleau-Ponty, hoping to shed
some light on why he sees narcissism in the dynamics of the flesh.
I will argue that what he is calling *narcissism* is totally different from
the "narcissism" that appears in the texts of Descartes, Freud, and
Lacan. In fact, I will argue for something even stronger: that, in
the "narcissism" of the flesh, the "narcissism" of the monadic
metaphysical subject is actually reversed, overturned: turned, *au
fond*, into its very opposite, a communicative intersubjectivity. In
the "narcissism" of the flesh, there is, in effect, a dialectic of reflection, and this dialectic *deconstructs* the narcissistic structure of the
self, redeeming, at the very heart of "subjectivity," its primordial
sociality, its inherence in the reciprocities of a social world — a
"moral community" — from the very beginning.

Finally, in Part 4, I shall briefly draw out of this account, in
more or less summary form, some of its broader implications for
our present cultural debate over the future of individualism — the

modern self — and the "social embodiment" of freedom and justice — those processes of enlightenment which it has been the distinctive contribution of the philosophical discourse of modernity to argue for and instigate. In particular, I want to suggest how Merleau-Ponty's work enables us to discern certain aporias in Foucault's politics of the body-self and move beyond the critical impasse where this politics seems to abandon us. I also want to indicate how the retrieval of an incarnate *logos* in Merleau-Ponty's work can carry forward the Habermasian project: the project, that is, of overcoming a subject-centered rationality and articulating a principle of justice grounded in the rationality of communicative practices.

1. DESCARTES

There are many ways of reading, many ways of interpreting, the text of Descartes's *Meditations on First Philosophy*. Here, partly for the sheer pleasure of it, and not too seriously, I am going to suggest a "psychoanalytic" reading, displaying the logic of moments in the unfolding of his meditations as a psycho-logic of moments in the symptom formation of narcissistic pathology. Is there, then, in the kind of "reflection" and "speculation" that opened the discourse of modernity, a certain deep and irremediable narcissism?

Descartes began with a reflection that would forever separate him from what Husserl called the *natural attitude*: an innocent or naive faith in perception, trust in one's senses, unquestionable certainty regarding the nature of reality. We might see in this natural, prereflective attitude a striking similarity to the primary narcissism of childhood. However, by venturing to doubt all that he had once — in his youth — thought to be beyond the shadow of doubt, Descartes renounced this primary narcissism of the natural attitude.

Now, the methodic doubt he set in motion was intended to construct his "knowledge" on unshakable grounds and give it an unquestionable authority. Thus we see that, although he renounced the state of primary narcissism, he did this only in order to restore his faith in himself; his ambition was to achieve a more secure state of self-assurance — in other words, a more secure state of narcissism, the power of total self-determination, total self-grounding.

The "real" world is full of dangers. Limitless occasions for deception create fear, uncertainty, even temptation. How could there be certainty in knowledge and security in life unless life is reduced to the compass of unquestionable knowledge? Methodic doubt, systematic doubt, compelled Descartes to renounce the world. This renunciation seemed at first to put him in control; but, as we eventually can see, it also sentenced him to a solipsism, a monadological isolation, that was not without its own dangers. Instead of finding certainty, he found himself haunted by doubts that he could dispel only by telling himself that his withdrawal from realism, his withdrawal from the world, was merely theoretical, merely symbolic. Instead of finding ontological security within himself, as he expected, he found himself threatened by the possibility of annihilation. On the verge of being overcome by the enormity of his loss, he fell into a narcissistic rage, turning his ontological anxiety into a wild paranoia. He constructed an appropriate phantasy, which embodied his paranoia in an evil demon, a being "not less powerful than deceitful." His textual strategies betray the fact that he unconsciously sensed his vulnerability: unless there is a benevolent deity about whose existence and attributes he can be absolutely certain, his "unquestionable" first axiom, the proposition, *cogito ergo sum*, can at most secure his existence only if, and only when, he is actually thinking it. Thus, the extremity of his narcissistic withdrawal from realism very quickly put him in an essentially depressive position: his grandiose renunciation of all that is uncertain threatened to cut him off from God; and his peculiar self-absorption so isolated him from others that, when he looked out his window, all he could see were self-moving machines instead of people.

The meditations of the Cartesian ego exemplify the disorder of secondary narcissism. The hyperconscious phantasy of the "malin génie" disguises a very real ontological anxiety: an anxiety from which Descartes escaped only because he was quickly seduced by another fantasy — this time, an *unconscious* fantasy whose narcissism he did not suspect. In the "arrogance" of the Cartesian proof that God exists, in a proof whose steps are to be found within the unquestionable *cogito,* all the "symptoms" by which the DSM-III diagnoses cognitive disorder can be recognized: a grandiose sense of self-importance and uniqueness; delusions of omnipotence and unlimited success; and exhibitionistic need for constant attention, for unconditional benevolence and admiration from the most important of all beings; characteristically paranoiac and defensive responses to threats thought to jeopardize self-esteem and the integrity of the self; problems of self-identity; extreme self-centeredness and self-absorption; and a deficient capacity for empathic responsiveness and social interaction. When he looked at the world — at a piece of melting wax, for example — all he could really see was himself, the activities of his own mind. The world was nothing but a mirror for the self, a self ultimately transparent to itself, and not needing, for self-knowledge, the real mediation of others.

Descartes withdrew from the world into a state of total self-absorption, taking himself, or rather, his methodically reduced self, as object. In terms of psychoanalysis, this withdrawing and self-absorption would be seen as a response to a "narcissistic wound": losing certainty in the midst of the world, the ego withdraws into itself, attempting to find in its self-absorption the security and self-possession denied by the world. Thus, using only the resources entirely contained within this unique and solitary self, he brought forth a dazzling — but in the final analysis delusionary — demonstration that the benevolent God of tradition actually does exist. But what was this feat, if not a thinly disguised exhibition of his own godlike omnipotence? Did it not, in a sense, claim to imitate, and therefore rival, the creative acts of God? Did it not put the *ego cogitans* at the very center of the discourse on truth and being, usurping the sacred place — the place of absence — once occupied by God? Did it not, in effect, make the *ego,* rather than God, the ultimate ground of all truth and all being?

Descartes moved out of the position that, following Freud, we have characterized as "primary narcissism" only to take up a position in which we can recognize the distinctive attitudes of a pathological "secondary narcissism": withdrawal from the world, excessive self-absorption, demonic self-doubts and anxieties, fantasies of omnipotence and omniscience. The Cartesian *cogito* is an ego that assumes it can ground knowledge, truth, and reality within its own unquestionable experience. It is an ego that claims to know itself totally and with absolute certainty — although, to make this claim, it has had to split off from its embodiment, its extension and dissemination through the flesh, and to deny, with a "metaphysics of presence," its mortal inherence in temporality. Released from all material impediments, it even claims the spiritual power to bring forth (the idea of) God's existence from within its own experience. More tragically, it must also be an isolated, self-contained substance, a monad, whose delusions of self-sufficiency and independence seriously limit and distort its capacity to relate itself to others. In Descartes, the narcissism essentially constitutive of the ego creates an affective and epistemological abyss between self and others. No sense of community can join together what has been separated by this abyss.

2. LACAN

For Lacan, as, later, for Kohut, "secondary" narcissism is seen as constituting a necessary phase in the process of self-development. The phase in question is called *narcissism* because it engages the child in a self-reflective process of "mirroring" that eventuates in the emergence of a coherent body-self image. In a paper entitled "The Mirror Stage as Formative of the Function of the 'I' as Revealed in Psychoanalytic Experience," presented in 1949 to the Sixteenth International Psycho-Analytical Congress in Zurich, Lacan attempted to argue for a theory of ego formation on which he had been working for many years and which he first put into writing in a 1936 paper — already anticipating some of his late criticisms of Freud's ego psychology and the theory of narcissism. Lacan figures in our story for a number of reasons. One of them is that he played an important role in Merleau-Ponty's thinking about "The Child's Relations with Others" and that his paper on the mirror stage undoubtedly encouraged Merleau-Ponty to make use of the images and concepts of narcissism in articulating the dimension of the flesh in *The Visible and the Invisible*.

For the sake of the record, it should be noted here that Lacan drew on the research of Köhler, who reported in 1925 on chimpanzee reactions to their mirrored images, and on the work of Henri Wallon, who reported in 1931 on the mirror experiences of children. It should also be noted that the American psychiatrist Harry Stack Sullivan devoted many years of clinical research to the mirroring process in mother-child relationships, and that he was writing and lecturing on this subject from 1944 to his death in 1949. *The Interpersonal Theory of Psychiatry*, finally published in 1953, assembles some of his lectures from the period 1944–1947, a period in which the problems of mirroring are of central importance for him. I do not know whether Lacan was aware of or, if aware, then familiar with, this ground-breaking work by Sullivan. I like the fact that Sullivan conceptualizes the problems in mirroring in interpersonal terms, rather than, as Lacan sees them, in terms of an objective mirror. This difference between them is important, because Lacan's analysis — his vision of narcissism — leads only to a negativity, whereas Sullivan's, like Merleau-Ponty's, leads us to see the beginning schematization of social perceptions basic to our ethical and political life.

In summarizing Lacan's theory, I am going to rely on *Lacan and Language*, the excellent guide to his *Ecrits* written by John P. Muller and William Richardson. According to these authors, Lacan's 1949 paper on mirroring is an attempt to exhibit "the role of the image in the development of the subject and the manner in which social experience evolves" (*Lacan and Language*, p. 29). Lacan argues that "the newborn is marked by a prematurity specific to humans, an anatomical incompleteness evidenced in motor turbulence and lack of coordination. This state of fragmentation becomes camouflaged through the infant's jubilant identification with its reflection, experienced as a powerful gestalt promising mastery, unity, and substantive stature" (ibid., p. 6). In their reading, then,

> Lacan's principal thesis is that the newly born human infant, initially sunk in motor incapacity, turbulent movements, and fragmentation, first experiences itself as a unity through experiencing some kind of reflection of itself, the paradigm for which would be self-reflection in a mirror. This normally occurs between the ages of 6 and 18 months. This mirrorlike reflection, then, serves as the form that informs the subject and guides its development. So it happens that there is an "identification" between infant and its reflection "in the full sense that

analysis gives to the term: namely, the transformation that takes place in the subject when he assumes an image." It is this reflected image of itself, with which the infant identifies, that Lacan understands by the "I." The consequences of this conception are manifold. (ibid., p. 29)

But there is a problem, a danger, latent within this process: "Since this reflection (whose prototypical image is as seen in a mirror) is an external form, to identify with it as ego means to install a radical alienation and distortion in the very foundation of one's identity" (ibid., p. 6). As we shall see in Part 3, I will argue that although Merleau-Ponty also discerns an "alienation" here, and therefore the possibility, or danger, of a "distortion in one's identity," his unique contribution to the discourse, a contribution of the utmost significance, is to show that this alienation is not *essentially* a "distortion" — that, on the contrary, it can be, and for the most part is, a way of awakening and eliciting the social, and indeed pro-social, foundations of the child's identity.

Now, to be sure, there is a case to be made for Lacan, and in *Logics of Disintegration*, Peter Dews argues it well: "[For Lacan,] the reified, monadic identity of the ego can never be entirely over-come, but, to the extent that it can be, such overcoming takes place through the interplay of identity and non-identity, of conscious ego and unconscious subject, which characterizes the field of intersub-jectivity. Alone among the prominent French thinkers of the 1960s and 1970s, it is Lacan who explores the communicative formation — and deformations — of the self" (p. 235). Nevertheless, Lacan's analysis of the narcissistic mirroring process seems at times to draw near the self-defeating position for which Louis Althusser used to argue: that the subject is nothing but an effect of specular ideology, and the child a mere reflection of the social structures within which he receives his mirroring. Here we can see the significance of Sullivan's analysis. Sullivan assumes that the primary mirroring will be interpersonal, and he shows in great detail how it works and how its working can be disturbed. I think it much to his credit that he makes this crucial assumption. Lacan, by contrast, assumes that the primary mirroring of the child's embodied self involves the mediation of real mirrors. His "realism," here, is unfortunate, because, whenever this mirroring of the child involves a real mir-

ror, rather than another person, for example, the parent functioning in a mirroring way, there is also, in addition to the basic
alienation-effect, that is, the fact that the child's identity as a
coherent bodily unity is achieved by mediation through a
"medium" outside itself, a certain "primitive distortion" in the ego's
experience of reality, "for the reflection in the mirror is an inversion
of what stands before the mirror" (Richardson and Muller, p. 31).
For Lacan, these alienations and distortions are extremely significant, because their operation within the process through which the
structure of the ego is constituted means that the ego will always be
predisposed to experience and relate to others in a pathologically
narcissistic way; that is, with a certain paranoia, exaggerated
defensiveness, and unprovoked aggressivity — with an attitude of
closure, rather than an attitude of trust and openness. (See his
paper on "Aggressivity in psychoanalysis.")

In *The Philosophical Discourse of Modernity*, Habermas
characterizes the gaze that is privileged by the paradigm of objective knowledge. The gaze of subject-centered reason is an imper-
sonal third-person observation, for which "everything gets frozen
into an object" (p. 297). In part, Lacan thinks of the mirroring as
an alienation because, even when he situates the mirroring in an
interpersonal relationship, he tends to frame the exchanges and
reflections of the gaze in which the child's body is mirrored in
terms of this paradigm — the very same paradigm that compels
Descartes to say, in his *Meditations*, that, when he looks out the window, all he sees, strictly speaking, are hats and coats, and that, for
all he knows, what he sees may be nothing but a group of robots.
Merleau-Ponty thinks of the gaze in very different terms: terms
that correspond to the Habermasian model of a reason which is
intersubjective, communicative, and embodied in reciprocities.

In sum, then, I think that we should *reject* the Lacanian inversion argument, as it assumes, contrary to fact, and indeed rather
perversely, that the mirroring process is mostly and primarily an
experience with real mirrors, whereas it is, mostly and primarily,
an experience of interpersonal relationships. But I also think we
should *heed* the alienation argument — although, as I shall argue in
Part 3, this second argument must be *corrected*, for it sees only the
moment of negative sociality in the dialectics of narcissism and

overlooks the radically transfigurative moment, the moment of
"redemption" that Merleau-Ponty brings to light in his hermeneutical phenomenology of reciprocating gazes: visions gathered,
through their intertwinings, transpositions, and reversibilities, into
the communicativeness — the communion — of the flesh. In the
dimension of the flesh, there is a radical deconstruction of the ego,
the metaphysical subjectivity of our historical culture. Here, then,
contrary to what Lacan is constrained to believe, the alienations of
the mirroring process can be redeemed. Merleau-Ponty shows us a
possibility that Lacan does not conceive: how narcissism itself can
be transformed.[3]

3. MERLEAU-PONTY

Peter Dews points out that, for Adorno, "it is the deepest need and
impulse of the self to open itself to its other — indeed, only by
doing so can it truly become a self, by acknowledging the moment
of non-identity in its own identity" (p. 141). This is precisely, I
think, what Merleau-Ponty was trying to show in his hermeneutical phenomenology of the narcissistic moment in interpersonal relationships. Narcissism, for him, is a seduction of the
ego, drawing it out of itself into a process of education: it is an
alienation that can be reappropriated. Because the other is the
medium through which this takes place, the being that is achieved
constitutes an identity informed by a differentiated recognition of
the other as both same and different: sharing a universal flesh, yet
also irreducibly and absolutely different.[4] Many people (Plato and
Rousseau, for example) have seen the roots of *autonomy* in the
child's relations with others. But the significance I see in Merleau-
Ponty's work is that it sees (and hears) the dialectic of socialization
and individuation *in* the narcissism of mirroring (and echoing),
and demonstrates that the roots of *justice* are always already inherent in the body's order, the body's need for, and responsiveness to,
these earliest relationships.[5] There is a structuring of mutual
recognition, a structuring of reciprocity, in the mirror of the flesh.
    The principal concern of Merleau-Ponty's essay on "The
Child's Relations with Others" is the argument that human beings
are not self-contained, self-sufficient subjects contingently and

externally related to one another, but beings who are formed, from the very beginning, in and through their social interactions. "I live in the facial expressions of the other, as I feel him living in mine" (p. 146). When, in a nursery, one infant starts to cry, the crying spreads to the other infants. Within seconds, they are all crying. At an extremely young age, long before the visual system is completely stabilized, an infant will respond to the smile of the mother by smiling back in return. For the child living in this symbiotic relationship, there is no aware, coherent sense of bodily differentiation from the mothering one; and yet, sociality is already constitutive, forming and informing, long before the emergence of a personal ego. Thus, in the prepersonal state Freud called "primary narcissism," there is, as Merleau-Ponty says, an "anonymous collectivity," an "initial community," social interactions already articulating the experience and comportment of the infant (ibid., p. 119).

In fact, sociality — responsiveness to others — is so primordially inherent in the infant's bodily nature that adults commonly catch children "attributing to others what belongs to the subject himself" (ibid., p. 148). Normally, of course, processes of differentiation progressively structure the child's experiential field: "my body" takes shape as a substantial, objectified, coherently bounded presence, and "I" become identified with, and assume my identity as, "this body." But, as Alford points out, "It is the parents' ability to respond to the child as though he possessed a coherent, integrated self that teaches the child that it *is* such a self" (p. 45). This development is dependent upon appropriately sensitive and mature social interactions: "there must be a consciousness of the reciprocity of points of view in order that the word 'I' may be used" (Merleau-Ponty, "The Child's Relations," p. 150).

Close or intimate interactions with others involve the child in a process of mirroring: the child sees herself reflected in and through the gaze, gestures, and postures of the other; the other, whom she sees, sees her and reflects back how she is being seen. Gradually, if the mirroring is not for some reason distorted or disturbed (e.g., because one of the parents is schizophrenic or does not really love the child), the child will develop a firm sense of her body as a coherent whole and an originating center of action: she will develop a stable "corporeal schema."

Children need the mirroring of close interpersonal relationships. And they need this mirroring to be accurate, honest, and
sincere. Lacking "inner self-experience," lacking any reflectively
constituted sense of self, they need (to see) what reactions they
bring out in others. For it is only *through interacting with others*, only
through experiencing their accurate mirroring, and developing a
capacity for reflection, that children can constitute for themselves a
private, characterological "interiority" of feelings, thoughts, sensations, and intentions: experiences with public names about which
they may be confident, even though there is a sense in which the
referents will never be publicly observable. This reflective social
mirroring, however, is an ambiguous process, because, at the same
time that it enables children to sense themselves, and constitute
themselves as integrated egological centers, it also subjects them to
the possibility of a certain alienation, forming them in conformity
to the images of their others. The self, born of reflection, is also
vulnerable: it can be possessed and alienated by it. Thus, in "The
Intertwining — the Chiasm," Merleau-Ponty took note of the fact
that "Narcissus was the mythical being who, after looking at his
image in the water, was drawn as if by vertigo to rejoin his image
in the mirror of the water" (*The Visible and the Invisible*, p. 136).

Merleau-Ponty's phenomenology of the flesh implicitly
challenges the Lacanian analysis, which can see in the mirroring
only these two polar moments. I am arguing that, in the "narcissism" of the flesh that his hermeneutical phenomenology brings
to light, we see the constitution of a form of subjectivity radically
different from the form our systems of metaphysics and psychology
have made familiar: a subjectivity whose identity is not necessarily
centered in egological experience; a subjectivity that the mirroring
has decentered, but not produced through a process that leaves it
in a state of absolute alienation. Whereas Descartes, Freud, and
Lacan can see in the mirroring of narcissism only the shaping of
an egological, egocentric identity, Merleau-Ponty sees in it the
limning of a larger, nonegological identity, radically decentered by
its dialectical experiencing of the intertwining of self and other.
And, whereas Lacan can see in this mirroring only a process of
alienation that imposes the deep disintegration of social conformity
as the price for a shallow but coherent embodied identity, Merleau-

Ponty sees in its deeper corporeal dimensions a compelling experience of our primordial sociality: a disclosure that enables the bodily ego that mirroring has brought forth to complete its passage through secondary narcissism, and that consequently *frees* it to continue its individuation, beyond socially imposed roles, by taking part in the communicativeness and reciprocity of an embodied social existence.

In the process of socialization, children are indeed drawn out of themselves. For Merleau-Ponty, this means that children are subject to a process of alienation. Here he is in agreement with Lacan. But he begins to differ from Lacan when he examines the significance of the fact that, since this alienation takes place as an *interpersonal* process of mirroring and reflecting, it shows children that they are already, and were from the very beginning, social beings, beings who, by grace of their embodiment in and as a "universal flesh," are already internally ordered for, internally readied for, the "transcendences" of social interaction. This self-knowledge encourages, in turn, further steps of individuation — a process the maturity of which is a function, in part, of the child's responsiveness to this self-recognition, the disclosure of a primordial sociability.

What does this "primordial sociability" mean? In a paper replying to Lefort, Martin Dillon asks whether the presence of the other is internal to the body-self, an "immanent phenomenon," or whether it is, instead, external, and therefore effects an "encroachment" and "transgression." He argues for the latter. I see the matter differently. Although I can see the logic of this argument, my answer is different. First of all, I must contest the use of words such as *encroachment, transgression* and *alienation.* These words come from, and only make sense within, a discourse (such as Husserl's) that posits the metaphysical priority of the subject and conceptualizes it as a self-contained monad. These words, words that figured in the work of Husserl, Wallon, and Lacan before they were taken over by Merleau-Ponty, implicitly contradict the very thesis we are presumably trying to establish, viz., that the body (the embodied subject) is *not* an essentially unorganized, autistic, self-contained entity, but is already organized, from the very beginning, for social interaction. If the body (the embodied subject) is *inherently* interactional, oriented from the very beginning toward the engagement and development of its sociability, then the child's initiation into social relationships cannot be an alienation; nor is the presence of others an encroachment and transgression. These words do not narrate the inherent nature of the situation. What they describe is possible as pathology: distortions in the structures of mutual recognition; disruptions and disturbances in the processes of communication within which children may find themselves bound. Thus I dispute the premises behind the question Dillon asks.

The point that calls for phenomenological work is not that the presence of the other draws me out of my present state, but rather that it enables me to see myself as *always already social* — as having *already been* social, social from the very beginning. This new and deeper self-recognition then enables me to make further steps toward a mature individuation, integrating and balancing strong needs for autonomy and equally strong needs for solidarity.[6]

In "The Intertwining — the Chiasm," Merleau-Ponty asserts that "there is a fundamental narcissism in all vision" (*The Visible and the Invisible*, p. 39). Going beyond Descartes, Kant, and Hegel, for whom reflexivity is a relation of consciousness to itself, Merleau-Ponty affirms, in perceptual experience, the operation of a different reflexivity: a relation of flesh to flesh he calls *reversibility*. "Every reflection," he writes, "is after the model of the reflection of the hand touching by the hand touched" (*The Visible and the Invisible*, p. 204). And he characterizes this reflexivity as a form of "narcissism." But he locates this reflexivity in the flesh of the world, not in the privacy of the mind. So, as we shall see, instead of postulating, like Descartes, what is, in effect, a "ghost in the machine," he uses hermeneutical phenomenology to disclose a dialectic of reflexivity taking place in the *intertwining* of subjectivity and world: "my eyes which see, my hands which touch, can also be seen and touched," and "therefore, in this sense, they see and touch the visible, the tangible, from within" ("Interrogation and Intuition," *The Visible and the Invisible*, p. 123).

For Merleau-Ponty, "The essential notion for such philosophy is that of the flesh, which is not the objective body, nor the body thought by the soul as its own (Descartes)" (*The Visible and the Invisi-*

ble, p. 259). But now, "The flesh is a mirror phenomenon" (ibid., pp. 255, 256; also see "The Intertwining — the Chiasm," p. 139). The flesh is the formative medium of the object and the subject (ibid., p. 147). It is the elemental matrix, the texture, the field or dimensionality of our being: that "medium" in the depths of which subject and object, simultaneously coemergent, are forever unified, and through which they are continually mirroring one another.

Now, in Descartes, the method of withdrawal and self-absorption, as we have said, is an attempt to achieve a state of self-sufficiency, or self-containedness, that would make it possible for the ego to reflect on itself and claim absolute epistemic self-evidence — self-grounding transparency — for the immanent *cogito*. But, for such self-evidence, such epistemological unquestionableness, to be possible, there would have to be a perfect temporal *coincidence* between the conditions of knowledge and the circumstances of being, a coincidence between the existence of the knower and the presence of the known. How this is possible, if the mind is supposed to mirror itself, remains a problem that none of the old "speculative" philosophies can settle, as self-mirroring requires a *splitting* of the self. Although Merleau-Ponty sees a kind of "narcissism" in the phenomenon of mirroring, he displays the fact that his mirroring is a dialectic that recognizes the impossibility of a Cartesian narcissism — a narcissism of total coincidence.

Because individuation (identity) always takes place in a dialectic relationship to socialization (nonidentity), there is, in the mirroring "narcissism" of the flesh, "a sort of dehiscence," an *ecstasy* (or *écart*) that "opens my body in two" (*The Visible and the Invisible*, p. 123). There is, then, no possibility of "fusion": the Cartesian "return to immediacy," the Cartesian "search for an original integrity," can be regarded only as the philosopher's narcissistic delusion (ibid.). *In his later work, Merleau-Ponty showed that he was as much an enemy of the "metaphysics of presence" as Derrida has been.* However, unlike Derrida, and like Heidegger, he would not see "presence" as *totally* wrongheaded; and he struggled, instead, against its metaphysical capture — its reification and totalization — in order to revise and reformulate, in the *extases* of perceptual experience, the metaphysical concept of presence. We must not be misled by his mythopoetic references to a "narcissism" of the flesh and jump to the conclusion that, because the narcissistic position of the Cartesian ego is used to justify the claims of a "metaphysics of presence," the "narcissism" that Merleau-Ponty espouses in the texts of *The Visible and the Invisible* is likewise bound up with an argument for this metaphysics.

In his "Working Notes," Merleau-Ponty observed that, "To touch *oneself*, to see *oneself*,... is not to apprehend oneself as an object, it is to be open to oneself, destined to oneself (narcissism) — Nor, therefore, is it to reach *oneself*; it is, on the contrary, to escape *oneself*, to be ignorant of *oneself*. The 'self' in question is by divergence (*décart*), is [an] *Unverborgenheit* of the *Verborgen* as such, which consequently does not cease to be hidden or latent" (*The Visible and the Invisible*, p. 249). It is essential to note, here, that the "narcissism" to which this passage alludes is *not* the immediate narcissism of Cartesian self-absorption and epistemic coincidence, but rather the mediated narcissism of a passage through the *écarts*, the ecstatic disseminations, of the flesh: I see myself mirrored in the body of the other; I see myself from the viewpoint of the other, as the other sees me. I *need* the other as my mirror, if I am to see and know myself; and in the mirroring, I get to *see* this — this passage — through alterity. "In fact," he argues, "I do not entirely succeed in touching myself touching, in seeing myself seeing; the experience I have of myself does not go beyond a sort of *immanence*; it terminates in the invisible. ... The self-perception is still a perception, i.e., it gives me a *nicht urpräsentierbar* (a non-visible, myself...)" (ibid.).

In brief: "I am a self-presence that is an absence from self" (ibid., p. 250). My subjectivity can never be a pure self-presence, an identity unmediated by nonidentity. Reflection can be integrating; but the integrity it forms cannot be the simple, fixed oneness that metaphysics wants. Judged, therefore, from the standpoint of our metaphysics of presence, what reflection effects is always a disintegration. It is true, however, that, according to Merleau-Ponty, I can *encounter* myself only because I am always partially invisible: "narcissism" is an experience of oneself that is made possible only because our bodily mode of being-in-the-world makes a Cartesian presence — my self-absorption and coincidence with my self — *not* possible.

In "The Intertwining — the Chiasm" (p. 134), Merleau-Ponty contends that "he who sees cannot possess the visible unless he is possessed by it." But to be "possessed by" the visible is to be a *cogito* dispossessed: an ego not in total possession of itself; an ego not totally present to (for) itself. Now, we might call this an *alienation*. Lacan does. But there are different kinds of alienation, and the "alienation" for which Merleau Ponty wants to argue is not the Lacanian. What Lacan calls to our attention is an incipient pathology of self-development. According to his analysis, the mirroring bestows on the child an *egocentric* identity. But, for Lacan, this identity is really an illusion, a sham, because in truth it represents a certain irremediable disintegration: the child's unconscious conformity to an alien image.[7] The "self" formed in this way is little more than a pattern of socially imposed roles: an ego, rather than a growing, authentic self. As Dews observes, "socialization depends on a mutual recognition of subjects, however distorted" (*Logics of Disintegration*, p. 198). Lacan understands this. Nevertheless, he sees in the dialectic of mirroring a disguised form of social violence: the child gains an ego but loses the life of the "self."

Now, I do not want to deny, or even to underestimate, the possibility, the danger, against which Lacan wants to warn us. He has certainly called attention to a phenomenon that Freudian psychoanalysis did not consider: a phenomenon, I would add, the very existence of which it could not acknowledge without radically calling into question its tacit normative commitment to an egocentric psychology. But the point I want to make, here, is that the "alienation" that Merleau-Ponty brings to light is an alienation through which we are *bodily decentered*, drawn out of our (egocentric) identities, and projected into a social existence with many possibilities for individuation. Lacan sees only the negative moment in the dialectic. And he seems to give weight to the assumption, which Peter Dews ascribes to poststructuralism, that "identity can never be anything other than the suppression of difference" (see *Logics of Disintegration*, p. 170). Merleau-Ponty acknowledges the negative, but also sees a field of more positive existential possibilities: authentic alternatives, inscribed in the very ambiguity of the dialectic, to the social imposition of identity and the suppression of all difference.

Let us return to a point in the text of "The Intertwining — the Chiasm" (p. 139), which I already quoted, picking up, this time, some of the words that precede it. Merleau-Ponty argues here that, "since the seer is caught up in what he sees, it is still himself he sees: there is a fundamental narcissism in all vision." This argument then continues:

> And thus, for the same reason, the vision he exercises he also undergoes from the things, such that, as many painters have said, I feel myself looked at by the things, my activity is equally passivity — which is the second and more profound sense of the narcissism: not to see in the outside, as the others see it, the contour of the body one inhabits, but especially to be seen by the outside, to exist within it, to emigrate into it, to be seduced, captivated, alienated by the phantom, so that the seer and the visible reciprocate one another and we no longer know which sees and which is seen.

This does not mean that the seer and the seen coincide — nor does it mean a state of fusion, the seer's total identification with the other. What makes this visionary experience a form of "narcissism" is that, in seeing the other, I am still seeing myself. But this narcissism is not Cartesian: it is not self-absorption, autism, or solipsism, a total disconnection from the world. On the contrary, it is, as he says, a "seduction," a "captivation," or an "alienation." And yet, this so-called alienation is not of the Lacanian type, because here, in the dimensionality of the flesh, the alienation shatters the moment of closure and becomes an opening for reciprocity, an occasion for the recognition of kinship or affinity: our "universal flesh" (*The Visible and the Invisible*, p. 137). In seeing myself reflected in and by the other, I can see the other's bodily being interwoven with my own. For Merleau-Ponty, the process of socialization, for which he unfortunately uses the word *alienation*, does not involve the social imposition of egological structures on a totally docile, passive body; nor does it impose order on a turbulent, totally chaotic body of drives, but rather, on the contrary, it makes possible a self-developing socialization, eliciting from the deep order of our embodiment its inherent capacity to turn experiences of social relationship into an assumption of the *position* identified with the other.

The principal concept Merleau-Ponty uses to interpret the nature of the flesh is "reversibility." It is the "reversibility" of the

flesh, he says, "which is the ultimate truth" ("The Intertwining —
the Chiasm," p. 155; also see pp. 141–154). *Reversibility* names very
precisely the experience about which we have been thinking: "We
no longer know which sees and which is seen." It names an experience that can serve as our ground for the cultivation of those
reciprocities so necessary for ethical life. In his "Working Notes"
(pp. 261–65), he says: "The chiasm, reversibility, is the idea that
every perception is doubled with a counter-perception..., is an act
with two faces; one no longer knows who speaks and who listens."
Because of the transpositions and reversals they effect in our
perception, the very same perceptual reflections that arouse our
narcissism also in the end double-cross it.

This reversibility manifests "the intertwining of my life with the
other lives, of my body with the visible things, by the intersection
of my perceptual field with that of the others" ("Interrogation and
Dialectic," *The Visible and the Invisible*, p. 49). Because of this "intertwining," my body "discovers in that other body a miraculous pro-
longation of my intentions" (*Phenomenology of Perception*, p. 354).
What I call *my body* is not only an extended material substance; it is
also a texture, a field — "a field open," as he says, "for other Narcissus" ("The Intertwining — the Chiasm," p. 141). Belonging to the
intertwinings of a "universal flesh" (p. 137), my body is "prolong-
ed," into and through the flesh of all others. This elemental "intercorporeality" (p. 141) is what enables each of us to enter into the
dialectics of narcissism and grow beyond it, learning from our
recognition of ourselves in the face of the other not only the basic
truth of our primordial sociality, but also, and more specifically,
that from the very beginning, social coexistence is transposition
and reversibility. Consequently, as a reflective moment in deeply
felt experience, the "narcissism" of the flesh leads to a self-
understanding that *reverses* and *double-crosses* narcissism as an in-
veterate tendency of the ego to inflate itself at the expense of its
response-ability in relation to others. Because of this "narcissism" of
the flesh, we are entwined with others, seduced into a vision of
ourselves as already inscribed in a dialectic of transposition and
reversibility. And what this double-crossing moment of recognition
in reversibility can teach us is *the root meaning* of reciprocity, a basic
sense, as Merleau-Ponty put it so well, of "an ideal community of

subjects, of intercorporeality" (*Themes from the Lectures at the Collège de France, 1952–60*, p. 82).

In "The Intertwining — The Chiasm," we come across a thought of momentous significance — a thought, however, that has not yet[8] been adequately explored: "We will...have to recognize an ideality that is not alien to the flesh, that gives it its axes, its depth, its dimensions" (p. 152). Even the infant body is always already informed by ideality, by the operative schematism of an ideal ethical community, an ideal body politic. This schematism — rudimentary, to be sure, and never an assured automatic development — inheres in organismic principles that are woven into the body's tissues, its musculature, its organs and limbs of perception and action: an incarnate dream, born of the flesh. There is, already, in the flesh, a certain *logos*, a certain *legein*, an inscription, as it were, of reason, always already laying down for us, and gathering us toward, an ethical and political assignment.[9] Our reason — the rationality in the social and political ideals of the Enlightenment — does not spring into being *ex nihilo*; it can be found already inscribed in the communicativeness of the flesh: it is the *logos* that is articulated in the transpositions and reversibilities of perception, and that constitutes, thereby, our initiation into the justice of reciprocity.

Our universality is as much ingrained in the flesh as our urge toward individuation: both are axes of ideality, prescribing their further actualization and development. But our life-in-common, our intercorporeality, is primary; a certain bodily schematized solidarity precedes our individuation; the flesh of our solidarity precedes, and indeed is the very ground of possibility for, the so-called alienations, the *écarts*, induced by vision and its reflections. These "alienations" can contribute to our individuation; but they can also contribute, at the same time, to the maturity of our socialization — for only through the "alienations" of the self-other dialectic can we learn about the primacy of our solidarity and achieve a social order that turns into living reality the ideality toward which our initial solidarity already points.

This ideality expresses the fact that the body has — is — an order of its own. The order of the body orders food when it is hungry; it orders sleep when it is tired. Analogously, the order of the body, though rudimentary, already orders autonomy and solidarity, individuation and reciprocity, which carry forward the initially schematic order of the body (see Gendlin's "A Philosophical Critique of the Concept of Narcissism"). This order is a kind of Archimedian *point d'appui* for measuring, evaluating, and — when necessary — resisting the social imposition of meaning. Lacan can see in the mirroring of the body image only a process of alienation, because he sees the infant body as without any inherent order of its own. But this empirically false assumption about the body's formation of an identity subjects it to an extreme test of relativism: because the body is without any internal order, it has no basis for measuring, evaluating, and resisting the imposition of an inimical social identity. So Merleau-Ponty argues that the body enjoys an inherent order. But his argument goes even further, because he demonstrates that this order is an order of intercorporeality — an order that orders reversibility and structures in an orientation toward fulfillment in structures of mutual recognition. Thus, Merleau-Ponty's phenomenology is more enlightened; it serves processes of enlightenment and contributes, at the same time, to a critical social practice, for it brings to light a body that can resist the forms of subjection and violence which Lacan's relativism makes him powerless to fight.[10] The body knows the difference between reason and domination, and if we pay attention, it can *tell* us the difference.[11] Nietzsche, Bataille, and Foucault perpetuate the old metaphysics when they regard the body as the absolute *other* of reason. Metaphysics cannot be overcome, nor can the dominations it legitimates be defeated, by an embrace of the body as reason's absolute other.[12]

5. JUSTICE IN THE FLESH

In *Culture and Domination*, John Brenkman locates some of the self-defeating assumptions in the "immanent" social critique of Horkheimer and Adorno:

> Having counterposed in absolute terms a reason that serves the aims of "self-preservation" and a reason that would seek the "truth," and having made the former the driving force of civilization as a whole, Horkheimer and Adorno narrow the resources of social and cultural

critique to the supposed upsurge of the non-instrumentalized, resistant energies of "nature" (the external world, the body, the unconscious). By their own account, however, this countermovement to instrumental reason is impervious to conceptualization of discursive thought. It can expressively indict the prevailing social order, but it cannot generate categories of social analysis. (p. 16)

I would like this chapter to show that our bodies are indeed capable of generating categories of social analysis — categories, moreover, with a critical edge. "Intercorporeality" and "reversibility" are categories derived from the flesh of our experience; and they bespeak a social order that calls into question all social systems where domination prevails over principles of mutual recognition and participatory justice.

Beginning with *The Birth of the Clinic*, Foucault's work increasingly casts his critical thought in the language of a politics of bodies. This has turned out to be a very productive strategy. Nevertheless, it could have been — and could still be — even more productive, with a phenomenological understanding of the body-as-subject to counterbalance his critically powerful, but also critically self-limiting conception of the body-as-object.

We must steer a course between the Scylla of biologism and the Charybdis of historicism. Foucault's politics of the body alternates between a conception of the body that reduces it to a mass of wild, anarchic drives and a conception that reduces it to the effects of history. Whereas the second conception enables him to display the operations and effects of power, applied to the body-as-object, the first conception defeats all attempts to relate the needs and motivations behind resistance to the body's experience of oppression, as it denies the body any *logos*, any rationality, any capacity to articulate its sense of things and generate new categories for its experiences (see Gendlin's paper on narcissism).

In *Logics of Disintegration*, Dews argues that Foucault "gravitates towards a position" in which "the very aim of political action appears to be the abrogation of reflection and the cancellation of self-consciousness.... Foucault's position implies at the very least an extreme spontaneism...[and a] theoretically unelaborated notion of 'resistance,' a corporeally grounded opposition to the power which...moulds human beings into self-identical subjects" (p. 164). I concur with this criticism; but Dews is making a mistake when he suggests that what Foucault needs is a "positive theory of the libidinal body" (ibid.). What Foucault needs, rather, is Merleau-Ponty's phenomenological conception of the body-subject, which recognizes its deeply intersubjective nature. The body of experience is an active, interactive, and in fact extremely articulate body, capable of forming a keen sense of justice and grounding its resistance to power in a wisdom, a *logos*, that comes from its primal experiences of intersubjective reversibility — reciprocity and the absence of reciprocity.

In "The Subject and Power" (p. 216), Foucault said: "We have to promote new forms of subjectivity through the refusal of the kind of individuality which has been imposed on us for several centuries." I see Merleau-Ponty's phenomenology of narcissism as a significant contribution to this very project. I have attempted to show, for example, how a self-understanding based on our experience of ourselves as rooted in the elemental intertwinings and reversibilities of a "universal flesh" can *decenter* the egocentric subject that rules over the traditional discourses of epistemology and psychoanalysis, and can *deconstruct* the traditional sense of individuality.

Foucault uncritically assumes Nietzsche's conception of liberation, which equates it with the wild, unrestrained "self-expression" of the inherently uncivilized energies of instinct. Consequently, he learned nothing from Merleau-Ponty in regard to the body of experience, the body as body-subject. The body of experience is a meaningful body — and a body capable, not only of expressing itself in gestures and deeds, but also of articulating its experience in the concepts of language. It is not reducible to a mass of drives. Nor is it reducible to a material substratum for the application of power, which is the only other conception of the body that, despite his contact with Merleau-Ponty, Foucault ever recognized. I think this partly explains why Foucault could conceive of subjectivity only as a process of submission and subjection. He wanted to think of subjectivity in terms of its embodiment; but he could think of this embodiment only as an inarticulate body of disorganized drives, or else in terms of its position as an object of power — an object, as he says in "Nietzsche, Genealogy, History," that is "totally imprinted by history."[13]

"On the Genealogy of Ethics" connects "the moral notion of authenticity" to "the idea of the self as something which is given to us," so that "to be truly our true self" can be only to conform to a predetermined bodily nature (biologism) or else to conform to the requirements and conditions of the prevailing social reality (historicism) (Rabinow, p. 351). For Foucault, "authenticity" requires a fixed essence, the same for everyone. Thus, he sees it as *opposed* to the idea that "we have to create ourselves as a work of art" (ibid.). But it never occurs to him that, as Merleau-Ponty suggests,[14] the human *body* can be taken up by "practices of the self" and created, with *souci de soi*, as a work of art. It never occurs to him to recognize that "subjectivity" is embodied in a body of meaningful experience, a body capable of thinking for itself, generating phenomenological categories, and talking back to history — talking back, for example, to a "psychology or psychoanalytic science, which is supposed to be able to tell you what your true self is" (ibid., p. 362).

Habermas sees the problem, but only partially, because, despite his nod of recognition in the direction of an "embodied reason," he continues to think *without* the body. Criticizing Foucault, he observes: "From his perspective, socialized individuals can only be perceived as exemplars, as standardized products of some discourse formation — as individual copies that are mechanically punched out" (*The Philosophical Discourse of Modernity*, p. 293). The same point must unfortunately be argued against Foucault's conception of the body. This conception has, nevertheless, become very influential, while Merleau-Ponty's much more empowering account of embodiment has been virtually consigned to the shadows. Thus, for example, in paper titled "Foucault, Freud, and the Technologies of the Self," Patrick Hutton has asserted that, "To search the psyche for the truth about ourselves is a futile task because the psyche can only reflect the images we have conjured up to describe ourselves. Looking into the psyche, therefore, is like looking into the mirror image of a mirror. One sees oneself reflected in an image of infinite regress. Our gaze is led not toward

the substance of our beginnings but rather into the meaninglessness of previously discarded images of the self" (p. 139). Merleau-
Ponty's phenomenological account of narcissism refutes the claim
that the psyche can only reflect old images. What the phenomenology shows is, on the contrary, how reflection can generate new
images. Reflection effects this because of its embodied intersubjectivity: the psyche can always of course conjure up its own images;
but it can also form images in response to what it sees reflected in
the gaze of the other. What Hutton ignores in his account is the
intercorporeality of the reflections and their images. What he ignores,
then, are the surprises in the reversibilities of intersubjective
dynamics. And he ignores these things because he assumes a
monadological, still essentially Cartesian model of subjectivity,
reflection, and perception.

In the transpositions and reversibilities of the flesh, a new form
of subjectivity, a self that recognizes itself as essentially constituted
through social relationships of reciprocity, is in fact already being
schematized. Although of course only in a rudimentary and
preliminary way that needs to be appropriately cultivated, intercorporeality already schematizes the embodiment of a self deeply
rooted in an ethics of caring and open to the kind of communication necessary for the building of a society truly organized by principles of justice. By grace of the reversibilities we inevitably live, we
already have, in the dimension of the flesh, a *preconceptual understanding* of the reciprocity necessary for the kind of communication
a rational and just society requires.[15]

In his Introduction to Jürgen Habermas's *Lectures on the Philosophical Discourse of Modernity*, Thomas McCarthy observes that "The
critique of subject-centered reason is a prologue to the critique of a
bankrupt culture." Looking at this same culture, Christopher Lasch
pointed out its destructive narcissism. But the critical discourse on
modernity has many voices and registers. Here, confirming Vico's
contention, in *The New Science*, that our learned discourse already
contains many words "carried over from bodies and from the properties of bodies to signify the institutions of the mind and spirit," I
have tried to show that Merleau-Ponty's late work in hermeneutical
phenomenology introduces an understanding of the body that contributes a new vision of subjectivity to the contemporary para-

digms of epistemology, ethics, and political theory. What he shows is that, in the dimensionality of the flesh, in the intertwinings, reversibilities, and communications of its depths, there is already at work a "miraculous" dialectic, one that suggests the possibility — but of course no more than a possibility — of an alternative cultural direction. In the articulation of this dialectic, which Merleau-Ponty unfortunately borrowed the word *narcissism* to describe, the corporeal schema of a new form of subjectivity, deeply concealed, is brought to light, already in operation. Just as, for Habermas, the "ideal speech situation" is necessarily implied in the competency structure of speech itself, so the reciprocity that is necessary in the constitution of a rational and just social order is an organismic "fulfillment" implied in the structural transpositions and reversibilities that already organize and predispose the flesh.

The subject of a society organized in consonance with the body-self deeply schematized in the reversibilities of intercorporeality must await, however, another time, and another essay, to be examined further. Suffice it to say, perhaps, that the corporeal schema laid out in our intercorporeality constitutes a very difficult social task. The task it projects requires the most careful cultivation of a potential, a moral capacity, latent in the flesh. And it "calls to mind," as Habermas says (*The Philosophical Discourse of Modernity*, p. 68), "a relationship between persons in which the accommodating, identifying externalization of one partner in relation to the other does not require the sacrifice of that partner's own identity, but preserves dependency and autonomy at once" (also see Habermas, "Moral Development and Ego Identity"). It is by no means certain that we know how, individually and as a society, to respond to this gift of the flesh.[16] For this reason, I try to keep in mind what Merleau-Ponty once wrote about the contribution of philosophical enquiry to the discourse on modernity: "Philosophy is not a particular body of knowledge; it is the vigilance which does not let us forget the source of all knowledge" (The Philosopher and Sociology," in *Signs*, p. 110).

The moral values, social ideals, and political principles of Enlightenment Humanism did not suddenly appear *ex nihilo* in the modern world. Most people would say, I think, that they formed, rather, in response to historical conditions. I agree. But I would like to add that they carried forward, life-affirmingly, values that are inherent in, and constitutive of, our most universal organismic capacities. In "The Idea of Equality," Bernard Williams argued that some of the capacities with which we are endowed as human beings, for example, our capacity to feel pain and our capacity to perceive suffering in others, give rise to moral claims, claims on ourselves and others, that we should not disregard or neglect. In this study, we have brought to light a "source" of moral and political "knowledge." We have seen an organismic basis for the principle of reciprocity. We have seen how reciprocity, a necessary condition of social justice, may be said to carry forward and satisfy that need which an organismic reversibility, visible even in narcissism, primally inaugurates — and for which it demands the most vigilant, most enduring recognition.

CONCLUSION

In a recent essay on "The Return of Values," sociologist Alan Wolfe observed that, "The major question facing a revival of moral sociology is whether it is possible to posit ties that can hold people together without subjecting them to historical traditions or political decisions over which they have no control" (*Tikkun*, p. 63). My aim in this chapter has been to show that the nature of the human body holds the beginning of an unexplored answer to this question. Against Nietzsche, Freud, Lacan, Bataille, Foucault, and Lyotard, I have argued for the following propositions:

1. It is not true that the only order in the human body is an order totally imposed by society, and that its order — human nature — is nothing but the accumulated historical effect of political controls.[17] This is historicism, and it must be rejected.

2. The human body has — is — an order of its own. This order has not been widely recognized. However, as Dews points out, "the cost of this separation and denial is the perpetuation of the blind coercion of nature within the self."[18]

3. The nature and order of the human body cannot be reduced to biological processes and automatisms.[19] Biologism is just as false and self-defeating as historicism, and it too must be rejected.

4. The body's order is *already* pro-social: therefore, the body's pro-social behavior is not, and does not need to be, totally introduced by the work of society.

5. Society's work of socialization, and its vision of moral development, should respect, and be responsive to, the primal order already inherent in the child's body. If pro-social behavioral tendencies *are* already present in the biological programming of the child, then education can indeed be what its Latin etymology calls for: a process of *bringing out* and *drawing out*. But if human beings are innately mean, nasty, and brutish, aggressive, and hostile, then, of course, education for civilization must be a process of imposing restraints.

6. The body's order is, as Gendlin (1987) words it, the life-affirming order of "carrying forward."

7. Reciprocity is a socially produced discursive order; it is also the only order we know of that adequately carries forward the surprising reversibilities in which the body's own order is manifest. All political systems should be at least consistent with the normativity of our biological order; but we have no a priori reason to suppose that there is one and only one political system which could harmoniously fulfill this order and which would be uniquely fated or prescribed. Our biology does not, and cannot, totally determine any specific political arrangements. Nevertheless, given the fact that the order of our bodies is an order structured by reversibility, it is clear that *what the body needs for its fulfillment* is a social order governed, at the very least, by forms of reciprocity and an ethics of communicative rationality.

8. In the phenomenology of "narcissism" that Merleau-Ponty brings to light, we can see our awakening to the ethics of reciprocity; we can see it taking shape in the character of the body's primal order.

9. Working for social justice today calls for "promoting new forms of subjectivity," as Foucault finally argued — and this means collaborating with the inherently pro-social order of our bodies to achieve in society at large a level of moral development in which questions of social justice, and the communicative procedures that reflection on these questions requires, are of paramount concern: a possibility we cannot recognize, I believe, without understanding

that neither the monadic ego (in the discourse of Cartesian meta-physics) nor the unruly body of drives (in the discourse of Freudian psychoanalysis) should continue to represent for us the distinctive social character of the embodied human self.

The story of Narcissus has been, for too long, a story of lost self-recognition. What Merleau-Ponty has shown us, I think, is that, because of our intersubjectivity, the chiasm that is our flesh, reflection becomes the double-crossing of narcissism, inducing the ego subject to acknowledge the truth of the other, and initiating the transpositions and reversals that ground in perception our under-standing of reciprocity and justice.

I want to give the last word to Merleau-Ponty. In *Phenomenology of Perception*, he writes: "In the experience of dialogue, there is consti-tuted between the other person and myself a common ground: my thought and his are interwoven into a single fabric... inserted into a shared operation of which neither of us is the creator... we are collab-orators for each other in consummate reciprocity" (p. 354).

NOTES

This is a revised version of a paper presented in October 1987 at a ses-sion of the Merleau-Ponty Conference, held at the University of Rhode Island. For their critical comments and suggestions for revision, I am especially grateful to Edward Casey, Martin Dillon, Eugene Gendlin, Joel Kovel, Roger Levin, Samuel Mallin, and Thomas McCarthy.

1. See William Galston, "Aristotelian Morality and Liberal Society," an unpublished paper read at the 1982 annual meeting of the American Political Science Association in Denver, cited by C. Fred Alford, in *Nar-cissism: Socrates, the Frankfurt School and Psychoanalytic Theory* (New Haven: Yale University Press, 1988), p. 1.

2. See Alford, *Narcissism*, p. 160. Alford argues that there is a positive or progressive side to narcissism, as well as a pathological side; and he characterizes the healthiness of narcissism as the self's quest for unity, wholeness, and perfection. Like Alford, Merleau-Ponty would emphasize that this quest can be furthered only by developing ourselves in reciprocating relationships with others.

3. In *Eros and Civilization*, Herbert Marcuse suggested that one

could see in the phenomenon of narcissism the utopian image of a reality principle different from Freud's. Alford comments (*Narcissism*, p. 140): "it is probably more fruitful to approach the whole issue of a 'different reality principle' from the perspective of narcissism than from that of drive theory." Neither Marcuse nor Alford have convinced me that the theory of narcissism is any better than drive theory, as a basis for conceiving a less "repressive" social reality, but I cannot take the space to argue the point here.

4. Merleau-Ponty's phenomenology of ambiguity helps us to appreciate Habermas's point that "Subjects who reciprocally recognize each other as such must consider each other as *identical*, insofar as they both take up the position of subjects; they must at all times subsume themselves and the other under the same category. At the same time, the relation of *reciprocity* of recognition demands the *non-identity* of the one and the other; both must also maintain their absolute difference, for to be a subject implies the claim to individuation." See J. Habermas, "Sprachspiel, Intention und Bedeutung," p. 334, in R. W. Wiggershaus, ed., *Sprachanalyse und Soziologie* (Frankfurt: Suhrkamp, 1971).

5. See Seymour Fisher and S. E. Cleveland, *Body Image and Personality* (Princeton, N.J.: Van Nostrand, 1958), p. 206: "The whole concept of body-image boundaries has implicit in it the idea of the structuring of one's relationships with others." Also see S. Fisher, "Body Image," in *International Encyclopedia of the Social Sciences*, ed. D. Sills (New York: Collier-Macmillan, 2nd ed., 1972), vol. 2, pp. 113–16.

6. "The reconciled condition would not annex what is other, but would find its happiness in the fact that this other retains its distance and its difference within the permitted intimacy, and that it remains beyond heterogeneity and sameness." See J. Habermas, *The Philosophical Discourse of Modernity*, p. 68. Habermas is quoting, here, from Adorno's *Negative Dialektik*, vol. 6 of the *Gesammelte Schriften* (Frankfurt: Suhrkamp, 1973), p. 192.

7. I say *alien image*, because the image formed within me comes to me through the other — and in a certain sense, it therefore *represents* and *belongs* to the other. See Peter Dews, *Logics of Disintegration* (London, New York: Verso, 1987), p. 228. He argues that poststructuralism thinks of individual identity as formed only through submission and the passive internalization of authority, rather than through interactive identification with others. This way of conceptualizing identity formation turns it into a process of disintegration.

8. But see my trilogy, *The Body's Recollection of Being* (London and Boston: Routledge, 1985), *The Opening of Vision* (New York and London: Routledge, 1988), and *The Listening Self* (New York and London: Routledge, 1989).

9. See Martin Heidegger, *Early Greek Thinking* (New York: Harper and Row, 1975). Heidegger interprets *legein*, the verb form of *logos*, as meaning "gathering" and "laying down." Habermas calls for a conception of reason that recognizes it as always embodied (see *The Philosophical Discourse of Modernity*, p. 317). Because "reason" is an established meaning for *logos*, I am exploring, in this paragraph, the *legein* of the *logos* as the embodiment of reason, developing this question in relation to Merleau-Ponty's recognition of an ideality inherent in the flesh. I identify this ideality as reason and claim that Habermas's "communicative reason" is an ideal born in the reversibilities of the flesh.

10. I am grateful to Martin Dillon for reminding me, in a letter dated 22 February 1988, that I had made this argument elsewhere in other papers, and for urging me to make it again, at this point, in the present chapter.

11. Merleau-Ponty's phenomenological disclosure of a communicative rationality already schematized in the flesh contests what Horkheimer and Adorno, in *Dialectic of Enlightenment* (New York: Seabury, 1977), p. 119, call Nietzsche's "merciless doctrine of the identity of domination and reason," by showing a rationality already in our bodily nature that is not only *other* than domination, but moreover *in protest* against it. The body is less easily fooled, less often deceived, when it comes to the difference between reason and domination, than the "consciousness" of our old metaphysics! When I listen I can hear the voice of reason, speaking its wisdom in and through my body.

12. See J. Habermas, *The Philosophical Discourse of Modernity* (Cambridge: MIT Press, 1987), p. 311: "A different, less dramatic, but step-by-step testable critique of the Western emphasis on *logos* starts from an attack on the abstractions surrounding *logos* itself, as free of language, as universalist, and as disembodied. It conceives... of the logocentrism of Western thought, heightened by the philosophy of consciousness, as a systematic *foreshortening* and *distortion* of a potential always already operative in the communicative practices of everyday life, but only selectively exploited."

13. Michel Foucault, "Nietzsche, Genealogy, History," in *Memory,*

Counter-memory, Practice (Ithaca, N.Y.: Cornell University Press, 1977), p. 148.

14. See Merleau-Ponty, *Phenomenology of Perception* (New York: Humanities, 1962), p. 150: "The body is to be compared, not to a physical object, but to a work of art."

15. Recent empirical research in psychology confirms this. See the works by Bar-Tal, Bullowa, Eisenberg, Fisher, Kohlberg, Lerner, Mussen, Staub, Stern, Sullivan, Yarrow, Whiting, and Winnicott cited in the Bibliography.

16. For two provocative readings relating to this question, see Francis Barker, *The Tremulous Private Body: Essays on Subjection* (London: Methuen, 1984) and Peter Stallybrass and Allon White, *The Politics and Poetics of Transgression* (Ithaca, N.Y.: Cornell University Press, 1986), esp. pp. 1–43.

17. See Gad Horowitz, "The Foucaultian Impasse: No Sex, No Self, No Revolution," *Political Theory* 15, no. 1 (February 1987): 61–80: "Foucault's anti-essentialism leads him to reject prematurely, as unacceptably essentialist, all notions of a significant transhistorical, depth-psychological...dimension of human experience" (p. 61). He argues that "There is a transhistorical, depth-psychological truth, but it is not sexuality in Foucault's sense. ... The trans-historical truth cannot be abolished by fiat, but that doesn't make this trans-historical truth an 'essence'" (p. 71). Also see Patrick Hutton, "Foucault, Freud, and the Technologies of the Self" (p. 127). Hutton, summarizing Foucault (accurately, I believe), says: "for Foucault, there is no such thing as a human nature. There are *only* the linguistic and institutional artifacts left behind by successive generations as each took up anew the task of creating categories to explain its perception of the human condition." Biological essentialism, legitimating reactionary politics, needs to be refuted; it is not only bad politics, but bad biology. However, the other extreme — historicism — is equally bad politics, and equally false.

18. Dews, *Logics of Disintegration*, pp. 138–39. Dews, here, is talking about Adorno. "The fundamental theme of *The Dialectic of Enlightenment*" is, he notes, "that the conscious self can only emerge through a separation from nature and a denial of its own internal basis."

19. In *Au Juste* (Paris: Christian Bourgeois, 1979), Jean-Francois Lyotard conceded, finally, that "it is not true that the quest for intensities or things of that kind can provide the substance of a politics, because there is the problem of injustice" (see *Au Juste*, pp. 170–71). Dews argues

that Lyotard is — or anyway, was — mired in "an abstract opposition between repressive order and 'emancipatory' disorder" (*Logics of Disintegration*, p. 143). I do not know what position Lyotard now holds, but Dews is certainly right to reject a position that "can only equate the ego with repression and the disorder of the drives with liberation" (Ibid., pp. 140–41). I hope Lyotard has abandoned this analysis.

BIBLIOGRAPHY

Adorno, Theodor, *Negative Dialektik, Gesammelte Werke*, vol. 6. Frankfurt: Suhrkamp, 1973.

Adorno, Theodor, and Max Horkheimer, *Dialectic of Enlightenment*. New York: Seabury Press, 1977.

Alford, C. Fred, *Narcissism: Socrates, the Frankfurt School, and Psychoanalytic Theory*. New Haven: Yale University Press, 1988.

Barker, Francis, *The Tremulous Private Body: Essays on Subjection*. London and New York: Methuen, 1984.

Bar-Tal, Daniel, *Prosocial Behavior: Theory and Research*. New York: John Wiley, 1976.

Brenkman, John, *Culture and Domination*. Ithaca: Cornell University Press, 1987.

Bullowa, M., ed., *Before Speech: The Beginnings of Interpersonal Communication*. Cambridge: Cambridge University Press, 1979.

Cohen, Richard, "Merleau-Ponty, the Flesh and Foucault," *Philosophy Today* 28 (Winter 1984).

Derrida, Jacques, "Cogito and the History of Madness," in *Writing and Difference*. Chicago: University of Chicago Press, 1978.

Descartes, Rene, "Meditations on First Philosophy," in E. Haldane and G. Ross, eds., *The Philosophical Work of Descartes*, vol. 1. New York: Dover Publishing, 1955.

Dews, Peter, *Logics of Disintegration: Post-Structuralist Thought and the Claims of Critical Theory*. London, New York: Verso, 1987.

Dillon, Martin, "Merleau-Ponty and the Psychogenesis of the Self," *Journal of Phenomenological Psychology* 9, nos. 1–2 (Autumn 1978).

Dillon, Martin, "Merleau-Ponty and the Reversibility Thesis," *Man and World* 16 (1983).

Eisenberg, Nancy, *The Development of Prosocial Behavior.* New York: Academic Press, 1982.

Fisher, Seymour, "Body Image," in *International Encyclopedia of the Social Sciences* 2, ed. D. Sills. New York: Collier-Macmillan, 1972.

Fisher, Seymour, and Cleveland, S. E., *Body Image and Personality.* Princeton: Van Nostrand, 1958.

Flynn, Bernard, "Descartes and the Ontology of Subjectivity," *Man and World* 16 (1983).

Foucault, Michel, "My Body, This Paper, This Fire," *Oxford Literary Review* 4 (Autumn 1979). English translation by Geoff Bennington of an appendix to the second (1972) edition of *Histoire de la folie* (Paris: Plon, 1961).

Foucault, Michel, "The Subject and Power," in H. Dreyfus and P. Rabinow, *Michel Foucault: Beyond Structuralism and Hermeneutics.* Chicago: University of Chicago Press, 1982.

Foucault, Michel, "What Is Enlightenment?" in Paul Rabinow, ed., *The Foucault Reader.* New York: Pantheon Books, 1984.

Foucault, Michel, "On the Genealogy of Ethics: An Overview of Work in Progress," in Paul Rabinow, ed., *The Foucault Reader.*

Foucault, Michel, "Technologies of the Self," in Luther Martin, Huck Gutman, and Patrick Hutton, eds., *Technologies of the Self.* Amherst: University of Massachusetts Press, 1988.

Freud, Sigmund, "On Narcissism: An Introduction," *Standard Edition of the Complete Works of Sigmund Freud*, vol. 14. London: Hogarth Press, 1957.

Freud, Sigmund, *The Ego and the Id.* New York: W. W. Norton, 1962.

Freud, Sigmund, *Introductory Lectures on Psycho-Analysis*, Part III: *General Theory of the Neuroses*, Standard Edition, vol. 16. London: Hogarth Press, 1963.

Freud, Sigmund, *New Introductory Lectures on Psychoanalysis*, Standard Edition, vol. 22. London: Hogarth Press, 1964.

Freud, Sigmund, "The Splitting of the Ego in the Process of Defence," in Standard Edition, vol. 23. London: Hogarth Press, 1964.

Galston, William, "Aristotelian Morality and Liberal Society," unpublished lecture at the 1982 annual meeting of the American Political Science Association in Denver, Colorado.

Gendlin, Eugene, "A Philosophical Critique of the Concept of Narcissism: The Significance of the Awareness Movement," in David M. Levin, ed., *Pathologies of the Modern Self: Postmodern Studies on Narcissism, Schizophrenia, and Depression*. New York: New York University Press, 1987.

Gilligan, Carol, *In a Different Voice: Psychological Theory and Women's Development*. Cambridge: Harvard University Press, 1982.

Habermas, Jürgen, "Sprachspiel, Intention und Bedeutung," in R. W. Wiggershaus, ed., *Sprachanalyse und Soziologie*. Frankfurt am Main: Suhrkamp Verlag, 1971.

Habermas, Jürgen, "Moral Development and Ego Identity," *Communication and the Evolution of Society*. Boston: Beacon Press, 1979.

Habermas, Jürgen, *Knowledge and Human Interest*. Boston: Beacon Press, 1979.

Habermas, Jürgen, *The Philosophical Discourse of Modernity*. Cambridge: MIT Press, 1987.

Horkheimer, Max, and Theodor Adorno, *Dialectic of Enlightenment*. New York: Seabury Press, 1977.

Horowitz, Gad, "The Foucauldian Impasse: No Sex, No Self, No Revolution," *Political Theory* 15, no. 1 (1987).

Hutton, Patrick, "Foucault, Freud, and the Technologies of the Self," in Luther Martin, Huck Gutman, and Patrick Hutton, eds., *Technologies of the Self*. Amherst: University of Massachusetts Press, 1988.

Kernberg, Otto, *Borderline Conditions and Pathological Narcissism*. New York: Jason Aronson, 1975.

Kohlberg, Lawrence, *The Philosophy of Moral Development*. New York: Harper and Row, 1981.

Kohlberg, Lawrence, *Essays in Moral Development*, Vol. 2. *The Psychology of Moral Development*. San Francisco: Harper and Row, 1984.

Kohut, Heinz, *The Restoration of the Self*. New York: International Universities Press, 1977.

Lacan, Jacques, *The Language of the Self.* Baltimore: Johns Hopkins University Press, 1968.

Lacan, Jacques, "The Mirror Stage as Formative of the Function of the I as Revealed in Psychoanalytic Experience," in Alan Sheridan, ed., *Ecrits: A Selection.* New York: W. W. Norton, 1977.

Lacan, Jacques, "Aggressivity in Psychoanalysis," in Alan Sheridan, ed., *Ecrits: A Selection.* New York: W. W. Norton, 1977.

Lasch, Christopher, *The Culture of Narcissism: American Life in an Age of Diminishing Expectations.* New York: Routledge & Kegan Paul, 1987.

Lerner, Melvin J., and Sally C. Lerner, eds., *The Justice Motive in Social Behavior: Adapting to Times of Scarcity and Change.* New York: Plenum Publishing, 1981.

Levin, David Michael, *The Body's Recollection of Being.* London and Boston: Routledge & Kegan Paul, 1985.

Levin, David Michael, "Psychopathology in the Epoch of Nihilism," in D. Levin, ed., *Pathologies of the Modern Self: Postmodern Studies on Narcissism, Schizophrenia and Depression.* New York: New York University Press, 1987.

Levin, David Michael, "Clinical Stories: A Modern Self in the Fury of Being," in D. Levin, ed., *Pathologies of the Modern Self.* New York: New York University Press, 1987.

Levin, David Michael, *The Opening of Vision: Nihilism and the Postmodern Situation.* London and New York: Routledge & Kegan Paul, 1987.

Lyotard, Jean-Francois, *Au Juste.* Paris: Christian Bourgeois, 1979.

MacIntyre, Alasdair, *After Virtue.* South Bend, Ind.: University of Notre Dame, 1981.

Marcuse, Herbert, *Eros and Civilization: A Philosophical Inquiry into Freud.* Boston: Beacon Press, 1955.

Marcuse, Herbert, "On Hedonism," *Negations: Essays in Critical Theory.* Boston: Beacon Press, 1968.

Marx, Karl, *Early Writings.* London: 1963.

McCarthy, Thomas, "Introduction" to Jürgen Habermas, *Lectures on the Philosophical Discourse of Modernity.* Cambridge: MIT Press, 1987.

Merleau-Ponty, Maurice, *The Phenomenology of Perception.* Atlantic Highlands, N.J.: Humanities Press, 1962.

Merleau-Ponty, Maurice, "The Child's Relations with Others," in *The Primacy of Perception*. Evanston, Ill.: Northwestern University Press, 1964.

Merleau-Ponty, Maurice, *The Visible and the Invisible*. Evanston, Ill.: Northwestern University Press, 1968.

Merleau-Ponty, Maurice, *Signs*. Evanston, Ill.: Northwestern University Press, 1964.

Merleau-Ponty, Maurice, *Themes from the Lectures at the Collège de France, 1952–1960*. Evanston, Ill.: Northwestern University Press, 1970.

Mussen, Paul, and Nancy Eisenberg, *The Roots of Caring, Sharing and Helping*. New York: W. H. Freeman, 1977.

Piaget, Jean, *The Moral Judgement of the Child*. New York: Macmillan, The Free Press, 1965.

Rabinow, Paul, ed., *The Foucault Reader*. New York: Pantheon Books, 1984.

Richardson, William, and John P. Muller, *Lacan and Language: Reader's Guide to Ecrits*. New York: International Universities Press, 1982.

Schwartz-Salant, Nathan, *Narcissism and Character Transformation: The Psychology of Narcissistic Character Disorders*. Toronto: Inner City Books, 1982.

Staub, Ervin, Daniel Bar-Tal, Jerzy Karylowski, and Janus Reykowski, eds., *Development and Maintenance of Prosocial Behavior*. New York: Plenum Publishing Co., 1984.

Stern, D., *The First Relationship: Infant and Mother*. Cambridge: Harvard University Press, 1977.

Sullivan, Harry Stack, *The Interpersonal Theory of Psychiatry*. New York: W. W. Norton, 1953.

Vico, Giambattisa, *The New Science*. Ithaca, N.Y.: Cornell University Press, 1984.

Whiting, B., ed., *Six Cultures: Studies of Child Rearing*. New York: John Wiley, 1963.

Williams, Bernard, "The Idea of Equality," in P. Laslett and W. G. Runciman, eds., *Philosophy, Politics and Society*. Oxford: Basil Blackwell, 1962, second series.

Winnicott, Donald, *Play and Reality*. Baltimore: Penguin Books, 1980.

Wolfe, Alan, "The Return of Values," *Tikkun* 1, no. 2 (1986).

Yarrow, Marian, "The Emergence and Founding of Pro-Social Behaviors in Young Children," in R. Smart, ed., *Readings in Child Development and Relationships*. New York: Macmillan, 1977.

4

Imperatives

Alphonso Lingis

All consciousness is consciousness of something; this Husserlian formula designates intentionality as the essence of consciousness. Is this "apodictic insight," like the laws of natural science, undecidably a law or a definition? The "something" in question toward which an awareness is intentionally turned is an object determined by scientific thought as empirically real; it is also a perceived pattern, a figment of the imagination, a proposition formulated in language, a number, the ego. But in perception, according to Merleau-Ponty's phenomenology, the something is a *thing*, an integrated, intersensorially consistent, graspable and manipulatable, real thing. The perception "devoted to things" shows that we exist-in-the-world. A figure against a background — that is not a contingent trait of perception; it is the definition of perception, Merleau-Ponty writes at the beginning of *Phenomenology of Perception*. Is this a psychological law, contingent then and admitting exceptions? Or is it a definition of what psychology will take to be perception?

Or is objective science, which represents objects, intrinsically dependent on the perception that presents things, such that it has to represent perception as presenting things? Then, why does science have to be objective, have to represent objects?

Merleau-Ponty finds, in the segmentation of the contemporary domain of sciences, a crisis in the very concept of objectivity. Conceptual models that reflect perceptual structures enter into the organization of the diverse segments of empirical research. Does this development show that the notion of *thing* rather than the notion of *object* is the imperative model for the scientific representation of the universe?

THE IMPERATIVES IN THINGS

The self that forms in our body, in the sensitive-sensible *element* that moves itself, moves toward *things*. If a momentary pattern in the

91

road is not confirmed by more visibility, I doubt that I was really seeing; if a brief cry heard in the night is not followed by another sound or something visible, I doubt that there was anything and that I had heard. If, observing her more, I doubt that this woman has anything really engaging or seductive about her, I doubt the reality of my love. If, among the colors and sizes and shapes of things, my perception discerns the real properties from the colors, sizes, and shapes distorted by the medium, the distance, or the perspective; if I see the sheets of paper scattered on the floor under the desk as white even though they reflect light-waves objectively measurable as gray; if I see the snow in the troughs as white seen through blue shadow — it is because my perception is finalized toward seeing coherent and consistent things, maintaining their properties as they endure. I see the reflection not as a patch of gleaming color on the rim of the iris, but as an immaterial radiance playing over the sphere of the eye, which is brown and white. I feel as heavy as two weights the one distributed over a broad expanse of my body, the other applied wholly upon a small area, and felt with two quite different systems of resistant tendons and muscles, the one laid on my stomach, the other hung from my finger. I feel the grain and composition of the wood beneath the carved form of the statue that is felt as put on the subsistent ligneous substance. My perception is this power to attain from the first the inter-sensorial coherence and consistency of a thing, a transcendent essence or way of being that no intersensorial exploration will ever make definitively given.

The distorted, phantomal, or illusory appearances are distinguished in perception from the real properties because perception *has to* perceive things, coherent and consistent beings. The things *have to* not exhibit all their sides and qualities, have to compress them behind the faces they turn to us, have to tilt back their sides in depth, and not occupy all the field with their relative bigness, because they *have to* coexist in a field with one another, and that field has to coexist with the fields of the other possible things. The double monocular images dissipate as my eyes advance to the sight of a real thing; the visual form of a furry animal disappears and is not reworked and integrated into the form of the porous rock that materializes as I get closer. Some sensory patterns disconnect from the map of reality and float like phantoms before it, because they do not fit into the coherence and consistency of the world.

Seeing is believing; the visible form of a furry animal gave itself out as a pattern in the world and in the real, but not as the real or true being itself, it was provisional, attendant upon confirmation through more seeing. The apparition of the real is not composed out of such appearances, for when I step closer it dissipates to give place to the more dense apparition of the porous rock. Yet real or true being is not something apart from these always presumptive appearances, since what motivates the dissociation of the furry animal form the real world is not an apprehension of the logic and necessities of the field, but the subsequent apparition in its place of the rock whose visibility persists. The "belief" in the reality of the first appearance is "revoked" only by being transferred to the next. More exactly, there are not successive acts of judgment; one takes as real the consistent appearance that forms on the sensible levels of the world.

The world in which we perceive extends in a space-time that is not a priori apprehendable in the formula for Euclidean or non-Euclidean geometrical dimensions and the objective time of successive moments. It extends on *levels* — the level of the light that our gaze adjusts to and sees with as it looks at the illuminated contours that surface as reliefs on the level, the level of the sonority our hearing attunes to as it harkens to sounds and noises that rise out of it, the level of the tangible our posture finds as our limbs move across the contours and textures of tangible substances, the levels of verticality and of depth and of rest that emerge as our position becomes functional in a layout of tasks. The level is found sensorially, by a movement that does not grasp at it as an objective but adjusts to it, is sustained by it, moves with it and according to it. The time of the perceived world also has to be conceived as a level. The time of the world is not a dimension $t+1$ projected by a conceptual operation in which we locate the present moment, in which all that is perceivable is presented. The future and the past extend like horizons, but not horizons we view: levels on which we find ourselves embarked and that sustain the configuration of the present. Our perceiving organism presents itself in the course of the world, where the present moment is not a closed form that reproduces itself along a linear dimension but a relief on a level of futurity and passage. The future extends not as a unit about to displace the present moment but as a directive toward which and with which we turn. The present as it passes does not subsist in the form of a closed moment that has, as Husserl put it, undergone simply the modification of distance; it loses its particularity, veers into generality, is no longer before us as an object of perception or an object of recall, but becomes the angle and the momentum with which we now envisage what is there. The world is not a framework, an order, or an arrangement, but a nexus of levels. The levels are not dimensions we can survey from above; we find them not by moving toward them but by moving with them. They are determinate not as an extension we can survey or a periodicity we can diagram but as a style we catch onto by moving with it and catching on to how each scene and each moment varies the last and launches a variation in its turn. As we catch onto the style of a writer or a conversation not by understanding the axioms from which each proposition is derived but by catching on to the rhythm, the tempo, the scope of the shifts, the range of the variations and repartees. The world holds the fields in which we perceive together in a consistency and coherence that is not formulable as a set of universal laws but apprehended as a style caught on the move and engendering variants by which we recognize the visible, the tangible, the sonorous realms beneath the monocular images, the will-o' the-wisps and the mirages.

The reality of the sensible levels, of the world — which is not the evidence of constitutional laws and necessities — gives to any thing in the world the evidence of its being real. The apparition of the sensible world is not that of a true representation, since all of the beings it presents and contains are given as real contingent upon subsequent perceptual confirmation, and since the coherence and compossibility of the fields of our various senses and of the transtemporal and intercorporeal field is never given and formulable, but is known only in the continuous transitions by which each field opens upon the next. But the reality of the sensible field is not effectively doubtable, since every doubt we can have and every dissillusioning we can experience concerns only particular configurations within it, and we doubt the reality of any appearance only by believing more in another perceptible configuration. Any more intelligible or more coherent representation we could have of the universe, including that of the universe of fully determinate objectivity that we posit as the ideal term of all our scientific investigations, could not be more certain or more real than the field we perceive, for every such representation is a re-presentation, in the linguistic formulations and calculus of our reason, of the field of our perception, and has to verify its calculations of what is real by controlled observations of the perceivable.

THE WORLD AS AN IMPERATIVE

What then is this finality that makes our perception *have to* perceive things and *have to* perceive a field of compossible things, a world? It is not a determinism; we can see without necessarily seeing things and without necessarily seeing a world. We can see monocular images and not binocular visions of things; our eyes can get caught up in phantasms and pre-things, in the caricatural doubles and mirages the sensible levels and planes also engender. Our look can record only the contours and finish our desires and our obsessions, our loves and our hatreds have put on the nodes in the fabric of sensible reality; our eyes and our hands can touch only the shapings culture and industry have left on the levels of the natural world. We can take refuge from the planes of sensible reality in a dream-space; we can drag fragments of things into a delirious space without levels and consistent dimensions; we can, as in advanced states of melancholia, settle in the realm of death.

The things do not subsist as givens but as tasks to which perception finds itself devoted. The things arise as reliefs on the levels of the world that extend about them and harbor other things to which they turn their lateral sides and that invite us as standpoints from which those sides can be seen. To reach the things we have to displace ourselves to those other standpoints in the landscape the other things mark out for us. The levels extend the world as a system where the things witness one another and each contributes to the consistency and coherence of all. The thing ordering the direction of our perception leads us to the consistency and coherence of the levels; the levels that we can reach only by subjecting ourselves to them conduct us to things. The things are not given in perception but order it as tasks; the world, nexus of levels, exists not as a perceptual given but as an imperative.

The directives with which the world extends are not given in perceptual presentation, nor in conceptual representation. The world is not given in the consistency and coherence of a saturated set of universal and necessary laws. We cannot derive the position and structure of the things the course of the world brings out of a blueprint our theory can represent. As we turn toward a thing we do see sketched out on the side it turns to us prefigurations of its other sides, and we see about it the other things whose consistency witnesses those other sides; but to reach those other sides we have to displace ourselves to see it from the standpoints the surrounding things fix for us, and in the time the displacement takes the side we have now left behind may discolor, bulge or shrivel, or disintegrate. Our very exploratory movements about it leave their marks on it. It would take an indefinite expanse of time to make each of its sides face us, and each thing the course of the world presents disintegrates in the course of time. A thing is before us as a task and a reality embedded in the subsistence of the world inasmuch as it is closed in itself and harbors secrets and surprises. The world order that sustains it, the levels that maintain it, are presented not as a framework surveyed but as directives pursued. The very representation we formulate, the set of formulations with which we represent its coherence and consistency as universal and necessary laws, is the way our theoretical reason seeks to follow its imperatives.

THE A PRIORI EXTERIORITY
OF THE IMPERATIVE

The imperative from which all hypothetical imperatives derive their imperative force is as a fact. It is the first fact. Kant argued that it is the imperative laid on thought to think consistently and coherently that makes the empirical facts recognizable as facts. The ultimately imperative is ungroundable and unrepresentable. The imperative itself is not a principle the mind would formulate or a program the mind would set before itself in a representation. Every principle with which reason represents what is imperative is consti-

tuted by a mind that is bound already to think according to principles. The imperative is not, as in Heidegger's interpretation of
Kant, the program the mind would formulate of a project that our
existence is. The force of the imperative is prior to the representation with which one makes its formulation present before oneself.
The imperative weighs on the mind as an exteriority prior to the
exteriority of the world of extended objects it presents.

Kant argues that thought is itself the original locus of the
imperative. He explains that the consistency and coherence of the
phenomenal field derives from the ordering activity of the understanding that combines with sensation to produce perception of
objects, and from the ordering activity of reason that relates coexist-
ing and successive objects. Thought that understands correctly and
reasons rightly is thought that represents coherence and consistency,
which represents objects according to their universal and necessary
structure and represents the coexistence and succession of objects
according to their universal and necessary order. Thought can
think something, can actualize itself as thought, only by thinking
according to the universal and the necessary. This imperative is not
a psychological necessity, which could be explained by representing
the innate structure and determined relationship between the
psychic apparatus and its objective environment. Such an explanation would itself be a work of thought and would have already
presupposed that thought subjected to the imperative in order to be
consistent and coherent. As soon as thought thinks it finds itself
subjected to an imperative to represent the universal and the
necessary. Thought is obedience. But it must command the perception and the motility that collect content for its ordering activity.
Thought is commanded to be in command.

For Merleau-Ponty, thought finds itself commanded to think
the consistent and the coherent because it is destined to think of
real things and the real world. Thought is not constitutive of
perception; it is a representation of the layout of things presented
in perception. It is not only the content of things, but their forms
that command thought. The imperative laid on the receptivity of
the spontaneity of understanding is itself grounded in the imperative laid on a sensibility that can actualize itself as perception only
by being receptive to the levels and ordering axes of the world and

perceiving things compossible within the world. Perception seeks in the sensorial patterns things that direct its intentionality and pursues the levels in which they are arrayed and that command it as an ordinance. The subjection of the mind to an imperative is first the subjection of perception to the imperatives in things and to the imperative ordinance of the world. It is the subjection of the subject to the exterior not as a material pressure that affects its sensory surfaces as sensations and affects its movements as reactions, but as an ordinance that directs the intentional focus of its sensory powers and its exploratory positions and movements. The imperative is first in the world, to which the sensitive-sensible flesh finds itself ordered, prior to any formation of dream-images, appearances that are not appearances of things, desiderata, implement structures, or organizing principles for its representations. The exteriority of the force of the imperative, not presented in the mind that represents the formulation of law it commands, is the exteriority of the world. It is the world not as a multiplicity of identifiable things a posteriori affecting the mind, but as an ordinance a priori laid on the mind. Or, more exactly, laid on our existence, which exists as destined for the world.

THE IMPERATIVE IS PRACTICAL

For Kant, the imperative is elucidated as an imperative for rational autonomy. The imperative, first seated in the understanding, commands thought to actualize itself, commands it to be in command, to command the sensory-motor organs that collect content for thought, and to disengage the activating will in our composite sensible nature from the lures of objects given as sensuous. As our practical powers manipulate things, they must arrange them not as so many sensuous lures but as intelligible structures. The imperative, as an imperative laid on a composite agency, becomes an imperative to act on the phenomenal field to order external nature in conformity with the rational representation of the universe thought constitutes in obedience to its own a priori imperative. Reason, then, by virtue of its own imperative, has to become practical.

For Merleau-Ponty, the world-imperative is received not in our understanding in conflict with our sensuality, but in our postural schema that integrates our sensibility and mobilizes our efficacity. The world-imperative commands our sensibility first to realize itself, as a praktognosis oriented to things. It commands our sensitive-sensible body to inhabit a world of things with the most centered, integral, and efficacious hold, from which every subsequent kind of comprehension will be derived. It orders our competence.

For perception is praktognosis. Perceived things are objectives. To perceive one has to look, one has to mobilize oneself and manipulate one's surroundings. To see a visible thing in real space is to feel how to get to it and how to handle it. The moon, as it rises over the planes and paths of the landscape in which I circulate, loses its determinate color and size, the mountain that I never address with a body intention of climbing floats as a phantom over reality, and become ultrathings, as Wallon classifies them, like the phantomal monocular images a motor intentionality mobilizing both eyes as one organ has not solidified into one integral vision of one thing. Sensation itself is behavior: to sense the green and the blue is to adopt a certain posture and to contract a certain muscular tonus; to hear a sound is to turn to it and to follow it. To synthesize the information collected in the diverse sense organs is to synergistically center one's surfaces and members and organs upon it. It is with a movement of one's hand that one perceives the texture and the grain of a surface; it is with a posture of one's mobile body that one perceives the position of a thing in the landscape, its up-down axis, its *sens* — its meaning and its orientation. Each perceived thing is a task and a means toward locating the next thing. Each profile of a thing is an objective for a body that has to center itself and a means for grasping the coherence and cohesion of something.

The engagement in the world, which is not a determination but an imperative, admits also a movement of disengagement from the sensible fields and levels of the world. "The relation between the things and my body is decidedly singular; it is what makes me sometimes remain in appearances, and it is also what sometimes brings me to the things themselves; it is what produces the buzzing of appearances, it is also what silences them and casts me fully into the world. Everything comes to pass as though my power to reach the world and my power to entrench myself in phantasms only came one with the other; even more; as though the access to the world were but the other face of a withdrawal and this retreat to the margin of the world a servitude and another expression of my natural power to enter into it."[1] The body that advances down and retreats from the levels at which things are found is the competent body, which can have objectives because the futures and possibilities of things are open-ended and because the imperative that makes each thing an objective is relativized by the next thing, and because the levels do not hold one unless one takes hold of them. The disengagement from the world is constitutive of its competence.

THE OBJECTIVE IMPERATIVE

The theoretical representation of the universe elaborated by science is a re-presentation of the perceived environment, which is not an amorphous medley of sensory givens but a field of things that emerge as tasks, ordinances commanding our postural focus, along levels that regulate our advance. The perceptual field is practicable, open to the initiatives of our sensory-motor powers, and open too to the manipulations, isolations, and experimentations by which the theorist selects and observes relevant data; it is open to the instruments the theorist uses to refine substances and the engineer to refine verifications. Theoretical practices are but one group among the larger number of initiatives our practical powers take in the perceptual field, to advance into it, to uncover things, to bring their possibilities and relationships to light. Empiricism in science means that every theoretical entity one constructs remains but hypothetical, an instrument of calculation, until it enables one to make predictions verified by observation, that is, by perceivable events in a practicable field. Atoms, electromagnetic fields, gravity — these are theoretical constructs that are not more real than the rocks, trees, birds, and fishes; they are theoretical instruments to represent the observed relationships between rocks, trees, birds, and fishes. Science does not find that the solidity and color of the rock is merely apparent; the subatomic particles moving at enormous velocity have as their sole justification the reactions one observes on the perceived rock. If one were to doubt that the rocks, trees, birds, and fishes were real, one would revoke into doubt at the same time the theoretical entities constructed by the natural scientists.

Science remains empirical when its theoretical elaborations, its microphysics and its cosmology, constructed perhaps for decades without experimental verification, one day programs the technological production of the prostheses that enormously expand the sphere of what is perceivable with the sense organs with which the human species has been genetically and culturally endowed, when the constructions with purely theoretical entities and with mathematics now cut absolutely free of their original moorings in geography and architecture design the technology that will equip the scientific observer to see like eagles and wasps, perceive with the sonar echolocation of bats and the sixth sense of fish, navigate with the magnetic or cosmic sense of migratory birds and insects, discern infinitesimal vibrations with the sensitivity of single cells or single electrons in those bats and fish.

Scientific observation does not only supersede natural perception to reach with the prosthetic organs technology has devised a more minute, more precise, and more stable percept; in recording its observations, it converts the percept into an *object*. The percept given in scientific observation is relocated in geometric space and metric time, indifferent to its contents, in which the object figures as the subsistent substrate of all its forms and attributes observation finds in the varying perspectives of the perceived field and at different moments of a wave of duration. The object is the simultaneous realization in a segment of cosmic time of all the aspects and facets that the perspectival and successive exploration of a thing will make determinate. Whereas real things in the perceived world are reliefs whose determinations form and eclipse across a wave of duration, the objects that furnish the scientific representation of the universe are represented as fully determined at each instant of their existence.

The scientist sets out to objectify his or her own body, with which he observes the perceived world. He will set out to do, over the time it takes, a complete itemization of all the contents and events of his body, and realize them simultaneously in an objective representation of his organism. He will set out to determine precisely the correlations between events in this object and the other determinate events of the objective environment.

About our bodies, now represented as objects in the midst of other objects in the objective representation of the universe, there is produced a field of perceived appearances, in which the surrounding things appear not as objects but as open-ended things forming on levels. The empirical psychologist will make observations of this perceptual field and record an objective version of it. She will determine its parameters; will record the patterns that take form within it, analyze its simplest component elements, which she takes to be elementary sense data, or sensations. She will then set out to correlate each point of color in the visual field with a physiological stimulus on the retina and nerve paths of the eye. She will show how physical events in the outside environment send physico-chemical and electromagnetic stimuli to the organism; she will record the physiological impulses in the afferent and efferent nervous circuitry of the objective body. She will then show how, projected in the brain, these physiological impulses result in psychic events, spots of color composing patterns in the visual field. The perceived patterns will be represented as effects of psychophysiological events in the objective body. The perceptual field will then figure as a segment of the objective representation of the universe. The empirical psychophysiologist will have determined how the objects of the external universe, the objects in her representation of the universe, produce that image of themselves which is the representation of the environment produced in perception.

There will remain for the cognitive psychologist to determine how the sensations associate among themselves according to psychological laws and produce general configurations, and how abstract concepts result from the association of sensations in the mind. She will one day determine how her mind produces out of its representation of the outside objects which is the perceptual field that second representation which is her objective representation of the universe. This psychology that constructs the world justifies itself with every advance in neurophysiology that maps on the neural substance of the organism localizations of the sensations with which the world is represented. It would explain the world order ultimately by the physiological imperatives of our own organism.

At the limit, the scientific theorist will produce one total objective representation of the universe, comprising an objective representation of all outside things given through perception, an objective representation of the scientist's own body that perceives those things, an objective representation of the scientist's own mind in which a perceptual field is produced representing in sensorial patterns a segment of the universe about that scientist, and a representation of the processes by which that scientist's mind produces his very science and his objective representation of all things.

But Merleau-Ponty argues that the theoretical objective, to represent the things we observe as objects and the field opened by our perception as a objective universe, is itself motivated by the structure of things that command our perception. To perceive is for my gaze to go out of my location to where the thing is, to inhabit it as it shows itself. On the contours of the side it turns to me I see adumbrated the other sides of that thing, sides it turns to things located alongside of it and behind it. My gaze is refracted to those places occupied by those other things, and already goes there to envision the thing from their positions. As each thing draws my gaze into its reality, it implants itself in a setting extended by the levels that support it and where the other things on those levels designate other perceivable sites from which it is perceivable. I do not only see the thing with the levels, with the light, with the verticality and repose of the field, rather I see it with the other things, which mark out viewing points on those levels. When I look at the giant sequoia before me, my vision attributes to it the other sides as they would be seen by the other trees about it, by the hills beyond and the river below and the clouds above; each of these other things, visible and real and a possible location for my look, guarantees for this tree all the sides now turned away from my gaze. This is the experience that makes me see each side of the thing as determinate, all of whose sides are kept determinate by the determinate forms of the other things of the world.

When I enter the luminous space of a room and look at this desk before me, presenting itself, establishing a moment of presence, it looks like it was there a moment ago and will be there in another moment. When the desk presents itself it also presents how it will go on being, how it was already. Something instantaneous, utterly unanticipatable and that vanishes at once, is a mirage, a phantom; it could not present itself as real. Each moment in which something is presented does not give itself out as the instantaneous correlate of my arising there and presenting myself. Each moment of duration invokes, as its witnesses, to anticipate and to confirm its presence, past and future moments. When I look at what is presented, I look out into the moments behind and ahead of it. The things appear embedded in the continuation of time; each present moment appears as fixed and identifiable in the interconnected moments of the course of the world.

Each thing that presents itself thus invites us to view it as something crystalized in a world of other things crystalized about it, in a fixed and identifiable moment on the axis of the time of the world. It invites us to situate it not within the hold of our body centered on it but within the system of the world and within the axis of its interlocked moments. Our own position, our own approach to it appear incidental to its being there.

And this is what motivates the scientific project of representing each thing as totally determinate now, within a universal system of outlying things themselves fully determinate now. It is what motivates the project of objectification, which represents the world presented in perception without levels extending indefinitely, without things exhibiting open-ended consistency in a time that can contain surprises, which eliminates from the representation of reality the structure of one determinate figure against a less determinate or indeterminate background, which represents the light, darkness, heat, sonority, rumble, silence in which things are found as themselves completely determinate multiplicities of completely determinate objects.

What the objectifying project of empirical science does is carry out the determination of each thing by the surrounding things, each moment by the preceding and following moments, all the way to the limit. In doing so it is commanded by the imperative that rules our perceptual life, which orients our perception toward the positing of things and of the coexistence of things.

THE APORIA

Merleau-Ponty's phenomenology makes perception a praktognosis, makes our existence a stand whose posture is directed upon objectives, makes our body occupied and laborious. He argues that the representation science elaborates of the objective universe is itself motivated by the imperative world levels that present things as objectives for competent bodies. Objective science is not only a practical project in that the theorist refines his substances and engineers his verifications with manipulations, isolations, and experimentations. Its objects themselves are objectives that represent the tasks things are for perception.

Yet the objectified representation of the universe is no longer a practicable world. The objective representation of the universe elaborated by science represents beings as in themselves totally determinate; it is a representation that renders as present their past and their future appearances. The sensible pivots are stabilized into points, the levels converted into lines, the horizons into planes, the depths into volumes, the space between things into potentially observable things, the murmur of silence into a multiplicity of tones. The body is converted into an exhaustively observable object determined from all points of view, where excitations in principle locatable at each moment as they travel the nervous circuitry result in temporally locatable psychic facts. Objective psychology represents the field of experience which that body maintains about itself as completely determinate, decomposable into psychic facts, sensations, which are in a constant relationship with the objective properties of external stimuli. Eventually the psychophysiologist would have to explain in terms of determinate correlations her own thought processes by which she produces the scientific representation of psychic facts, as the physicist produces his representation of the external stimuli. The scientist represents her body as an object agitated by outside forces triggering the ends of its nervous circuitry, and represents her own perceptual field and her objectified representation of the universe itself as ultimately produced by those outside objects. The theorist who has converted the world of levels with which she perceives into a representation of fully determinate objects whose perceptual possibilities are actualized, whose future apparitions are present, and converted the ipseity that forms in the reciprocal inscription of postural schema and body image into a representation of a psychophysical object, locates herself everywhere and nowhere, converts herself into a high-altitude absolute subject contemplating a body-object she no longer moves with. The original imperative that ordered a field of experience about her was laid on her body as a system of practical powers; when this imperative is carried out to the limit by the project of objectifying the universe, the scientist's own body, and the scientist's own mind, ends in a total disengagement from every practicable field, including the field of that praxis which is empirical observation.

This disengagement from the world is itself commanded by the world imperative. "Human life 'understands' not only a certain definite environment, but an infinite number of possible environments, and it understands itself because it is thrown into a natural world. Human behavior opens upon a world (*Welt*) and upon an object (*Gegenstand*) beyond the tools which it makes for itself, and one may even treat one's own body as an object. Human life is defined in terms of this power which it has of denying itself in objective thought, a power which stems from its primordial attachment to the world itself."[2]

THE SEGMENTATION OF THE
THEORETICAL UNIVERSE

The pursuit of the objective imperative issues in a split from the practicable field in which theoretical research must nonetheless effect its observations and its verifications. But Merleau-Ponty also sees in the science of our day the objective universe separating into discontinuous segments.

Psychology discovers, by its own methods, the unverifiability of the hypothesis of constancy between physiological impulses and the gestalts that form in the subject's field of perception. The region-specific concepts that it formulates to record those gestalts are not convertible into the concepts that record physiological processes. Physiology discovers, by its own methods, that the behavior of a living organism is correlative not with the objective properties of the external objects impinging on it but with their phenomenal properties, discovers it must, to understand behavior, correlate it not with the objective representation of the universe elaborated in physics, but with the sensory appearance of its environment the organism itself elaborates with its specific sensorium. The physiological environment presented to an organism disconnects from the physical universe represented by the physicist. Eventually physics, too, discovers as ultimate physical facts relational events that implicate the observer in the observed. The physical universe closes in about the physicist and disconnects from his own physiological environment and his field of perception.

The segmentation of the objective representation of the universe is fixed in the introduction of region-specific concepts and organizational models. Merleau-Ponty's phenomenology of perception was a theoretical project intended to fix a set of descriptive, and not objectifying, concepts and organizational models specific for the perceived field. Merleau-Ponty's thesis is that the new region-specific models we find in the physical segment, the physiological, the psychological, and the cognitive-science segments of contemporary science are likewise descriptive and not objectifying concepts and organizations models. And that they are in fact derived from the concepts and organizations specific to the field of perception. Not only in fact, obligatorily. For his thesis is that the scientific representation of the universe finds itself obliged, at a certain point in its elaboration, to return to the perceived world, not only to verify its calculations but to remodel its concepts.[3] And this imperative is intrinsically practical.

Merleau-Ponty's phenomenology of perception shows that it was able to elaborate descriptive concepts with which we were able to identify the structures specific to perceptual things, open-ended sensuous essences, which could not exist apart from the perceiving bodies for which their colors, their textures, their weights are real, and which could not exist as real things except by being always beyond what we grasp of them or determine of them. The phenomenology of perception was able to describe the real world in terms of levels and to differentiate this concept from the concepts of dimension, framework, and order. It was able to describe the per-

ceiver not as a psychophysiological object programmed by a priori
concepts but as a postural schema mobilized by perceived things
and engendering a body-image of itself as a thing among things.

In the scientific representation of the universe today, we find
concepts akin to these descriptive concepts.

This development is most advanced in physics. When physics
insists that what it can record is what it can operate on with its
instruments and its mathematics, it is defining physical entities not
as absolute objects but as correlates of our operations. The Einsteinian
theory of general relativity, the Heisenberg indeterminacy principle
force the physicist to take as ultimate entities not pure objects but
relationships between observer and observed. The physicist no
longer takes simultaneity or succession as absolutes, univocally
determinable. Physics today admits horizonal phenomena, properties without substances, collective entities or pure multiplicities,
entities without simple location.

In his first book *The Structure of Behavior*,[4] Merleau-Ponty traced
a similar transformation in contemporary physiology. Empirical
physiology was first based on anatomy. One analytically decomposed
the body and set out to determine with precision all its component
elements. One broke down the functioning of the body into
elementary reflex arcs, sought to correlate them with elementary
physicochemical or electromagnetic stimuli, and set out to explain
a movement, a gesture, or an operation as the sum of a multiplicity
of these automatic reflex arcs. This effort at an analytic explanation did not succeed. The sensory thresholds, which determine at
any moment the intensity and force of a stimulus that would
release a reflex arc, are variable; and they vary according to the
posture, the centering, the metabolic state of the whole organism.
When our bodies are centered on a task in front of us, the sensory
thresholds on our back are higher; it takes more pressure, more
intense cold or heat on our back before we feel it. The innervation
of our hand at any phase of a movement cannot be put in a one-to-
one correlation with external stimuli; it is, like a molecule of soap
on the surface of an expanding bubble, determined by the configuration of the whole, by the scope and sweep and rhythm of the
gesture. Each step we take is not only determined by the contours
of the terrain and by the air pressure, but also by the gait, that is,

the general rhythm we maintain when we launch our bodies into a continuous advance. We have to envision the position and movement of each of our parts not in function simply of the external pressures bombarding them but also in function of the postural axes they maintain and vary, in function of the gait they maintain, in function of the total diagram of a gesture, of an operation. To determine the physiological functioning of our body parts, our limbs, organs, glands, our body chemistry, and electrical fields, we have to envision our bodies as systems that do not tend to a state of rest, like inanimate things, but tend to maintain certain typical levels of tension, which are in correlation with the typical tasks our bodies maintain themselves in readiness for. We have to envision the functional organism not with the microscopic focus of the anatomist, but with the focus that takes in the whole posture of the organism and its correlates in its perceived environment. The concepts of posture, of gesture, of coordinated movement with which physiological behavior is theoretically represented are concepts derived from, rather than that constitute an objective replacement for, the way physiological behavior appears in the perceptual field of the physiologist.

The project of an objective psychology has likewise been transformed. The hypothesis of constancy, of a constant relationship between psychic sensations and physiological impulses and physical stimuli, could not be verified. It was found that the patterns that form in our field of perception could not be correlated with constellations of physical stimuli. Colors that form in our field of vision by contrast have no corresponding physical reality. The figure-ground organization of our field of perception does not correspond to anything physical on the retinas of our eyes. Distinctive regional concepts will be introduced to identify the typical patterns and structures within the field of perception. These concepts will no longer be objectifying, but descriptive of the open-ended structures of things as they appear in perception, of the levels of the perceived field that are not the dimensions in which objects are located.

The psychologist, in the name of the rigor of her own discipline, ends up describing the psychic field as a complex of nonobjects, appearances of open-ended things. The physiologist ends up not explaining the positions and movements of organisms by events in his objective representation of the universe, but correlating the postures, gestures, and operations of an organism as they appear in the field of perception of the physiologist and to that organism itself with the open-ended things that figure in the perceptual field of that organism. The specific structures of perceptual patterns and levels show through in the objects and dimensions of physics. Objectifying science was a praxis that would have ended up constituting a representation of the universe that made praxis inconceivable, but on the way finds that its representation of the objective universe re-presents the practicable format of world of perception. The cognitive psychology that set to explain the concepts of science itself as events in the objective universe ends up inscribing them in the field of postures and gestures. The scientist, motivated by the imperatives in things and in the practicable world to devote himself to elaborating an objectifying representation of the universe finds himself returning to a world of sensible levels in order to understand how he is commanded to pursue objectification, what operations his thought effects on the things given in his phenomenal field, and how he occupies a viewpoint, stands, moves, and sees.

INTERPRETING THE PRIMACY OF PERCEPTION

Merleau-Ponty then argues that there is nonetheless a universal field that contains all the segmented domains of empirical research. This field is not the universal form of objectivity; it is the perceived world. The region theoretically delimited as the physico-chemical sphere, that delimited as the physiological sphere, that delimited as the psychological sphere, that delimited as the cognitive sphere, are in fact all theoretically elaborated representations of sectors of the perceived sphere. The argument is not only that they draw their data from empirical observation; that is, from perceptions. It is also that the general form of all their new concepts reflects perceptual diagrams of apprehension. It would then seem that it is concepts, the identifying and organizing concepts that are region-specific, that segment an empirical domain from the continuity of nature. Yet all these concepts are perception derived. They should make possible a new continuity between the empirical regions they organize and segment.

Merleau-Ponty has linked the imperatives in things with the imperative the world is. The things arise as reliefs on the levels of the world that extend about them and harbor other things to which they turn their lateral sides and that invite us as standpoints from which those sides can be seen. The levels extend the world as a network of directives conducting us to things and to settings made of things. The thing ordering the direction of our perception leads us to the consistency and coherence of the levels; the levels we can reach only by subjecting ourselves to them conduct us to things. The levels pursued in whatever direction also lead us back to the things from which we started. When the music is over we pick up the thread of the world again as when we awaken to the visible again which continued uninterrupted during the interval of our sleep. As for Kant the imperative is inseparable from the form of universality and necessity, for Merleau-Ponty the imperative is inseparable from the consistency and coherence of one world. Our new scientific competencies, our prostheses technologically devised, which open up new theaters in the space of the world are continuous with the sensory-motor competency that dedicates our perception to things and to which the competent scientific observer returns.

The argument seems to us to have weak points. To argue that all theoretical regions are theoretically elaborated representations of sectors of the perceived sphere that for its part is one and encompassing is to argue that every empirical observed is located on the levels of the perceived landscape. And that it is only its re-presentation that relocates it on the axes of another space. Yet microscopic and macroscopic science has not only made more clear and distinct the things of the perceivable field, not only articulated its horizons, but changed its shape and its time. And if it is true that scientific observation differs from natural perception in that it narrows its focus, sets up its own controls, and determines what will count as verification, is it not also true that scientific observation segments, isolates, disconnects the field in which its perception is made from the levels of the natural world?

One transforms not only the hue, but the substance and location of a color by the focus, by reorganizing the scope and the field. Conversely, in transforming the clarity and distinctness of a perceived pattern, does one not disconnect its space from the space of the world? The segment of the wall seen through a tube loses its hue and its density and its surface, becomes a thin medium extending before the eye; the moon, whose size could be gauged when seen through a tube loses any measurable size when seen in the open sky. When one ceases to perceive the tones rumbling in the horns and on the skins of the drums and follows them as they relate to one another, the space of the music disconnects from the visual walls bounded by the walls of the concert hall. One shakes one's head as though awakening from a dream when the lights go on and one returns to the world of the visible and of things.

The objective representation of the universe programs the technology to contrive the prostheses that will enable the scientific observer, equipped by nature and by prior culture with only the sense organs specific to the human organism, to observe the data that would justify the theoretical hypotheses, and also to open new regions for exploration. The space of the micro- or macrophysicist accessible through her prostheses is not observable with the practices of the biologist; that of the biologist is not observable with those of the psychologist; that of the psychologist is not observable with those of the cognitive scientist. These new regions of data annexed to the world given to prescientific perception show structures that are, if not those of absolute determination in geometrical space and linear time in which objects are represented, also not those of the levels and durations in which the things of prescientific perception are found. Is not the segmentation of the theoretical representation of the universe also a segmentation of the regions of observation and a segmentation of the observing organism?

Would we not have to argue that the segmentation of the scientific representation of the world reflects a segmentation already at work in the world of perception, and a discontinuity in our competencies? If the new descriptive concepts and organizational concepts Merleau-Ponty has pointed to in the diverse regions of contemporary science are indeed so many abstract diagrams of perceptual syntheses and perceptual synergies, they are not simply variants of the things of prescientific perception and of the synergic postures with which those things are approached. To observe scientifically one has to develop new competencies, and one equips oneself with prostheses devised by technology. One obeys new imperatives.

The eyes that have to dissipate the monocular image and reach the thing have to "act as the two channels of a single Cylopian vision," the sensory-motor apparatus that has to dissipate the flux of reflections and shadows, perspectival deformations, mirages to come to grips with things has to "do but one thing at a time," has to stand and to move as a synergic and focused whole. The prostheses-equipped competencies of scientific observers become those of the eyes of eagles and wasps, of the sonar echolocation of bats and the sixth sense of fish, of the magnetic or cosmic sense of migratory birds and insects, of the sensitivity of single cells or single electrons in those bats and fish.

The imperatives that scientists find in the micro- and macrocosmic theaters they enter are no longer the imperatives the natural perception of our species found in things. These imperatives are recognized and obeyed with other competencies than those of our bodies competent to perceive things.

THE IMPERATIVE INCOMPETENCE

Is competence alone imperative?

What of the disengagement from things, and from the levels and planes that engender things, toward those refuges from the space of the world where the phantomal doubles of monocular vision, perceptual illusions, mere appearances, refract off the surfaces of things; what of the dream-scene, the private theaters of delirious apparitions, that realm of death in which the melancholic takes up his abode? What of the possibility of releasing one's hold on the levels, drifting into a sensible apeiron without levels, into that nocturnal oneiric, erotic, mythogenic second space that shows through the interstices of the daylight world of praktognostic competence?

We would like to argue that the world in Merleau-Ponty's sense — the light that forms a level along which color contrasts phosphoresce, the key about which the melody rises and falls, the murmur of nature from which a cry rises, the rumble of the city beneath which a moan of despair descends — these levels themselves form in a medium without dimensions or directions — the luminosity more vast than any panorama that the light outlines in it, the vibrancy that prolongs itself outside the city and beyond the murmur of nature, the darkness more abysmal than the night from which the day dawns and into which it confides itself. We want to propose that the world itself, in Merleau-Ponty's sense, is set in depths, in uncharted abysses, where there are vortices in which the body that lets loose its hold on the levels of the world, the dreaming, the visionary, the hallucinating, the lascivious body, gets drawn and drags with it not things, but those appearances without anything appearing, those phantoms, caricatures, and doubles that even in the high noon of the world float and scintillate over the contours of things and the planes of the world.

But we also want to say that if the sensibility is drawn into these vortices beyond the nexus of levels where the world offers things, it is drawn imperatively. Does not the visionary eye that is not led to the lambent things the light of the world illuminates obey another imperative in the light, the imperative to shine? Does not the vertigo that gives itself over to the abyss that descends and descends without end obey not the imperative of the depth to maintain surfaces, but another imperative that depth promotes and is: to deepen? Does not the hearing that hears not the particular songs, cries, and noises of the world, but the vibrancy beyond the corridors of the world, obey the imperative of hearing that it become vibrant?

And what of the imperative not to hold on to things and maintain the world, but to release every hold and to lose the world, an imperative which everyone who has to die, himself or herself, knows? There is in Merleau-Ponty's *Phenomenology of Perception* no word of this, only the imperative figure of an agent that holds on to things that are objectives and that maintains himself in the world. One dies of the world, and one dies into the world. The competence of the body casts it fully into the world and brings it to the things themselves; has not this competence also been a sending forth of its sensibility and its motor force into them, a taking leave of itself? In committing itself to them, does it not also disengage from them, and from its own powers, from its competence?

Heidegger had recognized the having to die with all one's own forces to be our very nature, but he equates it, dialectically, and to us incomprehensibly, with the resolute and caring hold on things and on the world. The care for things, the perception devoted to the sensible patterns that pass, is not only a presumptive apprehension of their integrated, intersensorially consistent, graspable and manipulatable, real structures. It is also a movement that lets the patterns pass, the reliefs merge into levels, the configurations dissolve into light and resonance and terrestrial density. It follows them as they pass, passes with them. We wonder if the one that dies to the things and the world does not know the imperative, not of becoming nothing, but of becoming elemental, following the light beyond every direction, following the depth that deepens without end, following the reverberation of the vibrancy beyond one's situation and every situation in the world.

NOTES

1. Maurice Merleau-Ponty, *The Visible and the Invisible*, trans. Alphonso Lingis (Evanston, Ill.: Northwestern University Press, 1969), p. 8.

2. Maurice Merleau-Ponty, *Phenomenology of Perception*, trans. Colin Smith (London: Routledge & Kegan Paul; Atlantic Highlands, N.J.: Humanities Press, 1962), p. 327.

3. Ibid., pp. 56–59.

4. Maurice Merleau-Ponty, *The Structure of Behavior*, trans. Alden L. Fisher (Boston: Beacon, 1959).

5

Merleau-Ponty's Deconstruction of Logocentrism

G. B. Madison

> Assertion [*die Aussage*, "judgment"]
> is not a free-floating kind of
> behavior which, in its own right,
> might be capable of disclosing
> entities in general in a primary
> way: on the contrary it always
> maintains itself on the basis of
> Being-in-the-world.
> — Heidegger, *Being and Time*,
> §33.

> No philosophy can afford to be
> ignorant of finitude, under pain
> of failing to understand itself as
> philosophy.
> — Merleau-Ponty, *Phenomenology
> of Perception*, p. 38

1. THE PRIMACY OF INDETERMINACY

After remarking in the *Twilight of the Idols* on how in logic "reality does not appear at all, not even as a problem, as little indeed, he said, "as does the question what value a system of conventional signs such as constitutes logic can possibly possess," Nietzsche proceeded to denounce one particularly "perilous" idiosyncrasy of the "philosophers." A suitable label for this idiosyncrasy would be *philosophical inversionism*. Nietzsche describes it this way:

117

They put that which comes at the end — unfortunately! for it ought not to come at all! — the "highest concepts," that is to say the most general, the emptiest concepts, the last fumes of evaporating reality, at the beginning *as* the beginning. It is again only the expression of their way of doing reverence: the higher must not be *allowed* to grow out of the lower, must not be *allowed* to have grown at all... [1]

Merleau-Ponty's entire philosophical enterprise was an attempt to subvert this sort of rationalist inversionism, this particular form of thinking that is synonymous with, that is indeed constitutive of, mainstream traditional philosophy.[2] The epithet that, early on, was attached to his philosophy — "a philosophy of ambiguity"[3] — sums up in a superbly succinct way the essential impetus of his thinking. For Merleau-Ponty's central project was that of rehabilitating and situating at the center of philosophical concern that which, in their search for the luminous *clarté* of the idea, philosophers and logicians (i.e., logocentric philosophers) have traditionally condemned, ignored, or sought to *aufheben* into the luminous univocity of the pure logos, of a self-transparent Reason: the vague, the indeterminate, the ambiguous. Far from maintaining that the essence of things and our experience of them is to be sought in the purity of the intelligible and transparent (univocal) idea, Merleau-Ponty insisted that "ambiguity is of the essence of human existence, [that] everything we live or think has always several meanings."[4] Ambiguity, he maintained, "is inherent in things (*PhP*, 172). When Merleau-Ponty affirmed that "ambiguity is not some imperfection of consciousness or existence, but the definition of them" (*PhP*, 332), he was in effect setting himself in opposition to Aristotle who had articulated the fundamental, guiding principle of philosophical and scientific thought (of which present-day, late modernist logicism and cybnerneticism claim, and rightfully so, to be the supreme embodiment) when he dogmatically proclaimed that "not to have one meaning is to have no meaning."[5] This paradoxical affirmation of ambiguity on Merleau-Ponty's part was the strategy by means of which he sought to realize his philosophical goal: the deconstructive inversion of philosophical inversionism.

What it means to characterize Merleau-Ponty's philosophy as a philosophy of ambiguity is something the (countertraditional) significance of which I do not believe we fully appreciate even today, some forty years after the publication of his major work. Since Merleau-Ponty's death (and, I suspect, in willful ignorance of what he effectively achieved), much talk has been expended on the demise of epistemological, foundationalist philosophy, of mentalist representationalism, and on the deconstruction of logocentrism and the "metaphysics of presence." The significance of Merleau-Ponty's work in regard to these postmodern themes has not, in my opinion, been duly acknowledged, nor does it seem to be generally realized that phenomenology, in Merleau-Ponty's hands, already accomplishes a decisive break with metaphysical logocentrism. That this is nevertheless the case is what I hope to suggest in this paper. I shall attempt to do so by setting out an imaginative reconstruction of a Merleau-Pontyean argument as to *the origin of logic.*

Before turning to this central issue, we should perhaps take careful note of how an attempt such as Merleau-Ponty's to confer philosophical status on the ambiguous is, in and of itself, a decisive repudiation of classical metaphysics. Ever since its inception, mainstream philosophy has been the attempt to determine precisely and to state unequivocally the exact nature of what is, of being, nature, reality. The guiding presupposition behind this enterprise (viz., the attempt to realize *episteme, scientia intuitiva,* "knowledge") is that being is, in its innermost reality, one and the self-same; it is something fully determinate in itself, well-rounded and complete (as Parmenides said). Being or reality (substance, *ousia*) is just exactly what it is, and not something else. When therefore, as Merleau-Ponty did, one privileges indeterminacy, one is, by that very fact, breaking with some 2,500 years of philosophical thought. To contest in this way the guiding principles of logical ousiology is to call into question the constitutive principles of thought itself, as it has traditionally been defined. Indeed, to privilege indeterminacy is to contest the primacy of the first principle of the "science of thought," of logic, this being of course, as Aristotle in effect proclaimed, the *principle of identity* (and its corollaries: noncontradiction and excluded middle).

Speaking of the "philosophers," Nietzsche said that for them "origin in something else counts as an objection, as casting a doubt on value."[6] Like Nietzsche, Merleau-Ponty sought to discredit the claims of rationalist or objectivist thinking — of what I am calling logocentrism — by exposing the genealogy of its various idea-products. In what follows I would like to show how, for Merleau-Ponty, the basic principles of logic do not stand on their own and are not, as Nietzsche would say, *causae sui* but have their origin in something existing outside of or prior to them, namely, our prelogical, perceptual experience of the world. To decenter logic in this way is, it should be noted, to deprive it of the value that logicists attribute to it, because, as they view the matter, logic cannot be of value unless this value is absolute, unconditioned, and nonderivative.

2. THE ORIGIN OF LOGIC

As is widely known, one of Merleau-Ponty's central theses in the *Phenomenology of Perception* has to do with the perceptual, bodily origin of all the "higher" formations of consciousness. In regard, for instance, to that most paradigmatic of rationalizing disciplines, geometry, Merleau-Ponty asserted: "The subject of geometry is a motor subject" (*PhP*, 387). It is not a pure, disembodied intellect that discovers within itself the ideal principles of geometry; it is a bodily subject engaged in a perceptual world that is the source of all those "external" verities labeled *geometric*. "Far from it being the case," he said, "that geometrical thinking transcends perceptual consciousness, it is from the world of perception that I borrow the notion of essence" (*PhP*, 388). When Merleau-Ponty says that "the certainty of ideas is not the foundation of the certainty of perception but is, rather, based on it" (*PhP*, 13), it is clear that his goal is the inversion of philosophical inversionism. He sums up his basic argument in the following way: "Our body, to the extent that it moves itself about, that is, to the extent that it is inseparable from a view of the world and is that view itself brought into existence, is the condition of possibility, not only of the geometrical synthesis, but of all the expressive operations and all the acquired views which constitute the cultural world" (*PhP*, 388). In short, "all consciousness is perceptual."[7]

Although Merleau-Ponty raised the question as to the "origin of geometry" and by implication extended what he says in this regard to "all the acquired views which constitute the cultural world," he did not specifically, in a systematic way, address the issue of logic. Nonetheless, I think it is possible to reconstruct what he would have said in this regard. It is simply a matter of following certain hints he provides his readers with in the *Phenomenology*: hints, as Derrida might say, as to the "prelogical possibilities of logic."[8] We can surely see what is at stake here: If logic has its origin in perception, then the "conditions of possibility" of logic are not themselves "logical." Logic itself is not, accordingly, self-grounding; it is not, and cannot be, a *foundational discipline*. The first principles of logic are not "self-evident." Whatever conviction they may carry is derived from, and is parasitical upon, the prelogical, perceptual life of the embodied subject. Now for the argument.

What I wish to show here is, put succinctly, that it is in our perceptual experience of the world that we first make an acquaintance with what later on, in higher flights of the abstractive and idealizing imagination, will ceremoniously be baptized "the principle of identity." Long before identity achieved, thanks to Aristotle, supreme metaphysical and logical status, it was, as it continues to be, the common experience of all embodied subjects. "Identity" is at bottom nothing other than a structural characteristic of the *perceptual field*. To see how this is so, let us recall some of the results of Merleau-Ponty's descriptive analysis of perception.

"To see an object," Merleau-Ponty writes, "is either to have it on the fringe of the visual field and be able to concentrate on it, or else respond to this summons by actually concentrating on it" (*PhP*, 67). To concentrate on an object, to become explicitly conscious of it, to see it as a specific, *identifiable* object, as a "this" rather than a "that," is to focus one's attentive gaze in such a way as to make of the hitherto vague, peripheral something-or-other the center of one's visual field. "The perceptual 'something' is always in the middle of something else, it always forms part of a 'field'" (*PhP*, 4). Thus, what constitutes perceptual experience is a *dialectic* of vagueness and clarity (vague surroundings — trailing off toward indeterminacy — and clear focus): unthematized, amorphous — or polymorphous — ground and explicit, well-defined figure, to speak in the terms of Gestalt psychology.

The important thing to note here is that a (specific) figure is *what it is*, and can be what it is (identity), only as standing out against a horizonal, relatively indeterminate background that is not, and *cannot*, as such, be a definite (identifiable) object itself: "It is necessary to put the surroundings in abeyance the better to see the object, and to lose in background what one gains in focal figure" (*PhP*, 67). To be sure, it is always possible for any aspect of the indeterminate background to become a definite, well-defined figure in its own right (this is, to speak in Husserlian terms, an eidetic feature of all perception), but in that case what had hitherto been a definite figure must itself, *by necessity*, recede into the vagueness of the horizon, *ceasing thereby to be a definite, self-identical object*. One object "cannot show itself without concealing others" (*PhP*, 68). As Merleau-Ponty says, "vision is an act with two facets" (*PhP*, 68). What we have to do with in perception is not a matter of presence (immanence) *versus* absence (transcendence), as the categories of logocentric thought would have it (cf. *PhP*, 80) or as the principle of excluded middle would seem to dictate (an object must be *either* present *or* absent; it must *either* be something definite *or* not be at all). It is not the case that perspectives are simply "opportunities" for an in-itself, self-same, subsistent object to display its (supposed) intrinsic permanence (cf. *PhP*, 90).[9] On the contrary, an object is, "in itself," *perspectival* (perspectoid). This amounts to saying that "Its presence is such that it entails a possible absence" (*PhP*, 90). This "entailment" is, to be sure, not logical but existential.

The important lesson that perception can teach us, therefore, is this: Presence — self-presence, an object's identity with itself (which is what makes it an object, a "substance") — is not the contrary of, not the metaphysical *opposite* of, absence.[10] Quite the contrary, presence is only on the basis of a possible absence, an absence that, therefore, is not external to it, but rather is its own innermost constitutive possibility.[11] Just as a figure cannot be the definite figure it is apart from its internal relation to an essentially indefinite background, a vague fringe realm of "determinable indeterminacy," as Husserl might say,[12] so likewise identity presupposes nonidentity and is inseparable from it. Identity is not therefore, a "logically primitive concept." Paraphrasing Merleau-Ponty, we could say: *Far from its being the case that logical thinking transcends perceptual consciousness, it is from the world of perception that I borrow the notion of identity*.[13]

We should perhaps take explicit notice of a couple of further philosophical consequences of "the primacy of perception" as they bear upon the issue of identity. The first has to do with that utterly basic notion, that of the "thing." *Was ist ein Ding?* Logical ousiology maintains that a thing, a *res* or substance, is that which exists in and of itself (*in se et per se*). A thing is that which is identical with itself; it is just exactly what it is: more, no less. We arrive in this way at the notion of the *absolute object*. What the return to perceptual experience teaches us, however, is the impossibility, that is to say, the nonsensicality, of an absolute thing, one that would be just exactly what it is, completely *other* than (independent of) everything it is *not*; that is, pure coincidence with itself, pure identity. The "completed," transparent object, Merleau-Ponty maintains, is an illusion of rationalist thought (*PhP*, 69). As we have seen, a thing can be a determinate thing only because of its internal relation to an indeterminate horizon; the "anonymous" horizon enters therefore into the very definition of the thing itself (qua focal figure). (We speak of a thing's continuing to be the "same" when in the course of ongoing experience a certain similarity of style is maintained between figure and background). Note, however, the consequence of this. If the horizon is open and indefinite, then, as Merleau-Ponty says, "through this opening...the substantiality of the object slips away" (*PhP*, 70).[14] The metaphysical notion of "substance" ("full presence," as Derrida would say) is possible only when in our thinking we *forget* what we had originally learned in our perceptual experience of the world.[15]

The second philosophical consequence of the primacy of perception concerns an equally primordial notion, that of the *world*. What we experience in our perceptual lives is a world. What, however, is "the world"? For objectivistic thinking the world is quite simply, as Merleau-Ponty so aptly put it, *"le grand Objet."*[16] It is itself a determinate *thing*, indeed, a super-thing, a totality, the sum total of (the finite number of) all independent, self-contained "things."[17] Such a "world," however, as Merleau-Ponty remarks, is merely an *idea* (*PhP*, 71); it is most certainly not anything of which we have ever had any actual *experience*. Such a concept is nothing more than a figment of the idealizing, abstractive imagination. It involves, in fact, a *double* forgetfulness in that it also rests on the forgetfulness of the experienced thing mentioned earlier. The world of our living experience, the perceived world is not a *universe*, "that is to say, a completed and explicit totality" — this being nothing more than a rationalist construction, *une entité métaphysique* (as William James would had said). In contrast to a universe, which exists only in the realm of logocentric ideality, a *world* is "an open and indefinite multiplicity of relationships which are of reciprocal implication" (*PhP*, 71).[18] The perceived world is an indeterminate — but infinitely determinable — horizon; it is, indeed, the "horizon of all horizons." As such, it is something that cannot possibly be thought by logical ousiology, something to which the latter remains cogenitally blind, operating as it does in accordance with the imperious principle of identity. This has significant ramifications, as we shall see a bit later on when we consider some of the implications of Merleau-Ponty's "genealogy of logic" as regards some contemporary embodiments of logocentrism.

3. LOGICAL FORGETFULNESS

One of the great merits of Merleau-Ponty's genealogical investigations in the *Phenomenology* is that they can serve to remind us of the incredible amount of "dying away from the self" (as Kierkegaard would say) that is called for if one is to become a successful, self-confident logician. What indeed is it that characterizes the transition from perceptual experience to logical thinking? The account that Husserl provides in his *Crisis* of the Galilean, mathematical *abstraction from* and *idealization of* the *Lebenswelt* is eminently applicable to the alchemy practiced by logicians who seek to transmute the base metal of perceptual experience into the pure gold of the transparent idea. What we have to do with here is a supreme case of philosophical inversionism.

After having operated his obfuscating abstraction from lived experience, arriving in this way at his "pure" concepts, the "logician" *turns around* and reads these abstractions *back into* the concrete reality of experience. In so doing he operates in accordance with what Marcel labeled "the spirit of abstraction"; that is, he not only abstracts from the concrete — a legitimate enough operation in itself, indeed, indispensable if one is to achieve intellectual "knowledge" of things, technological mastery over them — but he also surreptitiously *identifies* his abstractions with reality itself.[19] This is rationalist reductionism of the purest, most blatant sort; it amounts, as Husserl said of Galileo, "to [taking] for *true being* what is actually a *method*."[20] Or again, it is what James referred to as "the stock rationalist trick" that consists in taking "an idea abstracted from the concretes of experience" and then using it "to oppose and negate what it was abstracted from."[21] Thus it is that, as Nietzsche said, "philosophers" perversely take that which comes at the end, "the last fumes of evaporating reality," and place it at the beginning *as* the beginning. As Nietzsche so appropriately remarked of these "conceptual idolaters": "All that philosophers have handled for millennia has been conceptual mummies; nothing actual has escaped from their hands alive."[22] Rationalist inversionism is an insidious, highly contagious disease of the human understanding, and it was the prime target of both Husserl's "archeology" and Merleau-Ponty's "genealogy."

As Heidegger has shown, the logocentric "metaphysics of presence" assumes in our times the form of technologism. Unlike some critics of technologism, Merleau-Ponty was not, however, a philosophical Luddite. And unlike Heidegger Merleau-Ponty never sought to criticize and do away with "objectifying" thought as such. While he did indeed seek to call into question "the ontological value of the *Gegen-stand*," the pure object, he nevertheless insisted that "a return to pre-science is not the goal. The reconquest of the *Lebenswelt* is a reconquest of a *dimension*, in which the objectifications of science themselves retain a meaning and are to be understood as *true*" (*VI*, 182). The following text makes perfectly clear what might be called the "nondestructive" nature of Merleau-Ponty's deconstructive critique of objectivistic thought: "We are not asking the logician to take into consideration experiences which, in the light of reason, are nonsensical or contradictory, we merely want to push back the boundaries of what makes sense for us, and reset the narrow zone of thematic significance within that of non-thematic significance which embraces it" (*PhP*, 275).[23]

Merleau-Ponty's goal was not to destroy or even to transform logic — as if he thought that logic could or should take account of our prelogical experience. He was simply trying to expose the prelogical conditions of possibility of logic, conditions of possibility that logic itself must *necessarily* ignore,[24] The matter could be expressed another way. Like the notion of "pure sensation" of which Merleau-Ponty often speaks, the notions of the absolute, self-subsistent (atomistic) thing and of a universe perfectly determinate in itself (the sum total of all such "atoms") are, as he says, "illusions." They are fundamental "errors" of the understanding. The important thing to note, however (and this testifies to the subtlety of Merleau-Ponty's thought), is that these errors are "natural" ones; they are inevitable. As Merleau-Ponty says of "pure sensation" and the illusion "that causes us to put it at the beginning and to believe that it precedes knowledge": "It is the necessary, and necessarily misleading way in which a mind sees its own history" (*PhP*, 37). For Merleau-Ponty, *human understanding is of such a sort that it inevitably and necessarily tends to misunderstand itself*, to interpret itself to itself in objectivistic terms. "Human life is defined in terms of this power which it has of denying itself in objective thought, a power which stems from its primordial attachment to the world itself" (*PhP*, 327).[25] Accordingly, his philosophical objective was not that of inaugurating a non- or postmetaphysical mode of thinking, a post-epochal reign of aletheiological innocence. It was simply that of exposing what Sextus Empiricus called the "trickery of reason" and recalling to our attention the potentially misleading character of the objectifying categories to which we have recourse when we seek to achieve a theoretical understanding of our actual experience,[26]

Even though he had no intention of doing away with logic itself, Merleau-Ponty's "return" to perceptual experience is devastating to the logicist's belief that logic is the supreme means for understanding reality. When all is said and done, logic, as Nietzsche remarked in his customarily hyperbolic (and yet insightful) way, has nothing to tell us about reality and is, therefore, in this regard, worthless.[27] This should not, however, be taken to mean that it is altogether useless. Logic does have, to use Nietzsche's term, a certain "value" — and a very significant one at that. This value is not, however, "epistemological" or "cognitive" but, rather, *technological*. The technological value of logic lies in the fact that it can enable us to devise formal systems of reasoning which can be used to build bigger and better computers (or computer programs) with which to extend our anthropocentric mastery over nature. It should go without saying, however, that this undertaking itself — the attempt to achieve, by means of methodical thinking, the domination and control over nature and human nature dreamed of by Descartes at the beginning of our modern era — poses certain dangers to a properly human mode of being in the world.

4. THE HORIZONAL NATURE OF LANGUAGE

One of the contemporary embodiments of logocentrism that, as I said earlier, I would like to consider in order to draw out some of the implications of Merleau-Ponty's critique of logocentrism is that currently very trendy "research program" called *Artificial Intelligence*. Before doing so, however, a particularly complex issue should be addressed, if only in the most minimal of ways. This concerns the relation between, on the one hand, *perception* and, on the other, *expression* or *language*. One of the criticisms commonly addressed to Merleau-Ponty (indeed, one that he subsequently addressed to himself in *The Visible and the Invisible*) is that in the *Phenomenology* he does not clearly link up his discussion of perception with his discussion of language. In this book, the relation that obtains between perception and language remains, in my estimation, highly ambiguous (what exactly does it mean to speak of language as a "founded" phenomenon, to say that it "originates" in perception?).[28] It is, nevertheless, incumbent on me in this paper to tie the two together if I am going to be able to say something about various forms of logocentrism such as Artificial Intelligence, as these are all properly *linguistic* affairs.

  In order not to get bogged down in hermeneutical imbroglios, I am going to side-step the whole problematic issue as to the relation between perception and expression in Merleau-Ponty.[29] I will do so by asserting that, whatever the relation between them may be as far as Merleau-Ponty is concerned, the fact remains that a certain isomorphic relation obtains between perception and language. My thesis is this: just as in the case of perception, language is of an essentially "horizonal" nature; the notion of horizon is as indispensable for understanding language as it is for understanding perception. Let me attempt to say what I mean by that.

As human subjects, we are not only perceiving subjects, we are also speaking subjects. In fact, it could even be said — and I do not think that Merleau-Ponty would disagree — that we are the kind of perceiving subjects we are precisely because we are also speaking subjects.[30] That entity traditionally referred to as "man" is, in "essence," a language-using animal: *zoon logon ekon*, as the Greeks defined him. When I say "language-using animal" I do not mean by this something similar to what the objectivistic anthropologist means when he or she defines man as a "tool-using animal." Language is not a tool; it is not something ready to hand (*zuhanden*), something that one "possesses." As Merleau-Ponty often remarked, language possesses us. Language is the milieu in which, as understanding beings, we "live, move, and have our being"; language is the *world* we inhabit qua *human* beings, just as water is the elemental world of fish. The relation of the speaking subject to language is exactly of the same sort as the relation of the perceiving subject to the perceived world; in both cases what is indispensable to a proper understanding of the phenomenon in question is the notion of *horizon*.[31]

Ever since Plato philosophers have tended to view words as *signs* and have considered a language (a linguistic "system") to be the sum total of such signs, along with the syntactical rules prescribing the way in which these discrete sign entities may be related to one another. In this objectivistic, *partes extra partes*, view of language, the meaning of the "sign" is something external to it. A sign's meaning lies outside of it in its "referent," this being conceived of as either a well-defined, prelinguistic "Thought" (as the logician Frege would say) or a self-identical, atomistic thing in the "real" world. When we view language on the model of perception, phenomenologically described, everything changes, however.

Let us recall what we said about an "identical" thing being the result of a dialectical interplay between figure and background (i.e., all sorts of other possible "things"), about focal clarity and horizonal vagueness. A thing is not a definite thing, does not, as phenomenologists say, have the "meaning" (*sens, Sinn*) it has, except in relation to an indeterminate (but determinable) horizon, a horizon that therefore enters into the *internal* constitution of the thing itself. Exactly the same sort of thing can be said about language. There are strict parallels between, on the one hand, *thing* and *word* and, on the other hand *world* and *language*.

In regard to the word (or concept, the *verbum mentis*), it must be said that a word does not, as analytical thought would like to think, have meaning in and of itself. As Merleau-Ponty learned from Saussure, words do not have meanings apart from their diacritical, oppositional relation to all the other words in a language (which, let it be noted, is not to say that words have meaning *only* in reference to other words).[32] The definiteness of a word is therefore a function of the way it "profiles" itself against other words, the shadows it casts, the horizon of other determinable meanings in which it is situated. The figure-ground relation is fully operative here. As a more recent critic of logocentrism, Paul Feyerabend, observes: "concepts, just like percepts, are ambiguous and dependent on background."[33]

As in perception, so in the case of a natural language the basic phenomenon is not univocity but polysemia or multivocity ("ambiguity"). As we have seen Merleau-Ponty say, "ambiguity is of the essence of human existence, and everything we live or think has always several meanings." In fact, we should say even more. We should say that definiteness of meaning is itself made possible only by the semantic ambiguity that is characteristic of all natural languages. Pure univocity, pure identity of meaning, is only an idealizing or limiting concept, to be encountered only in artificially constructed, formalistic languages. But the peculiar characteristic of logistic languages is that they are not, strictly speaking, *about* anything; as in the case of mathematics above all, they never "express" anything other than themselves (no more than does the principle of identity, "A = A," have anything to say about anything other than itself). Pure identity of meaning, therefore, is not all that different from total meaninglessness. From this it follows that, by definition, a "world" in the phenomenological sense is something of which logistic languages know, and can know, nothing (Merleau-Ponty would say that the formalized language of mathematics — the "algorithm" — is a language that has broken with its roots in the perceptual world, with the *logos* of the perceived world).

The horizonal nature of the language in which we live is what accounts for the essential difference between this kind of language

and artificial languages. Language itself, Merleau-Ponty says (see
VI, 96), is a world in the phenomenological sense of the term. That
is, it is not a *totality*, not simply the sum total of all word-entities
that supposedly go to make it up. Unlike logistic languages that,
however extensive and "all-inclusive" they may be, are nevertheless,
by necessity, closed systems wherein one sign ideally never means
more than one thing and no two signs mean the same thing,
natural languages, characterized as they are by an open-ended
horizonality, are, in this sense, infinite. Grammarians (with the
notion of linguistic competence in mind) sometimes like to say that
the peculiar characteristic of our languages is that it is possible,
with a finite number of elements, to say a potentially infinite
number of new things. This is, however, a somewhat misleading
manner of speaking. A natural language is not something "finite."
Even in regard to vocabulary it is impossible, as a matter of principle, to draw up a complete list (a complete dictionary) of all the
"meanings" that a language "contains" (new "meanings" are being
constituted every minute).[34] "Can one," Merleau-Ponty asks, "count
up a language?" (*VI*, 199) One cannot, of course, and this is what it
means to speak of polysemia and horizonal indeterminacy. Even
though, as Merleau-Ponty said, "there is no experience without
speech,"[35] a natural language is most definitely not a closed system
in which speakers are imprisoned, which determines in advance
what can and what cannot be said (what is meaningful and what
is not meaningful — as is the case with formal languages).[36] As
Gadamer might say, the essential characteristic of a natural
language is that there is nothing that cannot, in principle, be said
in it (which is not to say that one could ever succeed in saying
everything that there is to be said about anything). Natural
languages are *infinitely expressive* (and reflect in this way the infinite
open-endedness of our experience of the "world").

Let us note, finally, that it is the "horizonal" character of natural languages which accounts for what is perhaps the most salient
difference between them and formalistic languages. Whereas there
are essential limits to what can be said in a logical language,[37]
indeed, whereas it is impossible for a logical language to speak
about itself (about its own enabling conditions) — it being necessary to pass to a higher-level metalanguage to do so — natural

languages are their own metalanguages. Not only are they infinitely expressive, they are also infinitely reflexive. As Habermas has remarked: "Owing to the reflexive structure of natural languages, ...the native speaker has at his command a unique realm of meta-communicative free play."[38] This unique feature of natural languages is due to that which, for logicism, is a defect and a deficiency; that is, their constitutive indeterminacy, the fact that, like the visual field, the field of linguistic meaningfulness can never be completely objectified, the fact that the background of indeterminate meaningfulness — polysemia — can never, in principle, be fully thematized.[39]

Let us now see what implications we can draw from all this.

5. LOGOCENTRISM AND ITS AVATARS

If anything can make plausible Merleau-Ponty's seemingly paradoxical thesis that human understanding necessarily tends to misunderstand itself, it is, surely, those two particularly rampant forms of logocentric objectivism that today go under the heading of Cognitive Science and Artificial Intelligence. It would indeed be hard to find two more thoroughgoing misunderstandings of human understanding than these. In their search for the universal algorithm, they represent a kind of innate, genetically programmed disease of the human mind or, at least, of modernist, Western, logocentric consciousness. Charles Taylor, who has been waging a valiant battle against the forces of analytic objectivism for a good number of years now, has expressed his amazement as to how this perverse form of thought blithely goes on to assume ever new forms, seemingly immune to the devastating criticisms that from Merleau-Ponty's time and before, have been brought against it. "Why," he plaintively asks, "is one spending this immense effort to show the inadequacy of what in the end is a wildly implausible view?"[40] The naturalistic, *partes extra partes* mode of explanation Merleau-Ponty attacked in *The Structure of Behavior* and *Phenomenology of Perception* would appear to be more alive and widespread than ever. Behaviorism may be pretty much a bygone fad among those social scientists who aspire to become "hard" scientists, but developments in computer technology have made possible a new objectivistic fad in the human sciences: the attempt to construct computational models of the human "mind," what H. L. Dreyfus calls "computer-Cartesianism."[41]

In light of these developments, a critique of objectivism is more urgent than ever. Let us see if we cannot find in Merleau-Ponty's critique of logocentrism some pertinent critical insights as regards the current mania for computer-based models of human understanding. Perhaps the most obvious lesson to be drawn from what was just said is that if human perceptual and linguistic experience is essentially of a "horizonal" nature, then Cognitive Science and Artificial Intelligence (whose working hypothesis is that the "mind" is a kind of formal automaton) are from the outset fundamentally misdirected pursuits — to the degree, that is, that, as in the case of "strong AI,"[42] they view themselves as something more than theoretical speculation relevant to computer technology and actually claim to provide an adequate understanding of human understanding. The reason of course is that these disciplines, if they are to exist at all, must attempt to translate human experience into formalistic, logistic (computational) languages (the only ones a computer is capable of "understanding" properly), and there is simply no place for *meaningful ambiguity* in these languages. As Taylor remarks, "There is nothing comparable to tacit knowledge in a machine."[43] That *machina rationatrix* which is the computer is a living embodiment of the sterile principle of identity, "the sterile noncontradiction of formal logic," as Merleau-Ponty would say (*PhP*, 19).[44] As such, there is nothing that it can possibly teach us about characteristically human forms of understanding. (Of course, to the degree that we think like a computer, as we oftentimes tend to do — such as when we do logic — computers can help us to "clarify" our thinking; computer programs can be devised to help people become better logicians.)

If what as humans we experience is not a "universe" but a "world," this means that human understanding is not fully formalizable. But if it is not formalizable, then it is also not understandable by means of formalized computer languages. If in the real world of lived experience there is always a background that cannot be thematized except in terms of a further background, the very project of Cognitive Science is fundamentally misplaced, in fact is an illusory undertaking, the vain pursuit of a metaphysical will-o'-the-wisp. Dreyfus has had some pertinent things to say in this regard. He remarks for instance on how computer researchers have come to realize that if they are ever to succeed in constructing a computer model which in any way approximates to the way humans actually do understand and act, they must find a way of treating "the broadest context or background as an object with its own set of preselected descriptive features." They must, in other words, find a way of *enframing* the horizon, transforming thereby the "world," the indefinite horizon of determinable indeterminacy, into a "universe," a collection of self-identical, determinate "things." As Dreyfus goes on to say: "This assumption, that the background can be treated as just another object to be represented in the same sort of structured description in which everyday objects are represented, is essential to our whole philosophical tradition." It is, as he so rightly remarks, a "metaphysical assumption."[45]

Let us conclude these brief observations on Cognitive Science and Artificial Intelligence by simply remarking that if the constitutive presuppositions of these disciplines are — as indeed they are — metaphysical in nature, having to do in particular with the modernist metaphysics of epistemological referentialist-representationalism,[46] then any critique that undermines this metaphysics undermines thereby all the various "research programs" (as empirical analysts are fond of calling them) informed by it. Merleau-Ponty's critique of logocentrism does, I believe, precisely this.

Another form of present-day logocentrism that I would like to comment on is that Movement (with a capital *M*, as some of its adherents refer to it) that goes under the heading of "informal logic" or "critical reasoning" (IL/CR). Given the present academic situation, there is no doubt that, as one apologist for the discipline remarks, "It is a good time to be in the critical thinking business."[47] Yet, were Nietzsche around today, he would likely view the whole project of IL/CR as a prime instance of philosophical "mummification" or "vampirism"[48] and the very idea of logical "knowledge" (a "knowledge" to be taught in its own right) as either vacuous or trivial. The question I would therefore like to raise is a properly

Nietzschean-critical one: what exactly is the purpose, as far as the teaching of philosophy is concerned, supposed to be served by these disciplines that claim to be context neutral?

Is the sought-after purpose of "critical reasoning" to enable people, by training them in the immense variety and subtlety of "illogical" forms of thought, to fend off "improper" arguments?[49] If this is supposed to be its justification, then it must be said that IL/CR embodies a particularly logocentric, agonistic conception of philosophy. Philosophy is viewed here not as a dialogical encounter with another person or with a text, with the aim of reaching "agreement," but as the monological concoction of "arguments" the net result of which is the irrefutable (and thus undiscussable) "demonstration" of some truth or other. But "argument" (in whatever variant of the logicist sense one wishes to understand the term) is not, and never has been, what philosophy is basically all about. Even when philosophers make use of an entire paraphernalia of argumentative devices, what counts ultimately is not the logical soundness of their "arguments" but their rhetorical persuasiveness. The rationalist's claim to have "demonstrated" something or other in a strictly logical fashion is in fact, as traditional rhetoric teaches us, one of the surest *rhetorical* means of securing the adhesion of one's audience.[50]

The very notion that philosophical "truth" can, or ought to be, logically "demonstrable" — and that, accordingly, we stand in need of a discipline such as IL/CR to lay down "rational criteria of truthfulness" — is expressive of an ideal which is itself eloquent testimony to the apparently ineradicable tendency on the part of human understanding to misunderstand itself; and it is thus itself, as it were, a "fallacy" to be exposed. Even when they have recourse to putatively "conclusive" arguments, philosophers are engaged not in an "argumentative" but in an *interpretive* enterprise. What counts is the persuasiveness (and comprehensiveness) of the view of things they manage to get across, by whatever means. What may be a "faulty" argument, from a logical point of view, nonetheless, may be philosophically enlightening.[51] Indeed, "logical" errors, like semantic or syntactical errors in ordinary conversation, often have no effect at all on the philosophical quality of the discourse and are normally not even perceived. (Conversely, we often experience difficulties with a philosophical, logically well-constructed "argument" and even refuse to go along with it, not for logical reasons, but for extralogical reasons of one sort or another). A truly great philosophical work is one that — even though it might contain 1,001 logical "fallacies" (furnishing thereby logicians with the wherewithal to prolong, Scheherazade-like, their professional existence) — is yet capable of enabling us to see the world in a new, less constrictive way. Postmodern philosophical discourse in particular often delibertely ignores the requirements of logic (e.g., the principle of non-contradiction), because what it wishes to say necessarily cannot be said by logic (in the eyes of many postmodernists it is no objection to an utterance that it be "inconsistent" or "improbable").[52] The important thing in the understanding of philosophical texts is to be able to cut through all the argumentative bric-à-brac and get at *die Sache selbst*, the issue at stake. No amount of training in the formalistics of argumentation will teach students how to do this. Indeed, encouraging them to nitpick[53] their way through philosophical works may permanently handicap them as far as philosophical understanding goes. Think, for instance, of those colleagues who, when called upon to their chagrin to teach a course in medieval philosophy, spend their lecture time attempting to poke logical holes in St. Thomas's proofs for the existence of God. Students may come out of such a course with a better acquaintance with Bertrand Russell's principles of logic, but they could hardly be said to have gained an understanding of Thomas's metaphysics. By the very nature of his project, which is essentially prescriptive rather than descriptive, seeking to specify what philosophical discourse *ought* to be (if it is to count as truly "rational") rather than what as a matter of fact it is, the informal logician is precluded from taking seriously what he or she nevertheless is forced to recognize is the case, viz., that the "charge of fallacy... is rarely logically compelling; it virtually never 'refutes' a point of view."[54] Were one to reflect seriously and systematically on *why* this is the case, one would find oneself engaged in a quite different undertaking from IL/CR; namely, *hermeneutics* or *rhetoric* — a discipline that can indeed claim to enable us to understand better philosophical and other modes of thinking.[55]

Perhaps, though, it will be said that the value of IL/CR is that it enables us not just to assess (or, as analysts like to say, "knock down") other peoples' arguments, but to think philosophically ourselves (IL/CR "seeks to enhance students' thinking ability in general, i.e., with regard to any particular subject matter"[56] If so IL/CR once again betrays its logocentric prejudices. To conceive of philosophical reasoning as a watered-down form of logical thinking — as the term "*in*formal logic" implies — is to operate with a conception of language foreign to the philosophical endeavor. Philosophy, unlike logic, operates with natural language and is fully dependent on its unique resources, in particular on the horizonal nature of language discussed earlier. To understand ("grasp") a philosophical concept is to appreciate the way a particular term acts as a crystalizing agent in a field of semantic, polysemic ambiguity. Contrasting the scientific and philosophical uses of language, Gadamer writes:

> In science, concepts like signs or symbols are chosen and defined. These have a purely communicative function, which is to insure that by means of them experience is designated in the most univocal way possible and thereby is made controllable. This is experience of the sort which allows univocal identification and therewith univocal symbolization. ...One can recognize the fact that this concern with definitions makes good sense when it is a matter of arranging component units of experience. But when it comes to philosophy, such a desire for defining gives one away as a dilettante. Philosophy must give ear to an older wisdom which speaks in living language.[57]

The way to teach philosophy — and the way one learns how to philosophize oneself — is not by means of an analytical "rational reconstruction" of "arguments," picking through the bare bones and disarticulating ("disambiguating") the bloodless, vampirized shell of what was once a living thought. What is required, instead, is that one plunge, or be plunged (learning in the process how to philosophize as one learns how to swim), into the overflowing, polysemic density of an actual, living *text*. Reading is not unlike perceiving. A text is itself a "world," a fringe realm of determinable indeterminacy in which one learns how to move about and orient oneself in much the same way that the embodied subject learns to inhabit the perceived world.[58] Philosophical concepts, like perceptual "things," neither exist nor are meaningful apart from their diacritical relation to all the determinable indeterminacies that surround them. Every philosophical text has, as Merleau-Ponty might have said, its own "perceptual" style; it is a kind of "matter-pregnant-with-form."⁵⁹ A philosophical education ought, therefore, to be one that enables students better to perceive that unique *style* which is what each and every philosophical text primarily is. In spite of all the promethean efforts expended in this area (with the aid of a great deal of government funding), we have yet to see a computer program that can produce anything resembling, in even the remotest of ways, a philosophical reading of, say, Leibniz, the great precursor of present-day attempts to devise a mathesis universalis, an *ars combinatoria*, a genuine *machina rationatrix*.

I realize full well that to maintain that "logic (formal or informal) is either largely or entirely irrelevant to critical thinking" (i.e., as I would say, philosophical thinking) is a "view that most rankles with members of the Informal Logic Movement"⁶⁰ ("all of us right-thinking people"⁶¹). I am not saying, however, as I believe that Merleau-Ponty would not say were he around today and could react to the latest instances of objectivism, that IL/CR is totally useless, anymore than is Cognitive Science or Artificial Intelligence. I am only saying — puzzling as I am still over Nietzsche's question as to "what value a system of conventional signs such as logic can possibly possess" — that, in the way it is generally conceived and taught, its usefulness or worth is not primarily philosophical.⁶² Indeed, to the degree that IL/CR is conceived of as a kind of lesser version of pure logic, as, so to speak, applied formal logic, dealing with argumentative "shortcuts," "rules of thumb," "figures of speech," and other such "lesser" modes of logical propriety, it, like Cognitive Science, perpetuates philosophical inversionism by upholding the foundationalist pretensions of logocentrism ("grounding" the *ratio* or the *logos* in, and identifying it with, the realm of abstract ideality and formal calculi — "the last fumes of evaporating reality"⁶³). As such, it is yet another embodiment of what Pascal called *l'esprit de géométrie* that, valuable enough as it is in itself, is nevertheless incapable of educating one in *l'esprit de finesse* (contextual flexibility) and inculcating a sensitivity for, as Gadamer would say, "productive ambiguity."⁶⁴

6. CONCLUSION

Unlike present-day "deconstruction," Merleau-Ponty's theoretical critique of logocentrism was animated by a definite, fully discernible practical purpose. What he was seeking to elaborate was a mode of philosophical discourse in which it would make perfectly good sense to speak of human freedom and dignity. For Merleau-Ponty the notion of "ambiguity" or "indeterminacy" was essential for an understanding of freedom, and for understanding as well how we create meaning in our lives, for understanding, in other words, human "transcendence," one of the most important themes in the *Phenomenology*. "Existence," he said, "is indeterminate in itself, by reason of its fundamental structures, and in so far as it is the very process whereby the hitherto meaningless takes on meaning" (*PhP*, 169). It could be said that for Merleau-Ponty a person's "dignity" consists in the fact that, as a bodily subject transcending purely natural being, he or she is a "meaning-giving," meaning-creating being in the world, an "animal" whose essential, defining feature is what Charles Taylor calls the *significance factor*.[65] Thus, we fundamentally misunderstand human beings when we view them objectivistically, as sophisticated "fact-processing" machines. Indeed, all attempts to construct machine models of human understanding owe their existence to a basic hermeneutical oversight: the fact that "facts" themselves are the result of the way humans creatively interpret the lived world of existential indeterminacy. Philosophical inversionism once again! Although computers may be said to register data, for these data to become "facts" they must be actively interpreted by a human overseer (or by a computer program designed by humans with human purposes in mind).

The "value" of Cognitive Science or of Artificial Intelligence, like logic or any other "science" in the modern sense of the term, lies, as I suggested earlier, not in its ability to provide us with a better understanding of ourselves or of what we call "reality" (i.e., "knowledge") but, rather, in its *technological* usefulness.[66] As one writer very pertinently remarks, "what we have to keep in mind is that we are dealing, not with the creation of 'artificial forms of intelligence', but rather, with the inexorable march of mathematical science."[67] That is, as I would express the matter, AI has no truth value but only a use value; it should be placed under the rubric not of *episteme* (as if it were within its power to tell us what human "intelligence" is) but of *techne* ("mathematical science"). To overlook this would be to fall prey to a "new Pythagoreanism," a new version of the old inversion that in fact inaugurated the metaphysical tradition and that took numbers to be the most real of things and identified the realm of artefactual necessity with "reality."[68] The critique of logocentrism maintains that mathematics has nothing to tell us about the nature of the world — even though it is a superb *instrument* for altering our environment. And yet, even though AI, rightly understood, is, so to speak, value neutral in "epistemological" terms, its real significance or worth lying solely in what it may contribute to the advancement of technology, to our ability to manipulate reality (including human reality), it is not for all that an innocuous intellectual endeavor and is not without posing a serious danger to a properly human mode of existence. Because the human being is a self-interpreting or self-defining being and because, in addition, human understanding has a natural tendency to misunderstand itself (by interpreting itself to itself in terms of the objectified by-products of its own idealizing imagination; e.g., in terms of computers or logic machines) — because of this there is a strong possibility that, fascinated with their own technological prowesses, moderns may very well attempt to understand themselves on the model of a computational machine and, *in so doing*, actually make themselves over into a kind of machine and fabricate for themselves a machinelike society (a "megamachine," as Lewis Mumford would say) structured solely in accordance with the dictates of calculative, instrumental rationality. (The power the human "mind" has of denying itself in technology is of exactly the same sort that, in the realm of sociopolitical praxis, human beings have of denying their basic freedoms — without which, as Merleau-Ponty well knew,[69] a properly human life is not possible.) As Merleau-Ponty wrote in "Eye and Mind," his very last publication:

> Today more than ever, science is sensitive to intellectual fads and
> fashions. When a model has succeeded in one order of problems, it is
> tried out everywhere else. ... Thinking "operationally" has become a
> sort of absolute artificialism, such as we see in the ideology of cyber-
> netics, where human creations are derived from a natural informa-

tion process, itself conceived on the model of human machines. If this kind of thinking were to extend its reign to man and history; if, pretending to ignore what we know of them through our own situations, it were to set out to construct man and history on the basis of a few abstract indices... — then, since man really becomes the *manipulandum* he takes himself to be, we enter into a cultural regimen where there is neither truth nor falsity concerning man and history, into a sleep, or a nightmare, from which there is no awakening (*PriP*, 160).

As a general rule (for the direction of our understanding), it would be well if we paid greater heed to Nietzsche who, with a vision as unclouded as that of Tiresias (but without, let us fervently hope, the curse of Cassandra), predicted the nightmarish, somniferous nihilism we are currently in the process of contriving for ourselves.

a 'world of truth' that can be mastered completely and forever with the aid of our square little reason. What? Do we really want to permit existence to be degraded for us like this — reduced to a mere exercise for a calculator and an indoor diversion for mathematicians? Above all, one should not wish to divest existence of its *rich ambiguity*: that is a dictate of good taste, gentlemen, the taste of reverence for everything that lies beyond your horizon,[70]

"Philosophers," to speak like Nietzsche, are not only, as they have been for some 2,500 years, mummifiers and vampires, they are also, in this technocratic day and age, *zombies*. Merleau-Ponty's critique of logocentrism is an echoing cry to us today not to fall prey to this form of incessant philosophical somnambulism, this regimen of the living dead. "The philosopher, "Merleau-Ponty asserted in the last lines of his inaugural lesson to the Collège de France in 1953 (but undoubtedly with an eye to things yet to come), the true philosopher, "is the man who wakes up and speaks."[71]

NOTES

1. F. Nietzsche, *Twilight of the Idols/The Anti-Christ*, trans. R. J. Hollingdale (Harmondsworth: Penguin Books, 1972), "Reason in Philosophy," §§3,4, pp. 36–37.

2. What in an earlier work (*Understanding: A Phenomenological-Pragmatic Analysis* [Westport, Conn.: Greenwood Press, 1982]) I referred to as *rationalism* (i.e., mainline, traditional philosophy; the "Tradition"), I am here calling *logocentrism*. The meaning I attach to this term, borrowed from Derrida, should become clear from the way it is used in the text. I shall not follow the logician's practice of defining my terms *before* using them. Like Feyerabend, I believe that the most fruitful discussions are those in which the meaning of a term or an idea emerges in the very process of applying it or arguing about it. Cf. Feyerabend, *Farewell to Reason* (London: Verso, 1987), p. 45.

3. By F. Alquié in 1947 in an article critical of Merleau-Ponty's project entitled "Une philosophie de l'ambiguité: l'existentialisme de Merleau-Ponty," *Fontaine*, no. 59; pp. 47–70. The epithet was subsequently taken up in a positive way by Alphonse de Waelhens in his sympathetic presentation of Merleau-Ponty, *Une philosophie de l'ambiguité: l'existentialisme de M. Merleau-Ponty* (Louvain: Bibliothèque philosophie de Louvain, 1951).

4. M. Merleau-Ponty, *Phenomenology of Perception*, trans. C. Smith (London: Routledge & Kegan Paul, 1962), p. 169; hereafter cited as *PhP.*

5. Aristotle, *Metaphysics*, 1006b8 (Ross trans.).

6. Nietzsche, *Twilight of the Idols*, p. 37.

7. M. Merleau-Ponty, *The Primacy of Perception*, ed. James Edie (Evanston, Ill.: Northwestern University Press, 1964), p. 13; hereafter cited as *PriP.* "All knowledge takes its place in the horizons opened up by perception" (*PhP*, 207).

8. J. Derrida, "Limited Inc abc...," *Glyph* 2 (1977): 235.

9. "To pay attention is not merely further to elucidate pre-existing data [as, one might say, a computer is capable of doing], it is to bring about a new articulation of them by taking them as *figures*" (*PhP*, 30).

10. "These two elements are not, properly speaking, contradictory. For if we reflect on this notion of perspective,... we see that the kind of evidence proper to the perceived, the appearance of 'something' requires this presence and this absence" (*PriP*, 16).

11. In "Limited Inc" Derrida argues in a properly Merleau-Pontyean fashion: "If one admits that writing (and the work in general) *must be able* to function in the absence of the sender, the receiver, the context of production, etc., that implies that this power, this *being able*, this *possibility*, is

always inscribed, hence *necessarily* inscribed *as possibility* in the functioning or the functional structure of the mark" (p. 184).

12. "The horizons are 'predeliniated' potentialities. ... The predelination itself, to be sure, is at all times imperfect; yet, with its *indeterminateness*, it has a determinate structure." E. Husserl, *Cartesian Meditations*, trans. D. Cairns (The Hague: Martinus Nijhoff, 1960), §19.

13. "The perception of one single thing lays forever the foundation of the ideal of objective or explicit knowledge which classical logic develops" (*PhP*, 322).

14. Merleau-Ponty goes on to say: "If it is to reach perfect density, in other words if there is to be an absolute object, it will have to consist of an infinite number of different perspectives compressed in a strict coexistence, and to be presented as it were to a host of eyes all engaged in one concerted act of seeing" (*PhP*, 70). As this condition cannot, of course, be met, is indeed nonsensical; the notion of an "absolute object" is nonsensical as well.

15. Speaking of this form of "forgetfulness" Merleau-Ponty says: "Thus 'objective' thought (in Kierkegaard's sense) is formed — being that of common sense and of science — which finally causes us to lose contact with perceptual experience, of which it is nevertheless the outcome and the natural sequel. The whole life of consciousness is characterized by the tendency to posit objects, since it is consciousness, that is to say self-knowledge, only in so far as it takes hold of itself and draws itself together in an identifiable object. And yet the absolute positing of a single object is the death of consciousness, since it congeals the whole of existence, as a crystal placed in a solution suddenly crystallizes it" (*PhP*, 71).

16. M. Merleau-Ponty, *The Visible and the Invisible*, trans. A. Lingis (Evanston, Ill.: Northwestern University Press, 1968), p. 15; hereafter cited as *VI*.

17. Wittgenstein's definition of the world as "the totality of facts" (*Tractatus Logico-Philosophicus*, 1.1) is a classic example of objectivistic thinking, just as was Russell's "logical atomism."

18. "We have the experience of a world, not understood as a system of relations which wholly determine each event, but as an open totality the synthesis of which is inexhaustible" (*PhP*, 219). The life-world, as Husserl said, contains "open, endless horizons of things unknown." *The Crisis of European Sciences and Transcendental Phenomenology*, trans. David Carr (Evanston, Ill.: Northwestern University Press, 1970), p. 149.

19. See Gabriel Marcel, *Man against Mass Society* (Chicago: Henry Regnery, 1962).

20. Husserl, *The Crisis*, p. 51. What occurs in Galilean science, Husserl says, is "the surreptitious substitution of the mathematically substructed world of idealities for the only real world, the one that is actually given through perception, that is ever experienced and experienceable — our everyday life-world" (pp. 48–49).

The notion of identity (A = A) ties in with that of equality. In *The Gay Science* (§111, "Origin of the logical") Nietzsche says: "The dominant tendency... to treat as equal what is merely similar — an illogical tendency, for nothing is really equal — is what first created the basis for logic." It is interesting to note that the early Husserl of the *Logical Investigations* was fully a victim of logicism when he maintained that "identity" is more basic than "alikeness." He corrected himself on this score in his later work, *Experience and Judgment*, which bears the subtitle: *Investigations in a Genealogy of Logic*. (See my *Understanding: A Phenomenological-Pragmatic Analysis*, pp. 126–27.)

21. W. James, "Pragmatism's Conception of Truth" in *William James: Writings 1902–1910* (New York: The Library of America, 1987), p. 586.

22. Nietzsche, *Twilight of the Idols*, "Reason in Philosophy," §1.

23. "There is... no destruction of the absolute or of rationality here, only of the absolute and the rationality separated from experience" (*PriP*, 27). What today goes under the heading of "deconstruction," however, is "deconstructive" in that it rejects the very notion of "experience" and thus finds itself without an alternate, nonmetaphysical way of understanding "rationality." That is, it lacks a nonfoundational basis on which to "reconstruct" rationality in a nonrationalistic way. It must be insisted in this regard that Merleau-Ponty's phenomenological recourse to "experience" does not, contrary to what Derrida often implies, signal an ongoing attachment to the "metaphysics of presence" of the sort still to be found in Husserl. See for instance *VI*, pp. 181–82. "This reflection is not, and cannot be, a limitation to the phenomenology of the *Erlebnisse*. The mistrust with regard to lived experience is philosophical — one postulates that consciousness deceives us about ourselves and about language, and one is right: this is the only way to *see* them. Philosophy has nothing to do with the privilege of the *Erlebnisse*, with the psychology of lived experience, etc."

24. "This thesis ['the perceived world is the always presupposed foundation of all rationality'] does not destroy either rationality or the absolute. It only tries to bring them down to earth" (*PriP*, 13).

25. "This paradox is that of all being in the world: when I move towards a world I bury my perceptual and practical intentions in objects which ultimately appear prior to and external to those intentions, and which nevertheless exist for me only in so far as they arouse in me thoughts or volitions" (*PhP*, 82). More recently Kurt Hübner has spoken of what we could call "the misunderstanding function" in the following way. "It appears to be an inextirpable characteristic of people to transform everything which in truth springs from their own invention and design promptly into an objective givenness. The history of physics is a process in which this confusion of our own free constructions with the ontologically real constantly repeats itself." *Critique of Scientific Reason* (Chicago: University of Chicago Press, 1983), p. 23.

26. Because Merleau-Ponty believed that human understanding necessarily tends to misunderstand itself, he did not believe in what today is everywhere and with a certain obviousness spoken of as the "end of metaphysics." Having its origin in Greek logocentrism, metaphysics, of course, is a historically and culturally relative phenomenon, finding its fullest expression in modern science and technology. Nevertheless, there is no reason to believe that it does not represent a natural tendency of the human "mind," a prime instance of human misunderstanding. If this is so, it would be idle to speculate on how me might step beyond the metaphysical "closure" so as to "enter into the event of Appropriation." (See Heidegger, *On Time and Being*, trans. J. Stambaugh [New York: Harper and Row, 1972], p. 41.) It would not make much sense to view modernity, eschatologically, as "the last epoch" and to view the "end of metaphysics" as the end of "epochal history."

If it does not make much sense, from Merleau-Ponty's perspective, to speak of the end of metaphysics or the end of history, it makes even less sense to speak about the "end of philosophy." This is because Merleau-Ponty never identified philosophy with metaphysics in the first place (such that a "releasement" from metaphysics would mean the overcoming of philosophy). To be sure, he vigorously opposed all forms of objectivistic philosophy and spoke of the need for "a complete reconstruction of philosophy" (*VI*, 193). But this is because he viewed this kind of philosophy as a *perversion* of authentic philosophizing. The true task of philosophy as he viewed it consists in effecting a "return" to and a recovery of our lived experience of the world, ourselves, and other people — a rediscovery of human finitude. "No philosophy can afford to be ignorant of finitude, under pain of failing to understand itself as philosophy." For Merleau-Ponty, philosophy was essentially a *critical* activity, and the *Phenomenology of Perception* is a superb example of the philosophical enterprise as he understood it. Because an "end of metaphysics" is unforeseeable, the task of philosophy qua critique of rationalism and qua defense of a wider conception of rationality is *never-ending*. If understanding inevitably tends to misunderstand itself, metaphysical illusion, to use Kant's words, is "inseparable from human reason, and..., even after its deceptiveness has been exposed, will not cease to play tricks with reason and continually entrap it into momentary aberrations ever and again calling for correction." *Critique of Pure Reason* (London: Macmillan, 1963), p. 58.

27. In addition to the remark from the *Twilight of the Idols* quoted at the beginning of the chapter, see also *Human, All Too Human*, trans. R. J. Hollingdale (Cambridge: Cambridge University Press, 1986) §11: "Logic...depends on presuppositions with which nothing in the real world corresponds, for example on the presupposition that there are identical things, that the same thing is identical at different points in time."

28. In those sections of the *Phenomenology* that deal directly with perception, Merleau-Ponty fails to follow up on the following suggestive remark. "But, once more, my human gaze never *posits* more than one facet of the object, even though by means of horizons it is directed towards all the others. It can never come up against previous appearances or those presented to other people otherwise than through the intermediary of time and *language*" (*PhP*, 69; emphasis added).

29. For a detailed treatment of the relation between experience and expression in Merleau-Ponty, see Michael T. Yeo, "Creative Adequation: Merleau-Ponty's Philosophy of Philosophy" (McMaster University, Ph.D. dissertation, 1987) as well as M. C. Dillon, *Merleau-Ponty's Ontology* (Bloomington: Indiana University Press, 1988) (Dillon emphasizes the, so to speak, non- or prelinguistic character of perception [conceived of as the extralinguistic "ground" or "origin" of language] more than I would care to). For additional remarks on the relation between perception and language in Merleau-Ponty, see my paper presented to the Thirteenth Annual International Conference of the Merleau-Ponty Circle (Villanova University, 1988), "Did Merleau-Ponty Have a Theory of Perception?"

30. For further remarks on this issue, see my essay, "The Philosophic Centrality of the Imagination: A Postmodern Approach," in G. B. Madison, *The Hermeneutics of Postmodernity: Figures and Themes* (Bloomington: Indiana University Press, 1988). Merleau-Ponty remarked, somewhat ambiguously: "there is no experience without speech, as the

purely lived through has no part in the discursive live of man" (*PhP*, 337). If, as Merleau-Ponty says, "man perceives in a way different from any animal" (*PriP*, 25), is this not precisely because man is, through and through, the "speaking animal"?

31. "Pure ideality is itself not without flesh nor freed from horizon structures; it lives of them, though they be another flesh and other horizons" (*VI*, 153).

32. "The linguists teach us that...the univocal significance is but one part of the significance of the word, that beyond it there is always a halo of significance that manifests itself in new and unexpected modes of use, that there is an operation of language upon language which, even without other instruments, would launch language back into a new history, and makes of the word-meaning itself an enigma" (*VI*, 96).

33. Paul Feyerabend, *Against Method* (London: Verso, 1978), p. 76. On p. 72 Feyerabend comments on the intimate link between perception and language.

34. A language may contain a finite number of *signs* but words are more than just signs; if one considers the "meanings" these words may have, then their number is indeed infinite.

35. See note 30.

36. On "algorithmic" languages see Merleau-Ponty, *La Prose du monde* (Paris: Gallimard, 1969), pp. 9–10. Among other things Merleau-Ponty remarks: "L'algorithme, le projet d'une langue universalle, c'est la révolte contre le langage donné. On ne veut pas dépendre de ses confusions, on veut le refaire à la mesure de la vérité, le redéfinir selon la pensée de Dieu, recommencer à zéro l'histoire de la parole, ou plutôt, arracher la parole à l'histoire" (p. 10).

37. The classic formulation of this characteristic of formal languages as regards number theory is Gödel's Theorem (1931).

38. J. Habermas, "On Hermeneutics' Claim to Universality" in K. Mueller-Vollmer, ed., *The Hermeneutics Reader* (New York: Continuum, 1985), p. 295.

39. "Il restera toujours, derrière nos propos sur le langage, plus de langage vivant qu'ils ne réussiront à en figer sous notre regard" *La Prose du monde*, pp. 164–64.

40. C. Taylor, *Philosophy and the Human Sciences* (Cambridge: Cambridge University Press, 1985), p. 5. "To take what is admittedly an

extreme case, once one has broken out from the world-view of a very narrow form of naturalism, it seems almost unbelievable that anyone could ever have taken a theory like behaviourism seriously. It takes a very powerful metaphysical set of preconceptions for one to ignore or over-ride so much that is so intuitively obvious about human life, for no valid scientific or explanatory reason. Behaviourism is out of fashion, so many readers may agree with my sentiments on this case. But I think that the situation is not all that different with the contemporary fashion of computer-modelled explanations. Their neglect of what I call...the 'significance factor' is so flagrant, and so bizarre, that only very strong preconceptions could mask it."

41. H. L. Dreyfus, *What Computers Can't Do*, rev. ed. (New York: Harper and Row, 1979). One of the characteristic features of Cognitive Science and Artificial Intelligence is that, because of their proclivity for analytic modes of thought, the dévotés of these disciplines turn a blind eye to the well-established insights of Gestalt psychology. Our remarks in this paper should suggest that if psychologists were not so oblivious to, for instance, the figure-ground phenomenon, the most basic perceptual phenomenon of all, Cognitive Psychology would be as dead an epistemological option as is old-fashioned behaviorism.

"[The] background, which need never have been made determinate, affects the appearance of what is determinate by letting it appear as a unified, bounded figure. ...Thus the figure has specific determinate characteristics only as that-which-is-not-the figure. This indeterminacy plays a crucial role in human perception. Merleau-Ponty points out that most of what we experience must remain in the background so that something can be perceived in the foreground. ...For a computer, which must take up every bit of information explicitly or not at all, there could be no outer horizon. Any information to be taken into account would have to be as determinate as the figure" (Dreyfus, pp. 239–41).

42. For a critical discussion of "strong AI," see John R. Searle, "Minds, Brains, and Programs" in *The Behavioral and Brain Sciences*, vol. 3 (New York: Cambridge University Press); reprinted in Douglas R. Hofstadter and Daniel C. Dennett, *The Mind's I: Fantasies and Reflections on Self and Soul* (New York: Basic Books, 1981).

43. C. Taylor, *Language and Human Agency* (Cambridge: Cambridge University Press, 1985), p. 188.

44. "Programmed behavior is *either* arbitrary *or* strictly rulelike [emphasis added]. Therefore, in confronting a new usage a machine must

either treat it as a clear case falling under the rules, or take a blind stab. A native speaker feels he has a third alternative. He can recognize the usage as odd, not falling under the rules, and yet he can make sense of it — give it a meaning in the context of human life in an apparently nonrulelike and yet nonarbitrary way.

"...Machines lack practical intelligence. They are 'existentially' stupid in that they cannot cope with specific situations. Thus they cannot accept ambiguity and the breaking of rules until the rules for dealing with the deviations have been so completely specified that the ambiguity has disappeared" (Dreyfus, *What Computers Can't Do*, pp. 199–201).

45. Dreyfus, ibid., p. 56.

46. Cf. Dreyfus, ibid., p. 196: "All AI research is dedicated to using logical operations to manipulate data *representing the world.*" Cf. also p. 205: "This assumption that the world can be exhaustively analyzed in terms of context-free data or atomic facts is the deepest assumption underlying work in AI and the whole philosophical tradition." Also p. 206: "the data with which the computer must operate if it is to perceive, speak, and in general behave intelligently, must be discrete, explicit, and determinate; otherwise, it will not be the sort of information which can be given to the computer so as to be processed by rule." And p. 212: "Thus both philosophy and technology, in their appeal to primitives continue to posit what Plato sought: a world in which the possibility of clarity, certainty, and control is guaranteed; a world of data structures, decision theory, and automation."

Hilary Putnam has also emphasized the key role that the metaphysics of referentialist-representationalism plays in Cognitive Science. The "working hypothesis of cognitive psychology today," he said, is that "the mind thinks with the aid of *representations*" and that it uses a formalized language "both as medium of computation and medium of representation." See Putnam, "Computational Psychology and Interpretation Theory" in Rainer Born, ed., *Artificial Intelligence: The Case Against* (London: Croom and Helm, 1987), pp. 2–3.

47. Harvey Siegel, *Educating Reason: Rationality, Critical Thinking, and Education* (New York: Routledge, 1988), p. 1.

48. "Philosophizing was always a kind of vampirism. Looking at these figures...[d]on't you sense a long concealed vampire in the background who begins with the senses and in the end is left with, and leaves, mere bones, mere clatter? I mean categories, formulas, *words.*" Nietzsche, *The Gay Science*, trans. W. Kaufmann (New York: Vintage Books, 1974), §372.

49. I am assuming that it is not the "sophistic" one of teaching people how to concoct "fallacious" arguments so as to better hoodwink their interlocutors — although one delightfully written book on the subject advertizes itself as supplying "advice on how to use the fallacy to mislead and to win an argument unfairly." See M. Pirie, *The Book of the Fallacy: A Training Manual for Intellectual Subversives* (London: Routledge and Kegan Paul, 1985). One textbook in informal logic by R. H. Johnson is revealing entitled: *Logical Self-Defense* (Toronto: McGraw-Hill Ryerson, 1983).

50. "Arguments are in fact but a special case of rhetorical tactics in general." M. C. McGee and J. R. Lyne, "What are Nice Folks Like You Doing in a Place Like This?" in J. S. Nelson, A. Mcgill, and D. N. McCloskey, eds., *The Rhetoric of the Human Sciences: Language and Argument in Scholarship and Public Affairs* (Madison: University of Wisconsin Press, 1987), p. 398.

51. An inverse parallel prevails as regards much of the AI literature. Whereas it is *philosophically* absurd to speak of the mind as a computer or to speak of computers "learning," such a mode of speech may serve a useful *technological* purpose in that it may spur on computer engineers to devising ever more sophisticated computer systems.

52. "The inventor of a new world view...must be able to talk nonsense until the amount of nonsense created by him and his friends is big enough to give sense to all its parts" (Feyerabend, *Against Method*, pp. 256–57). The whole section of Feyerabend's text from which this remark is drawn is very much in the spirit of Merleau-Ponty.

53. "What do we find in the informal logic classroom?...Everywhere attention is given to teaching the concept of an argument as a more or less complicated set of premises supporting a conclusion. The teacher seeks...a skill in the practical matter of recognizing the presence of such arguments in the discourse of their natural habitat and in extracting the arguments from the surrounding non-argumentative text and in displaying them in some perspicuous manner for later evaluation." J. Anthony Blair, "Current Issues in Informal Logic and Critical Thinking" in Alec Fisher, ed., *Critical Thinking: Proceedings of the First British Conference on Informal Logic and Critical Thinking* (University of East Anglia, 1988), p. 16.

54. R. W. Paul, "Teaching Critical Thinking...," p. 3; quoted in Siegel, *Educating Reason*, p. 17.

55. Groundbreaking work in this area of inquiry was done by C. Perelman and L. Olbrechts-Tyteca, *Traité d'argumentation: La nouvelle rhétorique* (Brussels: Editions de l'Institut de Sociologie de l'Université de

Bruxelles, 1970). Currently, much innovative work in the "new rhetoric" is being produced by the Project on the Rhetoric of Inquiry (POROI) at the University of Iowa, directed by Donald McCloskey and John Nelson. A representative number of essays on the "rhetoric of inquiry" (as opposed to the traditional "logic of inquiry) have been collected together in *Rhetoric and the Human Sciences* (see note 50).

56. Siegel, *Educating Reason*, p. 19.

57. H.-G. Gadamer, "Letter to Dallmayr," trans. Diane Michelfelder and Richard Palmer in D. Michelfelder and R. Palmer, *Dialogue and Deconstruction: The Gadamer-Derrida Encounter* (Albany: State University of New York Press, 1989), pp. 98–99.

58. "What then does language express, if it does not express thought? It presents or rather it *is* the subject's taking up of a position in the world of his meanings. The term 'world' here is not a manner of speaking: it means that the 'mental' or cultural life borrows its structures from natural life and that the thinking subject must have its basis in the incarnate subject. The phonetic 'gesture' brings about, both for the speaking subject and for his hearers, a certain structural co-ordination of experience, a certain modulation of existence, exactly as a pattern of my bodily behaviour endows the objects around me with a certain significance both for me and for others" (*PhP*, 193). See also *VI*, 190.

59. Let us, with the help of brackets, do a double, stereoscopic reading of the following text of Merleau-Ponty. "The perceived thing [philosophical concept] is not an ideal unity in the possession of the intellect, like a geometrical notion, for example; it is rather a totality [or a unity] open to a horizon of an indefinite number of perspectival views [interpretations] which blend with one another according to a given style, which defines the object [concept] in question [and which it is the object of text-interpretation to explicate]" (*PhP*, 16). On "style" see also *PhP*, 327.

Merleau-Ponty describes the way in which, as readers, we come to an understanding of philosophical concepts in the following way: "An as yet imperfectly understood piece of philosophical writing discloses to me at least a certain 'style' — either a Spinozist, criticist or phenomenological one — which is the first draft of its meaning. I begin to understand a philosophy by feeling my way into its existential manner, by reproducing the tone and accent of the philosopher. In fact, every language conveys its own teaching and carries its meaning into the listener's mind" (*PhP*, 179; see also *La Prose du monde*, p. 198).

Viewing the matter from the writer's point of view, it might be remarked that the process by means of which new philosophical "concepts are brought into being is none other than that of *metaphorical creativity*. Typical of the process is Aristotle's use of the word *ousia*. The philosopher produces his concept by taking a word that in its native habitat of ordinary language has a wide semantic range and separating out from the word's denotation or connotation, one single aspect that he then proclaims to be decisive — and exclusive; i.e., definitive. Thus, the condition of possibility of philosophical "univocity" is *forgetfulness* of a word's natural multivocity. (Aristotle was able to give a definitive [and decisive] answer to the question, "What is being?" only by losing sight of all but one of the possible meanings of "being.")

   60. Siegel, *Educating Reason*, p. 29.

   61. Ibid., p. 48.

   62. "A conventional algorithm — which moreover is meaningful only in relation to language — will never express anything but Nature without man. Strictly speaking, therefore, there are no conventional signs, standing as the simple notation of a thought pure and clear in itself. There are only words [*paroles*] into which the history of a whole language is compressed, and which effect communication with no absolute guarantee, dogged as they are by incredible linguistic hazards [*et qui accomplissent la communication sans aucune garantie, au milieu d'incroyables hasards linguistiques*]" (*PhP*, 188).

   63. Siegel voices the typical logocentric prejudice when he tells us that formal logic is "a paradigm of good argumentation," that it constitutes "an 'ideal type' of argument" (*Educating Reason*, p. 26). Even my colleague David Hitchcock is expressing a logocentric prejudice when he asserts (on what rational grounds?) that "reason is in fact the only sure ultimate guide to truth" (*Critical Thinking: A Guide to Evaluating Information* [Toronto: Methuen, 1983], p. 5). A whole host of countertraditional thinkers have hotly contested this. Even as rationalist a thinker as Thomas Aquinas otherwise was would have disagreed.

   64. See Hans-Georg Gadamer, *Dialogue and Dialectic*, trans. P. C. Smith (New Haven, Conn.: Yale University Press, 1980), p. 111. In my rereadings of Merleau-Ponty over the last few years, I have been much impressed by the far-ranging and deep affinities between Merleau-Ponty's phenomenology and Gadamer's hermeneutics. The similarities between their respective positions are all the more remarkable in that they are purely "accidental" (i.e., the position expressed by Gadamer in 1960 in *Wahrheit und Methode* had been arrived at in ignorance of Merleau-Ponty's work).

   65. See Taylor, *Language and Human Agency*, Chapter 8. Cf. also *PhP*,

pp. 193–94: "the human body is defined in terms of its property of appro-priating, in an indefinite series of discontinuous acts, significant cores which transcend and transfigure its natural powers. This act of trans-cendence is first encountered in the acquisition of a pattern of behaviour, then in the mute communication of gesture... speech causes a new sense to arise, if it is authentic speech, just as gesture endows the object for the first time with human significance, if it is an initiating gesture. Moreover significance now acquired must necessarily have been new once. We must therefore recognize as an ultimate fact this open and indefinite power of giving significance — that is, both of apprehending and conveying a meaning — by which man transcends himself towards a new form of behaviour, or towards other people, or towards his own thought, through his body and his speech." Cf. also *PhP*, p. 197: "[One's own body] is not a collection of particles, each one remaining in itself, nor yet a network of processes defined once and for all — it is not where it is, nor what it is [note the implication of this as regards the principle of identity] — since we see it secreting in itself a 'significance' which comes to it from nowhere, projecting that significance upon its material surrounding, and communicating it to other embodied subjects."

66. The following remarks by Dreyfus are suggestive as regards the inner link between scientific "knowledge" and technological know-how. "Alchemists were so successful in distilling quicksilver from what seemed to be dirt that, after several hundred years of fruitless efforts to convert lead into gold, they still refused to believe that on the chemical level one cannot transmute metals. They did, however, produce — as by-products — ovens, retorts, crucibles, and so forth, just as computer workers, while failing to produce artificial intelligence, have developed assembly pro-grams, debugging programs, program-editing programs, and so on, and the M.I.T. robot project has built a very elegant mechanical arm." Dreyfus, *What Computers Can't Do*, p. 303.

67. G. Shanker, "The Decline and Fall of the Mechanist Metaphor" in Born, *Artificial Intelligence*, p. 126.

68. See in this regard my essay, "Metaphysics as Myth," in *The Hermeneutics of Postmodernity*.

69. See Madison, "Merleau-Ponty and Postmodernity," in ibid., p. 72.

70. Nietzsche, *The Gay Science*, §373.

71. M. Merleau-Ponty, *Eloge de la philosophie* (Paris: Gallimard, 1953), p. 100: "*Le philosophie est l'homme qui s'éveille et qui parle...*"

6

Phenomenology and Metaphysics: Husserl, Heidegger, and Merleau-Ponty

Joseph Margolis

I

Borrowing a term from the grammar of semantics, we may say that the embedded use of two distinct radicals yields a metaphysics: (1) one through which, in speaking of *what* we speak of, we are committed to certain structures obtaining in what we take the limiting possibilities of our world to be; and (2) one through which, in *speaking* of what we speak of, we are committed to certain categories of discourse obtaining in what we take the limiting possibilities of discourse to be. Call the first *de re*, and the second, *de dicto*. We cannot disjoin our talk about the nature of things from our conceptual prejudices about the neutrality of the language we use in doing that; and we cannot speak of the syntactic uniformities of our language without implicating our symbiotized prejudices about the nature of things. We address an indissolubly languaged world and we speak an indissolubly worlded language. The *de re* and *de dicto* necessities asymmetrically drawn from the would-be disjunction of world and word obscure the tacit source they share. But if that is so, then a large, disputatious benefit is to be claimed at once: neither radical, taken separately, provides an adequate foundation for a science or a metaphysics of any sort; and every science and every metaphysics implicates each of these two radicals indifferently — though they are, indeed, altogether different from one another. One may say, provocatively, that this finding is shared by phenomenology and pragmatism, however different their particular practices may be.

Note that the disjunction says no word about cognitive access or privilege regarding world or speech. Metaphysics, in the standard lexicon of postphenomenological discourse, is pejoratively marked by *de re* presumptions or necessities *de re* informed by some

153

strong privilege of a naturalistic sort. Phenomenology, bracketing such *de re* or *de dicto* presumptions (bracketing naturalism), presumes to examine, even more deeply, *de cogitatione*, beyond that constituted disjunction, structures freed now from the "metaphysical" and "epistemological" naiveté *of the other*. Nevertheless, if our original term of art be allowed to serve its purpose (that is, the notion of artificially abstracted radicals), then there remains a prejudical "metaphysics" and "epistemology" embedded *in* phenomenology itself. For whatever is said to originate or constitute that disjunction is itself posited only within its constituted powers. Phenomenology seeks to probe the conditions of thinking (originary, precognitive, prethetic, transcendental, or however otherwise characterized as pristine or "prior") on which the seemingly stable bifurcation of *de re* and *de dicto* objectivities itself depends. *Metaphysics* and *epistemology* are therefore treated as terms of opprobrium restricted to the work of the latter. Nevertheless, insofar as it also proceeds discursively, phenomenology cannot fail to be infected, symbiotically, by the presumptive powers it means to "constitute."

The argument is a general one and does not depend on *any* particular elaboration of method. Wherever we presume to withdraw from the false fixed privilege of natural discourse about the world — whether as Hegelians, Marxists, phenomenologists, existentialists, hermeneuts, Frankfurt School advocates, poststructuralists, postmodernists, pragmatists, deconstructionists, genealogists, nihilists hardly matters — we do not and cannot withdraw from the rigors of enunciative discourse (whatever those rigors may be) and we cannot, adhering to the enunciative, fail to implicate the salient structures of the world we take ourselves to encounter. Husserl's presumption, at least in his sometimes obsessive search for the apodictic regularities of what *he* took to be the *de cogitatione* concerns of pure phenomenology, fails in a more modest way to eclipse all forms of metaphysics. For although there is indeed a metaphysics of privilege or presence that so many (following Husserl) have now routinely exposed, there is also a metaphysics of enunciative or assortoric utterance *whether or not there is the other*.

Now, *if* we yield on privilege of every sort — against naturalisms, objectivisms, functionalisms, transcendental arguments, foundationalisms, logocentrisms, structuralisms, ontotheologies, essentialisms, universalisms, traditionalisms, idealisms, modernisms, transparency and mirror theories, legitimations, apodictic phenomenologies, "archisms,"[1] totalizations, originary origins, and the like, then the bias of disjoining our original radicals stares us in the face. A languaged world or a worlded language serves as a convenient epithet to fix whatever we may suppose is the originary, incompletely penetrable precondition posited *from* the transient vantage of *whatever* bifurcated *de re* and *de dicto* (or *de cogitatione*) resources we assign ourselves. The analysis of subject and object — which, in effect, is the deeper, more familiar disjunction of the *de re* and *de dicto* radicals we provisionally allowed ourselves — *is* an analysis reflexively pursued under the banner of that very bifurcation. Either, therefore, an element of privilege infects every enunciation, or else the analysis of mere statement *can yield a metaphysics without privilege.*

Alternatively — now, more familiarly — Husserl's disjunction of naturalism and phenomenology, fairly vindicated in terms of exposing a metaphysics of privilege, vindicated by exposing certain obviously biased assumptions about the possibilities of first-order *de re* discourse,[2] can and even must be overcome if we admit a metaphysics of enunciation freed at least from the simplistic presumptions of the naturalists and objectivists Husserl exposed. The upshot is that, in a sense — monstrous as the terminological intrusion may appear to be — there *is* a metaphysics in Husserl's phenomenology. Just as we cannot separate analyses *de re* and *de dicto*, we cannot separate their cognitional preconditions from the contingent but symbiotic influence of our ordinary concepts in referential and predicative discourse; that is, from the normal contexts of distributed things. Hence, in abandoning privilege, we collapse the disjunction between naturalism and phenomenology — not in the sense that what Husserl treated as naturalism is what he also treated as phenomenology but rather in the sense that naturalism deprivileged *is* (now) naturalism phenomenolo*gized* and phenomenology deprivileged (against Husserl's own extreme temptation) *is* (now) phenomenology natura*lized*. To grasp the point is to grasp the intent with which, with somewhat oddly varying degrees of success, skill, scope, understanding, even awareness, both a privileged naturalism and a privileged phenomenology are opposed by

Heidegger, Merleau-Ponty, Derrida, James, Dewey, and, in a pop sense, Rorty. Of these, perhaps the most effective is Merleau-Ponty.

That is, *if* what we have been treating as merely heuristically disjoined radicals implicated in every analysis — implicated in an indissoluble way that cannot be represented in the idiom of those same radicals — answers to the indissolubility of every would-be analysis of whatever is cognized or cognizable and of what are the ultimate resources by which whatever is cognizable is cognized, then there cannot be any separable order of disciplines serially, perhaps hierarchically, addressed, first, to the natural world or to the natural world as it appears to discursively apt investigators and, second, addressed to the essential or limiting conceptual possibilities by which any analysis of the first sort may be guided or governed or grounded.

This is not to deny that inquiries similar to those just identified may be pursued. It is only to deny that the two sorts of inquiry may be disjoined from one another or that the second may attain a certitude or a form of knowledge more fundamental than that of the other. That there *are* relevant achievements of the second sort is a permanent tribute to Husserl's penetrating analysis of the opposition between phenomenology and what he usually understands in speaking of naturalism and empiricism, or "positive" or "objective" science. This is the point, for example, of that marvellous piece of rhetoric in which Husserl asks whether it is "nonsensical and circular" to attempt to explain "the historical event 'natural science'" by means of natural science itself.[3] On the other hand, Husserl's question is plainly linked to his own excitement at having discovered "a *science whose peculiar nature is unprecedented* . . . a science of concrete transcendental subjectivity, as given in actual and possible transcendental experience, a science that forms the *extremest contrast to sciences in the hitherto accepted sense.*" Of this, he says: "we are envisaging a science that is, so to speak, absolutely subjective, whose thematic object exists whether or not the world exists."[4]

There are, obviously, attractive false clues to be seduced by in this passage and in similar passages, and dubious presumptions are also embedded in Husserl's own way of viewing the highest phenomenological science. Husserl draws attention immediately to the threat of "a permanently solipsistic science" and to the prospects regarding how *that* provisional science "leads over to a phenomenology of transcendental intersubjectivity."[5] But it is certainly not clear that Husserl ever successfully overcame that solipsism, for example, even in *The Crisis*, which represents in a way his greatest but still inadequate concession to the historicity and social nature of human existence. In *The Crisis*, Husserl reconciles the solipsism of the "primal [constituting] ego" with the intersubjectivity of plural "I's" "among [so-called] transcendental others" by announcing that, in every apparently "always singular 'I,'" there is always in that "I," "'another I' that achieves ontic validity as copresent with his own ways of being self-evidently verified." We are to understand here that the "ontic" plurality of transcendental egos is, somehow, a pluralizing necessarily entailed in being "constituted in the world as a human being"; and yet, at the same time, we are to understand that "constituting the world" (that includes *that* plurality) is such that "the world... does not exist as *an* entity, as an object, but exists with such uniqueness that the plural makes no sense when applied to it. Every plural, and every singular drawn from it," says Husserl, "presupposes the world-horizon."[6] Correspondingly, every singular ego must be a pluralizable site of the ultimate constituting subjectivity (or Ego) regarding which singular and plural also make no sense. This is certainly close to the intended message of the fifth Meditation,[7] and produces an even deeper (but no longer merely human) solipsism.

Still, the solipsistic puzzle is *not* the pressure point we really want. It is rather the absence of number (the absence of individuatability) that is decisive in speaking of constituted *Lebenswelt* and constituting subjectivity, regardless of the fact that, elsewhere, Husserl is obviously content to pluralize active and cognizing subjectivities and *Lebenswelten*. For, it is incoherent to preserve phenomenology *as a critical discipline* when it is applied to the numberless. The restoration of number (or distributed reference) effectively naturalizes phenomenology and disallows any pretension of apodicticity. Heidegger abandons critical phenomenology altogether (or nearly altogether) *in* exploring the import of numberless *Sein* and *Dasein*; and Merleau-Ponty willingly risks the apodictic within critical phenomenology *by* numbering subjectivity. The effect is to force a convergence between phenomenology and pragmatism or

some other critical naturalism; that is, to trade on the difference
between a naturalism of privilege and a naturalism of enunciation.
This is overly compressed, of course, but it does capture the essential theme.

When Husserl speaks so engagingly of a science "whose
thematic object exists whether or not the world exists," we are not
to understand him as recommending a hierarchy of disjoined or
independent disciplines. Husserl's demarcation of the "absolutely
subjective" is marked off *in* the space of natural human thought,
experience, and activity with respect to the initial (and initiative)
data regarding which it is able to probe to more profound fixities
than might at first be imagined possible: it is an achievement that
can be grasped only by a deepening order of reflections that
"bracket" the progressively less confining contingencies and artifacts of each successive level of analysis. The trouble with Husserl's
project lies not so much with the supposed achievement of particular apodictic discoveries at the end of his exercises but rather with
the very rationale for thinking that, apart from plural, apparent
invariances yielded by appropriate reflection here and now, there is
a linear, progressive, sequential unity of such exercises (or a unity
that coherently collects every possible such exercise) that entitles us
in principle to suppose we are *approximating* (by such efforts) to
whatever may be the ultimate disclosures of the phenomenological
method itself.

The rejection of Husserlian optimism about such totalizing,
systematicity, progress, apodicticity (the principal versions of
Husserlian "privilege") — without rejecting phenomenological invariances of any particular kind — in a way, is the distinctive work of
Heidegger and Merleau-Ponty, possibly (in a rigorous sense) of
Merleau-Ponty preeminently. If we treat eidetic invariances (that
we seem able to approach) in just the terms by which we oppose
cognitive privilege — that is, *as* the ineluctably contingent functions
of an equally contingent preformational world or social history of
praxis, a precondition that is tacit, incompletely penetrable, changing, plural, capable of tolerating conceptual incommensurabilities,
itself something of an artifact constructed in the process of natural
activity and eidetic reflection, profoundly horizontal as affecting the
perception of invariance, constituting an endogenous barrier

against the discovery of contextless invariances, therefore in principle incapable of supporting Husserl's optimism about approx-
imative progress in understanding a uniquely constituted world or
constituting "I" such that "the plural makes no sense" applied to
"either" — then we are surely drawn to construing what remains of
phenomenology in a way that is more or less common ground for
such utterly different authors as Heidegger, Merleau-Ponty, Derrida, and James. The recovery of a *plural* with regard to whatever
may be *critically* posited as the pregiven conditions of natural discourse is incompatible in an elementary way with the notion of a
progressive phenomenology ranging over all possible reflection.
There is no such reflection. There is Husserl's essential vulnerability.

In an important sense both Husserl and Heidegger resist or
demote metaphysics. In Husserl, it takes the form of an opposition
to Descartes's notion of an "all-embracing" science, already in some
sense given, that "rests, *ordine geometrico*, on an axiomatic foundation
that grounds the deduction [of the entire system] absolutely."
Husserl makes it clear at once that he means to redeem a
Cartesian-like objective phenomenologically, by adhering to "the
general aim of grounding science absolutely," but only by gaining
that objective through a gradual process by which "it shall become
determined concretely."[8] Husserl gives up metaphysics and epistemology, therefore, in the Cartesian or objectivist sense; but, in
the argument sketched, he redeems (and is aware that he must
redeem) metaphysics and epistemology by way of an analysis of
assertoric discourse and the structural possibilities of thought that
underlie discourse and science and metaphysics. If, however,
Husserl cannot in principle appeal to conceptual resources genuinely deeper, more foundational, more authoritative than
Descartes's, then there is no dimensional or hierarchical difference
between naturalism and phenomenology: they are no more than
heuristically distinguished aspects of an indissolubly relentless
probing — which was the original point of our speaking of naturalizing phenomenology and of phenomenologizing naturalism.

Husserl, of course, believed that Heidegger was something of a
renegade — or no phenomenologist at all. Heidegger, unnamed but
clearly intended in Husserl's 1931 lecture, "Phenomenology and

Anthropology," according to Husserl, was set to redeem phenomenology, "true philosophy," by locating "its foundations exclusively in
man and, more specifically, in the essence of his concrete worldly
existence";[9] that is, by a complete reversal of the conceptual depen-
dencies Husserl originally favored in conceiving the distinctive
science of phenomenology. For, it was Husserl's view that psychology and anthropology, for example, "demand [that is, antecedently
depend upon] a science of transcendental subjectivity, a science of
a completely new kind [phenomenology], without which psychology and the other sciences cannot be grounded philosophically."[10]
The *Britannica* essay and Walter Biemel's discussion of Heidegger's
involvement in its revision make it quite clear that Husserl and
Heidegger disagreed fundamentally.[11] The essential point remains
that Husserl *could not* resist Heidegger's reversal if he did not
believe that phenomenology "was a science of a completely new
kind," an a priori science, a science that could yield a distinct sort
of apodictic knowledge. Thus he says:

> If this meaning [the meaning of the task of philosophy] is necessarily
> subjective [on the acknowledgement that "everyone feels that
> philosophy needs to be subjectively grounded"], the specific meaning
> of this subjectivity must also be determined *a priori*. It must,
> therefore, be possible to choose, once and for all, between anthro-
> pologism and transcendentalism without reference to any historical
> form of philosophy and anthropology (or psychology).[12]

In this sense, in insisting, as *we* have, that a metaphysics *is* implicit
in Husserl's phenomenology, we are going expressly contrary to
Husserl's own view of his work *and*, to that extent, agreeing with
Heidegger's general reorientation. For, Heidegger does not allow
the constituting (alethic) process between *Sein* and *Dasein* to function merely *critically* — to implicate number in the treatment of *Sein*
and *Dasein*; for his part, Husserl does intend the relation between
numberless *Lebenswelt* and subjectivity *to* function critically — but
that is impossible.

II

We need not agree with Heidegger, however. Heidegger begins
Being and Time also by opposing Descartes's project. Thus, very

quickly reviewing the history of Western metaphysics, Heidegger remarks:

> In the course of this history certain distinctive domains of Being have come into view and have served as the primary guides for subsequent problematics: the *ego cogito* of Descartes, the subject, the "I", reason, spirit, person. But these all remain uninterrogated as to their Being and its structure, in accordance with the thoroughgoing way in which the question of Being has been neglected. ...If the question of Being is to have its own history made transparent, then this hardened tradition must be loosened up, and the concealments which it has brought about must be dissolved. We understand this task as one in which by taking *the question of Being as our clue*, we are to *destroy* the traditional content of ancient ontology until we arrive at those primordial experiences in which we achieved our first ways of determining the nature of Being — the ways which have guided us ever since.[13]

Heidegger's solution lies with his analysis of "temporality" (*Zeitlichkeit*) and leads to displacing a Cartesian emphasis on cognition by means of attending to the precognitive structure of *Dasein's* career as essentially one of "Being-in-the-world" (*In-der-Welt-sein*). The decisive point is that Heidegger means to redeem a radically contingent metaphysics directly by what he regards as a phenomenological discovery of the essential preconditions of the "ontic" structure of man's (or *Dasein's*) self-understanding: the preconditions are "ontological" rather than "ontic," occupied with *aletheia*, the dialectic of *Vorhandenheit* and *Zuhandenheit*, the dialectic of the *existentiell* and the *existential*, the priority of temporality to historicality, the primordial potentiality of *Dasein*, what is not captured by notions of "presence," and similar themes.

What is distinctive in his account is that Heidegger regards metaphysics as concerned with "the meaning of Being,"[14] within which the ontic and ontological are already inextricably intertwined. As Heidegger puts it, "Dasein is ontically distinctive in that it *is* ontological" — it is "ontically distinguished by the fact that, in its very being, that Being is an *issue* for it."[15] Husserl apparently construes Heidegger as reversing the order he himself favored. But a more sympathetic reading, at whatever ulterior price, takes note of the fact that the "ontological" is teased out by Heidegger by an a priori reflection that does *not* rest on any psychology or anthropology (at least in Husserl's sense) but rather on a *mythic* conjecture regarding the constituting existential structure of *Dasein* in virtue of which any particular "ontic" (or empirical) assignment to human nature or the natural world may be understood and accounted for.

What is radical about Heidegger's notion is located here. For, since the speculation about the structure of *Dasein* is mythic — what else could we suppose is meant by *Dasein's* aptness for receiving the temporally sequenced primordial disclosures of *Sein* itself — the ontological structures attributed are "existentialia" rather than categories (roughly, the essential, as yet unstructured hermeneutic potency of a certain kind of being *vis-à-vis* other beings including itself) and are always, in particular circumstances, instantly interpreted in accord with the forestructuring powers of historically entrenched particular categories (that first organize our conceptual *and* active efforts).[16] In a word, the charm of Heidegger's account is simply that it exhibits the peculiar contingency of metaphysics — a fortiori, the contingency of phenomenology:

1. by displacing the cognitive with the precognitively and existentially active;

2. by construing the phenomenological characterization of the existential structure of *Dasein* as yielding only an invariance of a mythic sort that is *not* directly occupied with the categories of any would-be science;

3. by construing the articulation of all categories as conditioned in a radically contingent way by the preformative power of ulterior categories historically already in place in a world into which we are "thrown";

4. by construing the seeming system of the diachronic history of given sets of categories as phenomenologically open to transformations due to different but utterly unpredictable, utterly unsystematizable, disclosures of *Sein* and *Dasein* by which the fixity of given categories is radically risked.

Husserl was right to see the threat of Heidegger's revision; but it was not meant as a threat that did not attempt to preserve the apriority of phenomenology. It meant to preserve apriority by radically transforming it. It preserved the a priori at the price of denying *its critical capacity* for totalizing, for fixing the original sources of the essential, for recovering or approximating to the apodictic. *It preserved invariance but only as a mythic conjecture ventured at our own particular historical moment* — hence, only by abandoning phenomenological privilege. What is alien about Heidegger is that he is content to abandon the Husserlian pursuit of eidetic invariants. In fact, he effectively abandons any sustained interest in notions of truth other than that associated with the mythic "disclosedness" of Being.[17] He is not interested in invariances involving any mere conceptual *categories*, however generated. Hence, he shows how the phenomenological, the a priori, and the metaphysical can be reconciled while giving up altogether Husserl's new Cartesian venture. It is true that the supposed phenomenology of existentialia yields essential constraints on a pluralized *Dasein* that are not reducible to mere natural categories. And, in this, Heidegger traps himself, confuses metaphysics and phenomenology. Nevertheless, for one thing, *those* constraints are always and ineluctably articulated or interpreted in terms of the existentiell categories that form *our* conceptual horizon; and, for another, to preserve that distinction, Heidegger holds that we must construe the existential invariances we posit as conjectures regarding the originary mythic relation between *Sein* and *Dasein* and the bearing of that relationship on whatever critical ontic regularities we may venture. Existentialia never directly affect particular categorical claims, only their contingency with regard to *aletheia*. Those invariances are emphatically not *critical*, not conceptually *prior*, not *foundations*, not the *constituting* conditions of meaning Husserl insists on. If they were, Heidegger's program would disable itself. (Heidegger, however, is not entirely consistent here.)

This is the meaning of his having begun *Being and Time* with the question of "the Meaning of Being." *Being* is not constituted by *Dasein* but only disclosed to it; and plural entities (beings, *Seiende*) are not constituted by *Dasein* either, but constituted only in the mythic disclosure of Being to *Dasein*. Being has no inherent or discoverable or disclosable structure at all; what is disclosed of Being to *Dasein* is instantly pluralized (including *Dasein* itself) within the essential, "transparent" inquiry of each and every entity inherently capable of such inquiry; namely, each of us, each human person.

"Being" itself is not a concept or category for Heidegger; it is "what is really intended," "sought" (beyond all categories and all existentialia) in every inquiry of *Dasein*; it is ultimately a surd:[18]

> to work out the question of Being adequately [says Heidegger], we must make an entity — the inquirer — transparent in his own Being. The very asking of this question is an entity's mode of *Being*; and as such it gets its essential character from what is inquired about — namely, Being. This entity which each of us is himself and which includes inquiring as one of the possibilities of its Being, we shall denote by the term "*Dasein*."[19]

The conferring of meaning on beings is not accessible in a *critical* sense, as it is for Husserl; it is critically *lost* in the symbiotic power of Being to disclose itself as an order of plural beings to plural beings of a unique kind apt for receiving such disclosures. (That is surely the sense in which Derrida may be said to continue Heidegger's work.) The conferring or constituting of the world is *mythic* rather than *critical*: that is,

1. not managed by determinable concepts or categories;
2. not distributively assigned as the preconstituting structures of thought by which particular sets of discursive claims are understood to be referentially contingent options among a systematic and inclusive set of all possible such alternatives;
3. not in any regard constitutively prior to our natural discourse about the apparent world.

In being mythic rather than critical, the precondition alleged is also:

4. never other than global or holistic;
5. not concerned with the determinate use or alterability of concepts at all;
6. disposed to treat every apparent limit or necessity of conceptual schemes as an artifact of the serial disclosures of *Sein* to *Dasein* — which continues without end;
7. committed to construing every critical activity (Husserl's own, for instance) as a mere, though quite natural, occasion within the originary (mythic) disclosure of Being.

It is in this sense that Heidegger supposes that he does not violate the spirit of phenomenology, though he does not adhere to Husserl's untenably privileged phenomenological program. His maneuver also, therefore, yields a radical escape from Kant. In effect, Heidegger endorses the naturalizing of phenomenology and the phenomenologizing of naturalism — *at* Husserl's level of discourse; *and then* adds a mythic dimension to phenomenological speculation that expresses *that* symbiosis, the sense of the inherent limits of the critical search for eidetic necessities, as a "higher" comment on a mere moment in *Dasein*'s career. This may well be the point of Heidegger's indebtedness to Dilthey — which Husserl had noted. But it is *not* the restoration of the priority of the natural, the priority of psychology or anthropology, the use of number (or reference) in a preontized phenomenology. It is certainly the essential clue to the intriguing absorption in — almost fondness for — the bearable indescribability of Being that one finds in Derrida and other late post-Heideggerian thinkers.[20] Also, it must be remembered (or conceded), *Dasein* plays both a mythic and a critical role — indissolubly — because it is at once an "ontic-ontological" notion, a notion about a structured and particular *Seiendes* and about the phenomenologically invariant function that this entity is said to perform relative to what has no structure or number and is not conceptually capturable at all (but is only intended or presupposed in the essential functioning of *Dasein*): namely, *Sein*; hence, it categorizes an existentiale that may be universally assigned, as intended, in the existentiell career of every particular historically "thrown" human individual thereby individuated *as Dasein*. So the characterization of humankind incorporates Heidegger's vision of what *is* (he believes) invariant in human nature: namely, *the global concern for Being that yields nothing determinately invariant* but is predictably trapped into believing that it has discovered invariances at whatever levels of conceptual inquiry individuals happen to favor. There is no eidetic exercise of a Husserlian sort to confirm the discovery. The myth of the relation between *Sein* and *Dasein* apparently obviates its need.

Heidegger is disappointing, however. Because, having located the essential threat of arbitrariness and self-delusion in Husserl, he never returned to collect whatever distributed candidates for categorical invariance might be promising or instructive *within* the global dispensation of our own apparent ordered world. Either he remained uninterested in such matters, once the universalism Husserl pursued proved delusive; or else he became increasingly fearful that the slightest encouragement of a discursive critique of whatever sort might symbiotize naturalism and phenomenology suitably — Kantian, Frankfurt School, Marxist, Hegelian, pragmatist — would inevitably lead to the gloomy end of philosophy he himself predicted.[21] In any case, the exposé of the inevitable contingency of all would-be critical or necessary invariants would have yielded (and would still yield) an instruction of the highest benefit under the conditions of the flux Heidegger embraced. For example, the exposé of the limited scope of Euclidean parallel lines, the dispensability of the principle of excluded middle, the oddity of the Moebius strip, the puzzles of quantum superposition, the uncertainties of time travel, even the vagaries of Hume's contentions about numerical identity in general and personal identity in particular, and the indecisiveness of Husserl's own refutation of psychologism are of the greatest importance precisely *under* the conditions of (what we may now hint at as) phenomenological *salience* as opposed to eidetic *invariance*.[22] Husserl is recoverable in this regard — even if against his own presumption; but Heidegger is largely silent.

Nevertheless, in a certain distant sense, the point of Heidegger's florid myth is to restore phenomenology to a more limited role within a pregiven world that never exhausts the possibilities of its own disclosure and that never is transparent to the agents to which it is initially and forever legible. It restores the irreducible relationship between cognized world and cognizing subject for every set of determinate claims. It restores that relationship within a precondition that admits an endless genesis of discontinuous and incommensurable schemata and tacit sources of precognitive effectiveness that defeat at a single stroke every pretension of total system, originary source, apodictic confidence, cognitive hierarchy, and the detailed fit of world and word. In short, Heidegger is a realist of some sort, recovering a metaphysics sufficient at least to disallow Husserl's threatening idealism — or solipsism.[23] And yet, as soon as that is said, Husserl's own idiom of constituting subjectivity and constituted *Lebenswelt* sounds like a myth as well, within which the match of world and word or world and thought is not intended to disallow the actual independence of other selves or the independence of natural things but rather to ensure a context congruent enough for the endless, fabled pursuit of the constitution of *that* particular world we know — construed (now) as fitted within the limiting necessities of thought, themselves inexplicably fitted to that same world. So seen, Husserl's passion to define the powers of his unheard-of science of meanings obliges him to discount metaphysics or the fit of phenomenology to metaphysics; but then, he always admits the surd of the necessity of ultimate subjectivity's own would-be necessities: why should the world be fitted to "its" necessities and not to others? So seen, phenomenology's eclipse of metaphysics is plainly itself a metaphysics manqué — and a metaphysics acknowledged.[24]

III

Merleau-Ponty is the phenomenologically minded witness of just those strains between Husserl's and Heidegger's project. As we know, he is reported, with great regularity, to be "perhaps the greatest and most faithful disciple of Husserl's."[25]

But the compliment — is it really meant for Merleau-Ponty or for Husserl? — obscures the sense in which he is that disciple. It is not that he does or does not oppose Husserl: he does both, of course. It is just that at the end we really do not know exactly how Merleau-Ponty would resolve the questions he himself admits. He never brought his final account to a sufficient resolution for us to say. He may have abandoned *The Origin of Truth*. The usual picture offered claims, mildly enough, that he was drawn in his middle and later work to Heidegger and to a most unfamiliar Saussure against his earlier loyalty to Husserl, and that, "perhaps," he was returning at the end to a reconciliation with the themes of his earlier phenomenology. The posthumous publication of *The Visible and the Invisible* does not quite bear that out in a simple way. But more to the point, the relevant uneasinesses are already apparent in *Phenomenology of Perception*, the principal site of his orthodoxy.

Thus, in bringing the *Phenomenology* to a close with the final chapters on temporality and freedom — topics that provide for the greatest and clearest contrast between Husserl and Heidegger — Merleau-Ponty already remarks:

> The world is inseparable from the subject, but from a subject which is nothing but a project of the world, and the subject is inseparable from the world, but from a world which it projects itself. The subject is a being-in-the-world and the world remains "subjective" since its texture and articulations are indicated by the subject's movement of transcendence.[26]

Surely, this *is* the "chiasm" before its time. It is already to be found in Heidegger as well. Merleau-Ponty actually cites the relevant passage from *Being and Time* as a footnote to the passage just given: "If [says Heidegger] the 'subject' gets conceived ontologically as an existing Dasein whose Being is grounded in temporality, then one must say that the world is 'subjective.' But in that case, this 'subjective' world, as one that is temporally transcendent, is 'more Objective' than any possible 'Object.'"[27] Heidegger also says, even more pointedly in the same passage, that

> the significance-relationships which determine the structure of the world are not a network of forms which a worldless subject has laid over some kind of material. What is rather the case is that factical Dasein, understanding itself and its world ecstatically in the unity of the "there," comes back from these horizons to the entities encountered within them. Coming back to these entities understandingly is the existential meaning of letting them be encountered by making them present; that is why we call them entities "within-the-world." The world is, as it were, already "further outside" than any Object can ever be.[28]

But this, also, *is* Merleau-Ponty's chiasm — or, the half of it. For Merleau-Ponty's is a "double chiasm" (which Heidegger elsewhere also surely honors).

In the Working Notes added to the text of *The Visible and the Invisible*, Merleau-Ponty says very plainly:

> The chiasm is not only a me-other exchange (the messages he receives reach me, the messages I receive reach him). It is also an exchange between me and the world, between the phenomenal body

and the "objective" body, between the perceiving and the perceived: what begins as a thing ends as consciousness of the thing, what begins as a "state of consciousness" ends as a thing.[29]

That note was written barely two years before Merleau-Ponty's death. It is surely a return to the *Phenomenology of Perception*; but that is to say the *Phenomenology* was already chiasmic, occupied with the incvitability of rcconciling phcnomcnology with mctaphysics, symbiotizing phenomenology and naturalism.

Reconciling and *symbiotizing* are actually terms too tame for Merleau-Ponty; they are also, frankly, terms that must appear eccentric from his perspective. He construed the "ontology of the object" and the "ontology of the existent" — ontologies implicated in asymmetrical ways in naturalism and phenomology — as "monocular images" needing to be "taken over," integrated "in order to make of them one sole vision."[30] There can be no question about that. He himself, already in the Cartesian endeavor he always sought to understand and redeem, fixes our attention on "the 'strabism' [in effect, a certain monocularism] of Western ontology" and the "ontological diplopia" [in effect, a certain double vision] that are the hereditary disorders of the Western mind. Also, in outlining the Introduction to the projected *Origin of Truth*, he already announces the "necessity of a return to ontology" — by which he understands at least the plural binocularisms of

the subject-object question
the question of inter-subjectivity
the question of Nature.[31]

Nevertheless, there is a lacuna in his project that marks the "diplopia" he wished to overcome in Husserl.

The essential puzzle is this. The transcendental functioning of the subject's constituting the life-world yields the strabism of a seeming idealism or solipsism — with regard to the real world, with regard to the flux of the actual prescientific world the sciences presuppose. But its correction, the recovery of the preconstituted world *via* the naturalism or objectivism of the sciences, can yield only a "transcendental naiveté."[32] Still, the original "psychological" power *to* "constitute" the world transcendentally cannot itself be merely an artifact of *that* construction, and it cannot (in Husserl's argument) be satisfied with the Cartesian or Kantian resolution either. Husserl was already occupied with the paradox: "I myself," he says, "as transcendental ego, 'constitute' the world, and at the same time, as soul [as human subjectivity], I am a human ego in the world."[33] Naively but correctly put (that is, from *this* vantage), the transcendental ego seeks to understand how the human, natural, empirical ego discovers that it is a transcendental ego that, among other things, "constitutes" its own mundane self; and the psychological ego seeks to understand how it is objectified as a human being in the world, which it accomplishes by discovering the transcendental function it performs by which it does precisely that.[34] This is surely the "verbal vertigo" Marjorie Grene confesses to having experienced in reading Merleau-Ponty.[35] But, here, we have drawn the chiasmic theme *from Husserl's Crisis*.

The truth is, there is already, in *Cartesian Meditations*, evidence of a proto-chiasmic nagging that Husserl clearly intended to resolve in due course. In the fifth Meditation, Husserl remarks, in a context in which all three of Merleau-Ponty questions are clearly anticipated:

> Connected with this [that is, "the necessary parallel between explica-tions of what is internal to the psyche and egological transcendental explications"] is the fact that, a priori, every analysis or theory of transcendental phenomenology — including the theory whose main features have just been indicated, the theory of transcendental consti-tution of an Objective world — can be produced in the natural realm, when we give up the transcendental attitude. Thus transposed to the realm of transcendental naiveté, it becomes a theory pertaining to internal psychology. *Whether the two disciplines be eidetic or empirical, a "pure" psychology* — a psychology that merely explicates what belongs to a psyche, to a concrete human Ego, as its own intentional essence — corresponds to a *transcendental phenomenology*, and vice versa. That, however, is something to be made evident transcendentally.[36]

Husserl speaks of a "parallel" between the natural and the phenom-enological. Merleau-Ponty speaks rather of a "chiasmus," which suggests both the deeper worry on Merleau-Ponty's part (against Husserl) *and* his own plan for resolving the question. It is, one may say, the principal *philosophical* instance of Merleau-Ponty's fascina-tion with figure-ground puzzles. It is difficult to suppose that

Husserl would have been entirely willing to view his own endeavor thus. Hence, the quiet force of the final line of the citation just given: "That, however, is something to be made evident transcendentally" — which does not quite provide *for treating the transcendental itself as a "figure" within a larger "ground"*. The difference is certainly confirmed in Husserl's *Crisis*: what Merleau-Ponty diagnoses as a strabism nearly proves, in Husserl, to be a normal monocularism.[37] It could also issue in what Merleau-Ponty calls an "ontological diplopia" — at least to the extent that Husserl fails to grasp the full profundity of the chiasmic puzzle, as we have already remarked. But is it too much to say that Merleau-Ponty sees the threat of the weakness of Husserl's own analysis of it partly at least in terms of the symptomatic inadequacies of Sartre's use of phenomenology in *Being and Nothingness*? For what Merleau-Ponty remarked in Sartre was the strabism of the transcendental ego that did not and could not rightly grip the reality of the world or of others or even of one's own bodily reality.[38]

Merleau-Ponty's intuition is rather nicely captured by Paul Valéry (as Merleau-Ponty remarks). The truth is that Valéry helps only to fix the puzzle and Merleau-Ponty's conviction; at best, he offers no more then a clue to its resolution: what he says clearly begs the essential question though it indicates something of what we must say:

> for Valéry too [Merleau-Ponty says] consciousness of the body is inevitably obsession with others. "No one could think freely [says Valéry] if his eyes could not take leave of different eyes which followed them. As soon as glances meet, we are no longer wholly two, and it is hard to remain alone. This exchange (the term is exact) realizes in a very short time a transposition or metathesis — a chiasma of two 'destinies,' two points of view.[39]

The passage is almost miraculously planted by Valéry for Merleau-Ponty's use. It is also precisely the theme Merleau-Ponty finds *in* the Husserl *he* rescues in "The Philosopher and His Shadow." For there, presenting his own conviction but finding his bearings once again in a reading of Husserl's unpublished papers, Merleau-Ponty characteristically treats the perception of another person more or less on the model of a man's touching one hand with the other:

Man can create the alter ego which "thought" cannot create, because he is outside himself in the world and because one ek-stasis is compossible with other ek-stases. And that possibility is fulfilled in perception as *vinculum* of brute being and a body. The whole riddle of *Einfühlung* lies in its initial "esthesiological" phase; and it is solved there because it is a perception. He who "posits" the other man is a perceiving subject, the other person's body is a perceived thing, and the other person himself is "posited" as "perceiving." It is never a matter of anything but co-perception. I see that this man over there sees, as I touch my left hand while it is touching my right.[40]

That achievement must be the benefit of a structure in the natural, distributively describable order of things; it cannot merely or primarily or correctly or apodictically be recovered by a transcendental exercise *unless it is already, relative to the other, suitably located in the natural, psychological, social world of man — located there in a sense apt for a distributed finding. That* it must be located there if it is to be transcendentally discovered-that-it-must-be-located-there (*if* solipsism is to be avoided) is not the same as holding that *its being there* is transcendentally thus constituted (so as *to* escape solipsism).

Merleau-Ponty knows what the chiasmus signifies for *him*; but he is now uncertain, now certain, that what it signifies for him it signifies for Husserl. Furthermore, the fatal point is never quite rightly acknowledged in Husserl or in Merleau-Ponty; namely, that *we cannot recover the clue to the resolution of our philosophical diplopia unless, in a way that escapes the cognitive privilege (the "transcendental naiveté") of naturalism and objectivism, the distributed enunciative or assertoric findings of the sciences and human studies already preserve a realist import that is not merely an artifact of the transcendental, of what the transcendental requires of the psychological to secure the flux of the real world. If that* is psychologism or naturalism once again, so be it. Any other escape from the original diplopia can be little more than a strabism.

One powerful way of putting the point is to grant that the "ontology of the object" and the "ontology of the existent" *cannot be more than global (unnumbered) distinctions* unless they trade on the distributed empirical or natural findings of actual inquiry about the world. The "ontology of the existent" is, therefore, an *empty* posit if it is shorn of determinate and distributed claims; also, the "ontology of the object" is an *empty* posit if it is not applied to those same claims. It is also true that those claims remain, for their part, *blind* or fatally *privileged* if they are less or more than the alterable saliences with which our critical reflection may proceed in both directions. In that sense, *phenomenology and naturalism* must be reconciled if we are ever to overcome our transcendental and psychological diplopia.

This is the point of insisting on a distributed metaphysics drawn from the constative saliences of our presence in the world, tethered, to be sure, in a global way to the ontological functions of the transcendental and psychological egos that are in some sense one and different. Merleau-Ponty collapses, in effect, the mythic and critical functions of the chiasmic double. For him as for Husserl, the psychological or "natural" — the natural that is emphatically not the "naturalistic" (the "*naturlich*" but not the "*natural*,"[41] not the pale, denatured "shadows" of things grasped by a Cartesian abstraction) — is still the prior, untranscendental, un-"constituted" other that the transcendental itself must posit. In this sense — to suggest a gymnastic turn — Merleau-Ponty construes something like the *mythic* theme of Heidegger's *Sein* and *Dasein* as overcoming the diplopia of Husserl's transcendental and natural poles, but preserves *their* themes as well as their *critical* functions (in Husserl's sense) still within the robust space of the profound temporality of human existence.

All this may be put more trimly. First of all, the chiasmus of the transcendental and the natural, in Husserl's *Crisis* and in Merleau-Ponty's *Visible and Invisible*, are symbiotically matched mythic notions that, qua mythic, function only en bloc: that is, they serve to orient *any* critically pertinent claim within the dialectical limits of conceptual constitution and precognitive encounter, *but they do not and cannot as such yield any particular critical claim.* Second, critical claims reflexively test particular first-order claims addressed to the salient world within the limiting concerns of the chiasmus; hence, they are themselves always distributed and always addressed to distributed claims. Third, no hierarchy of cognitive aptitudes of any sort unites the mythic and the critical or unites critical and natural inquiry: every distributed claim reverberates through all the dimensions noted at the same level of thought or discourse, and anything less or more yields judgments that are merely blind or categories that are merely empty. Fourth and finally, every distributed claim must satisfy the minimal constraints of *enunciation*, whether or not it escapes the pretensions of *privilege*. That is, either all the uniformities of discourse involved in the recognition of kinds, the individuation of particulars, the divided ascription of common predicables, the reidentification of the same referents under change and within changing contexts do not as such entail cognitive transparency or privilege of any sort, *or* else there is no escape from privilege.

The phenomenological traditions running from Husserl to Merleau-Ponty has not altogether clearly sorted its commitment on that last distinction. For if it had, it would have seen at once that there must be a "naturalism" of mere *enunciation* — a naturalism meeting the minima of orderly reference and predication — quite different from any "naturalism" of *privilege* (which both Husserl and Merleau-Ponty inveigh against).[42] This is the sense in which phenomenology and naturalism must be reconciled — the sense in which a metaphysics suited to distributed claims is entirely possible and unavoidable, accommodates the holistic ontologies of the chiasmus, and resolves the chiasmic puzzle without restoring either the privilege of objectivism *or* the privilege of apodictic phenomenology.

IV

It is possible that Merleau-Ponty had something of the sort in mind. Certainly, he opposes the apodictic though not the search for invariances. He begins *The Visible and Invisible* saying

> We see the things themselves, the world is what we see. ... It is at the same time true that the world is *what we see* and that, nonetheless, we must learn to see it — first that we must match this vision with knowledge, take possession of it, say what *we* and what *seeing* are, act therefore as if we knew nothing about it, as if here we still had everything to learn [and second that philosophy must learn that] it is the things themselves, from the depths of their silence, that it wishes to bring to expression.[43]

He also says that Husserl sought "a way between psychology and philosophy — a mode of thinking ... which would be neither eternal and without root in the present nor a mere event destined to be replaced by another event tomorrow, and consequently deprived of any intrinsic value."[44] Nevertheless, there are no assurances about the "ante-predicative life of consciousness" we struggle to recover: it cannot help us or Merleau-Ponty in a *cognitive* way to think of "reawakening the basic experience of the world of which science is the second order expression."[45] The thesis exhausts itself in repudiating Cartesian presumptions. Whatever it may yield cannot be guessed except by reflecting on the contingent saliencies of an already languaged world. The notion that science is already "second-order" betrays a potentially illicit confidence on Merleau-Ponty's part (and on Husserl's as well) to the effect that the precognitive world can actually be cognitively recovered. But that "world," after all, is introduced only in a *mythic* way to orient our *critical* examination of an already thoroughly languaged world. The chiasmic complexities Merleau-Ponty had worried required that wherever the *mythic* (en-bloc) posit of the "real," "perceived," precognitive, unthematized, "wild" world is "described, and not constructed or constituted" (as the *Phenomenology of Perception* had already advised[46]), the *critical* (*distributed*) recovery of that primary world is never more than a posit (a second-order posit, in spite of Merleau-Ponty's own usage) with respect to the apparent metaphysics of constative discourse that it may in turn affect and alter. To say that is decidedly to favor the strategy Paul Ricoeur happens to have stressed (though not necessarily for his reasons): namely, that the Husserlian life-world — to which no number, no singular or plural attaches — must be replaced by plural, variable, historicized, open, potentially incommensurable life-worlds. That charge, of course, subverts altogether the intended force of Merleau-Ponty's remark that science is "the second-order expression" of *the* life-world.[47]

Having said that, we may suspect that there is a simpler way to redeem the strenuous exercises of phenomenology. Perhaps Husserl thought so too, particularly in expressing his admiration for William James. But there can be little doubt that Husserl's regard for James, fastened as it was to what Husserl took to be James's defeat of psychologism, is largely drawn to the latter's relatively unguarded and preliminary pronouncements on the invariant laws of thought irreducible to psychological association, somehow embedded in and recoverable from the saliences of perceptual experience. This is the point, of course, of James's well-known remarks on the invariant distinction between black and white.⁴⁸ It is certainly true that James draws from this example and others the affirmation of "necessary and eternal relations" that "form a determinate system, independent of the order of frequency in which experience may have associated their originals in time and space";⁴⁹ but, whether, with or against James (or Husserl), there *are* such "eternal" relations that we can discern, that is, not merely the first-order "indicative" invariances of the black-white contrast but also the second-order cognitional fixities alleged, or whether such second-order invariances are themselves quite contingent invariances hostage to the incompletely fathomable contingencies of plural life-worlds, is a question James never directly addressed or Husserl convincingly resolved.⁵⁰

It would certainly be possible to reconcile Merleau-Ponty's notion of the "tacit *cogito*" with the weakened phenomenological vision we are here barely sketching, despite his usual verbal "loyalty" to Husserl.⁵¹ In any case, really two fundamentally different strategies of phenomenology may be traced here. One yields the idealism, solipsism, diplopia, and strabism Merleau-Ponty wished to avoid that threatens the Husserlian corpus; the other recovers the binocularism of the chiasmic unity Merleau-Ponty wished to recover but never quite fashioned. Husserl draws William James to himself rather along the lines of the first strategy, given his own strong reading of the need to repudiate psychologism; but Merleau-Ponty's notion of "invariants" *could* be reconciled with the admission of plural life-worlds in the sense suggested — in which case, eidetically retrieved "essences" would have to be relativized to the constative structures reportable in such life-worlds.⁵² The fact is that, when he considers the *explanation* of the black-white invariance, James emphatically announces: "The only clear thing to do is to give up the sham of a pretended explanation, and to fall back on the fact that the sense of difference *has* arisen, in some natural manner doubtless, but in a manner which we do not understand."⁵³ Also, there can be little doubt that James, though he does not discuss Husserl or, in particular, the first strategy of reading

Husserl, would have repudiated that strategy in *A Pluralistic Universe*. For example, he says very plainly, attacking the "auto-intoxication...of the block-universe eternal and without a history," that "the only way of escape...from all this is to be frankly pluralistic and to assume that the superhuman consciousness, however vast it may be *has itself an external environment, and consequently is finite*."[54] A pluralistic universe, mythically rather than critically introduced (in the puzzling manner of Nelson Goodman, for instance, also said to be Jamesian in inspiration[55]), offers the essential ground for reconciling phenomenology and pragmatism — for reconciling, that is, a phenomenologized naturalism and a naturalized phenomenology. There is an open family of relatively "invariant" metaphysics to be located there. But such invariants would be no more than second-order saliences that have survived and continue to survive within the contingencies of human history. Still, that would already be quite a lot.

It would also be a prize gained at a considerable (though not unreasonable) price. We should have to concede that

1. No natural language is without enunciative resources, in particular, no natural language lacks referential and predicative facilities.

2. No first-order or second-order discourse (that is, scientific or critical or transcendental or legitimative discourse) can fail to be enunciative.

3. No enunciative discourse can function as such without employing distinctions of number. that is, no such discourse can fail to make distributed claims.

4. All referential discourse that disallows distributed claims (lacks number) functions in a mythic rather than a critical way, rhetorically posits a totalized context for first- and second-order discourse but ventures no such discourse itself.

5. Mythic discourse as such is conceptually parasitic on discourse that is fully enunciative.

6. Enunciative discourse as such is not cognitively privileged.

7. Discourse that is not cognitively privileged in any critical, transcendental, legitimative (second-order) sense cannot concede

any logical priority or hierarchical order among the cognitive sources of first-order, critical, or mythic claims.

8. A metaphysics of enunciative discourse, a metaphysics of the invariant structures of a languaged world or worlded language, is viable and even unavoidable, without implicating any cognitive privilege.

9. The invariants of enunciative discourse are themselves the provisional artifacts of whatever contingent preformative forces obtain, that, without privilege (under those same conditions), we speculate we collect critically or in a mythic way.

10. Findings 1–9 signify the equivalence of phenomenologizing naturalism and naturalizing phenomenology.

Among phenomenologists proper, it appears that Merleau-Ponty is the one most consistently and ardently disposed to favor these concessions. They are, in fact, the conditions for overcoming philosophical strabism and philosophical diplopia.

NOTES

1. Reiner Schürmann, *Heidegger on Being and Acting: From Principles to Anarchy*, trans. Christine-Marie Gros in collaboration with the author (Bloomington: Indiana University Press, 1987).

2. This may be taken to be the classic theme of the Husserlian sort of labor explicitly sketched in Edmund Husserl, *Phenomenology and the Crisis of Philosophy*, trans. Quentin Lauer (New York: Harper and Row, 1965). Lauer has brought together here the early essay "Philosophy as Rigorous Science" and the later essay "Philosophy and the Crisis of European Man."

3. Edmund Husserl, "Philosophy and the Crisis of European Man," in *Phenomenology and the Crisis of Philosophy*, p. 154.

4. Edmund Husserl, *Cartesian Meditations*, trans. Dorion Cairns (The Hague: Martinus Nijhoff, 1960), Second Meditation, p. 30 (pp. 68–69 in the marginal pagination).

5. Ibid.

6. Edmund Husserl, *The Crisis of European Sciences and Transcendental*

Phenomenology, trans. David Carr (Evanston, Ill.: Northwestern University Press, 1970), pp. 185–86, 143.

7. *Cartesian Meditations*, pp. 92–94 (pp. 124–25 in the marginal pagination).

8. *Cartesian Meditations*, First Meditation, pp. 7–8 (pp. 48–49 in the marginal pagination).

9. Edmund Husserl, "Phenomenology and Anthropology," trans. Richard G. Schmitt, in Roderick M. Chisholm, ed., *Realism and the Background of Phenomenology* (Glencoe, Ill.: Free Press, 1960), p. 129.

10. Ibid., pp. 129–30.

11. See "'Phenomenology,' Edmund Husserl's Article for the *Encyclopaedia Britannica* (1927)," rev. trans. Richard E. Palmer, in Peter McCormick and Frederick A. Elliston, eds., *Husserl: Shorter Works* (Notre Dame, Ind.: University of Notre Dame Press, 1981); and Walter Biemel, "Husserl's *Encyclopaedia Britannica* Article and Heidegger's Remarks Thereon," trans. P. McCormick and F. Elliston, in Frederick A. Elliston and Peter McCormick, eds., *Husserl: Expositions and Appraisals* (Notre Dame, Ind.: University of Notre Dame Press, 1977).

12. "Phenomenology and Anthropology," pp. 129–30.

13. Martin Heidegger, *Being and Time*, trans. John Macquarrie and Edward Robinson (New York: Harper and Row, 1962), p. 44 (p. 22 in the marginal pagination).

14. Ibid., p. 21 (p. 2 in the marginal pagination).

15. Ibid., p. 32 (p. 12 in the marginal pagination).

16. Ibid., pp. 69–70, 203–10 (pp. 44, 160–66 in the marginal pagination); see §44.

17. Ibid., §§ 7, 44.

18. Ibid., pp. 21–28 in the marginal pagination).

19. Ibid., p. 27 (p. 7 in the marginal pagination).

20. This is surely the point of Jacques Derrida, "Différance," *Margins of Philosophy*, trans. Alan Bass (Chicago: University of Chicago Press, 1982). See, also, Schürmann, *Heidegger on Being and Acting*, and John D. Caputo, *Radical Hermeneutics: Repetition, Deconstruction, and the Hermeneutic Project* (Bloomington: Indiana University Press, 1987).

21. Martin Heidegger, "The End of Philosophy and the Task of Thinking," in *Basic Writings*, ed. David Farrell Krell (New York: Harper and Row, 1977).

22. For a brief but relevant discussion of a number of these themes, see Hilary Putnam, "A Philosopher Looks at Quantum Mechanics" and "The Logic of Quantum Mechanics," *Mathematics, Matter and Method* in *Philosophical Papers*, Vol. 1 (Cambridge: Cambridge University Press, 1975); Michael Dummett, "Truth," *Truth and Other Enigmas* (Cambridge: Harvard University Press, 1978); Kurt Gödel, "A Remark about the Relationship between Relativity Theory and Idealistic Philosophy," in Paul Arthur Schilpp, ed., *Albert Einstein: Philosopher-Scientist* (La Salle, Ill.: Open Court, 1949).

23. See Martin Heidegger, "The Question Concerning Technology," trans. William Lovitt, in *Basic Writings*.

24. See, for example, Robert Sokolowski, *Husserlian Meditations* (Evanston, Ill.: Northwestern University Press, 1974), §41; and Suzanne Bachelard, *A Study of Husserl's Formal and Transcendental Logic*, trans. Lester E. Embree (Evanston, Ill.: Northwestern University Press, 1968), p. 222.

25. James M. Edie, *Edmund Husserl's Phenomenology: A Critical Commentary* (Bloomington: Indiana University Press, 1987), p. 63.

26. Maurice Merleau-Ponty, *Phenomenology of Perception*, trans. Colin Smith (London: Routledge and Kegan Paul, 1962), p. 430.

27. *Being and Time*, p. 418 (p. 366 in the marginal pagination).

28. Ibid., p. 417 (p. 366 in the marginal pagination).

29. Maurice Merleau-Ponty, *The Visible and the Invisible*, ed. Claude Lefort, trans. Alphonso Lingis (Evanston, Ill.: Northwestern University Press, 1968), pp. 214–15.

30. Editor's Note 2, cited from a lecture course of Merleau-Ponty's in *Annuaire du Collège de France, 58 année* (Paris, 1958), pp. 213–14, in Working Notes, *The Visible and the Invisible*, p. 166.

31. The phrase in Husserl's, of course. See *The Crisis of European Sciences and Transcendental Philosophy*, p. 193; cf. p. 204 and the rest of Part III B.

32. Ibid., p. 202.

33. Ibid., pp. 205–6.

34. Marjorie Grene, "Merleau-Ponty and the Renewal of Ontology," *Review of Metaphysics*, 29 (1976): 622.

35. *The Visible and the Invisible*, Working Notes, pp. 165–66.

36. *Cartesian Meditations*, Fifth Meditation, p. 131 (p. 159 in the marginal pagination).

37. See Appendix VI: "The Origin of Geometry," *The Crisis of European Sciences and Transcendental Phenomenology*, pp. 371–72. See, also, Ludwig Landgrebe, "The Problem of a Transcendental Science of the a Priori of the Life-World," trans. Donn Welton, *The Phenomenology of Edmund Husserl*, ed. Donn Welton (Ithaca, N.Y.: Cornell University Press, 1981).

38. See Merleau-Ponty, *Adventures of the Dialectic*, trans. Joseph Bien (Evanston, Ill.: Northwestern University Press, 1973).

39. Maurice Merleau-Ponty, "Man and Adversity," in *Signs*, trans. Richard C. McCleary (Evanston, Ill.: Northwestern University Press, 1964), p. 231.

40. "The Philosopher and His Shadow," *Signs*, p. 170; cf. p. 174; also, *Phenomenology of Perception*, p. 352.

41. Cf. "The Philosopher and His Shadow," pp. 161, 164.

42. See Joseph Margolis, *Texts without Referents: Reconciling Science and Narrative* (Oxford: Basil Blackwell, 1989), Chapter 3.

43. *The Visible and the Invisible*, p. 4.

44. Maurice Merleau-Ponty, "Phenomenology and the Sciences of Man," trans. John Wild, in *The Primacy of Perception*, ed. James M. Edie (Evanston, Ill.: Northwestern University Press, 1964), p. 92.

45. *Phenomenology of Perception*, Preface, pp. xiii, xv.

46. *Phenomenology of Perception*, p. x.

47. See Paul Ricoeur, "On Interpretation," trans. Kathleen McLaughlin, in Alan Montefiore, ed., *Philosophy in France Today* (Cambridge: Cambridge University, 1983).

48. See William James, *Principles of Psychology*, Vol. 2 (New York: Dover, 1950), pp. 641–44; and Edmund Husserl, *Logical Investigations*, trans. J. N. Findlay, from 2nd ed., 2 vols. (New York: Humanities Press, 1970), Investigation II (Vol.1, p. 420, n. 1.)

49. *Principles of Psychology*, Vol. 2, p. 661.

50. See, further, *Texts without Referents*, Chapter 3.

51. See *Phenomenology of Perception*, Part III, Chapter 1.

52. See *The Visible and the Invisible*, Chapter 3, for instance p. 11.

53. *The Principles of Psychology*, Vol. 2, p. 661.

54. William James, *A Pluralistic Universe* (New York: Longmans, Green, 1909), pp. 310–11; italics added.

55. See Nelson Goodman, *Ways of Worldmaking* (Indianapolis: Hackett Publishing Co., 1978).

7

The Text of the Speaking Subject:
From Merleau-Ponty to Kristeva

Hugh J. Silverman

The speaking subject speaks — but not always. The speaking subject is embodied, but that embodiment can be read as a text. The speaking subject divides itself and yet also brings together difference. The speaking subject is embedded in a difference between the semiotic and the symbolic or between indirect language and a pure language — or at least it seeks avenues to articulate itself in such terms. These characteristics of the speaking subject link together two philosophical enterprises that might on the surface appear to be radically different; namely, those of Julia Kristeva and Maurice Merleau-Ponty.

Julia Kristeva entered the philosophical scene in a significant way in 1969 with a volume of essays entitled *Semiotiké*. This was only two years after Derrida's initial contribution in *Writing and Difference*, *Of Grammatology*, and *Speech and Phenomena* and eight years after the death of Merleau-Ponty. Kristeva's major theoretical statement, however, came in 1974 with her *Revolution in Poetic Language*. Although portions of *Semiotiké* along with essays from a later volume *Polylogue* (1977) were collected in English as *Desire in Language*, the English translation of *La Révolution du langage poétique* did not appear until 1984 (ten years after its initial publication). As a *thèse d'état*, it was crucial that the volume be comprehensive, theoretically well-formulated, and embellished adequately with practical implications — and indeed the French version is precisely that. What was translated into English (as in German — though much earlier) is only the first (theoretical) portion of the book. Hence all the 'practical' readings of particular texts are left for a future translation.

What I propose to develop here is the role of the "speaking subject" as articulated by Merleau-Ponty from the time of *Phenomenology of Perception* (1945), as carried through *Consciousness and*

183

the Acquisition of Language (1948–49), as reformulated in *The Prose of the World* (1952), and subsequently, as elaborated in Kristeva's theoretical writings. Despite the commonality of concern with the "speaking subject," it would appear that the two discourses lack a common domain. Indeed Merleau-Ponty does not appear in the bibliographies of Kristeva's theoretical writings — even though Husserl, Freud, de Saussure, and Lacan are all fully represented. One would expect that her treatment of them would have traversed the thought of Merleau-Ponty — implicitly if not explicitly. And as the role of the *'speaking subject'* in Kristeva's writings is particularly dominant, she has admitted that she needs to examine the particular relation between her own notion of the 'speaking subject' and that of Merleau-Ponty.[1] I propose to explore what turns out to bring the two discourses into a common place of potential dialogue and exchange despite the obvious divergences.

A reading of the speaking subject in Merleau-Ponty and Kristeva will necessitate a consideration of (1) the relationship between Kristeva's semiotic-symbolic distinction and Merleau-Ponty's account of indirect language versus pure language, and (2) the signifying process in relation to the text of the speaking subject, or the subject 'in process' and 'on trial.'

1. SEMIOTIC-SYMBOLIC: INDIRECT-PURE LANGUAGE

According to Julia Kristeva, the "semiotic" and the "symbolic" are two modalities of the same signifying process. Language is formed by a signifying process. The type of discourse in question is determined by the particular modality operative at a particular time. Whether it is theory, narrative, poetry, metalanguage, or some other form of discourse will be determined by the specific functioning of the semiotic or the symbolic. Kristeva characterizes the relation between the two as a "dialectic." The nature of the dialectic itself needs clarification. Although there may be dominance of the one or the other (the semiotic or the symbolic) at any particular moment, they never operate in isolation from one another. They are not exclusive in that neither the semiotic nor the symbolic is totally independent of the other.

The terms *semiotic* and *symbolic* have long and complex histories. Kristeva wants to understand them in her own particular fashion. For Kristeva, the *symbolic* is tied up in the signifier (a word)-signified (a concept) relation. De Saussure calls this relation the "sign" and characterizes it as "arbitrary." However, he leaves room for bringing together a word and a concept as "motivated." Kristeva suggests that the motivated aspect of the relation lies in the unconscious drives (or *pulsions*) and the primary processes (of displacement and condensation) that underlie the surface 'arbitrarily thinking' of a particular signifier along with a particular signified. The association of the primary processes of 'displacement' and 'condensation' with 'metonymy' and 'metaphor' is already suggested in Lacan's reading of Jakobson and Freud. 'Displacement' involves a veering off to a contiguous signifier; hence, metonymy. 'Condensation' involves an overdetermination of the signified in its relation to the signifier. This crowding of signifieds onto a particular signifier is offered as a version of metaphor. Both metaphor and metonymy operate as symbolic elements in language. Thus the linking of the signifier and the signified in one of these ways interrupts the purely arbitrary account. It also brings out the syntactic and semantic aspects of language, aspects that Kristeva calls *symbolic*.

The symbolic — namely, "the syntactic and linguistic categories of a signifying process" — according to Kristeva, is "a social effect of the relation to the other, established through the objective constraints of biological (including sexual) differences and concrete, historical family structures."[2] The symbolic, then, is an effect of how one relates to other people as limited by differences that are set biologically, genetically, and within a determinate family context. The symbolic accounts for what arises within certain social and linguistic frameworks. There is just so much that the symbolic can accomplish within these frameworks. The symbolic is limited in what it can formulate, limited by its own structures, determinations, and motivations.

Furthermore, the symbolic operates as a scientific language in which the structures of discourse are rigidly defined, bounded, and set. The symbolic is the authoritative, assertive, definitive mode. It operates — and here Kristeva agrees with Lacan — by way of the paternal negation: the law of the Father (*le nom/non du père*).

The symbolic posits the subject. The subject does not (as Husserl would have claimed) constitute the symbolic. For instance, and this is one of Kristeva's major theses, when the phallic function becomes *the* symbolic function, speaking begins to take hold. Before the law of the father is introduced, the mother occupies the place of the phallic function. And when the phallic function becomes the symbolic function, the mother loses her special status. Prior to that time, "her replete body, the receptacle and guarantor of demands, takes the place of all narcissistic, hence imaginary, effects and gratifications; she is, in other words, the phallus" (*RPL*, p. 47). However, with the "discovery of castration," she loses her special status: the subject is detached from its dependence on the mother, "and the perception of this lack [*manque*] makes the phallic function a symbolic function" (*RPL*, 47). Because the phallus is itself a signifier it motivates a particular set of relations to gravitate toward a particular signified (or particular set of signifieds). In this way, the symbolic achieves its own particular formation.

Into the symbolic, certain elements of the semiotic intrude. The symbolic wants to affirm itself, define itself, give itself its own name. The semiotic irrupts into the symbolic while at the same time maintaining its autonomy, for the subject's position is retained as always in process and on trial (*en procès*). The layer of 'semiosis' that underlies the symbolic relation of the signifier to the signified is typically relegated to a pragmatics and semantics of language. Kristeva takes as her task to show that the semiotic has other dimensions.

Kristeva points out — in careful symbolic form — that there is, along with the ordering, law-like functions of the symbolic, another modality, namely that of "the Freudian *facilitation* and structuring *disposition* of drives, and also the primary processes which displace and condense both energies and their inscription" (*RPL* 25). These drives are described as "energy" charges and "psychical" marks. As such, they articulate what Kristeva calls a "*chora*." This key idea for Kristeva characterizes notably a "nonexpressive totality formed by the drives and their stases in a motility that is as full of movement as it is regulated" (*RPL* 25). The *chora* designates what is "mobile" and "an extremely provisional articulation constituted by movements and their ephemeral stases." The *chora*, "as rupture articulations (rhythm), precedes evidence, verisimilitude, spatiality, and temporality" (*RPL* 26). Further, she states that "the *chora* is a modality of significance in which the linguistic sign is not yet articulated as the absence of an object and as the distinction between real and symbolic" (*RPL* 26). Hence, the *chora* is more fundamental than — or underlies — the basic relation between the signifier and the signified. With the semiotic *chora*, difference and identity are not yet present; hence, certain differentiations do not yet pertain. For instance, one feature of the sign is that the signified does not necessarily designate an object that is present. The *chora* precedes this sense that the object is absent. The differentiation is not part of the semiotic functioning, for that itself would be a symbolic matter. Even the Freudian distinction between the real and the symbolic remains unspecified. This also means that the formation or establishment of the sign follows from the *semiotic* and its functioning.

What does it mean to say that the semiotic is more basic than the sign itself? For Kristeva, the semiotic is characterized by "flow and marks, by facilitation, energy transfers, the cutting up of a corporeal and social continuum as well as that of signifying material." And the *chora* is a "pulsating, rhythmic, nonexpressive totality" (*RPL* 40). Further descriptions of the semiotic include: "indifferent to language, enigmatic and feminine,...unfettered, irreducible to its verbal translation,...musical, anterior to judgement, but restrained by a single guarantee: syntax" (*RPL* 29). Understood metaphorically here, "syntax" structures the flow, channels experience, and gives shape to the symbolic content but does not determine it.

Where sign and syntax are features of the symbolic function, flow, energy, musicality, maternal, receptacle — in short, poetic language — can be ascribed to the semiotic. The semiotic practice of language highlights "nondisjunction" and continuity. It brings the bodily, material aspects of language in conjunction with the cognitive and formal aspects. The semiotic, however, does not stand apart from the symbolic but rather acts in concert with it.

The correspondence between Kristeva's account of the relationships between the symbolic and the semiotic and Merleau-Ponty's descriptions of pure language in relation to indirect language are striking. Whereas Merleau-Ponty's notion of indirect language was offered in two published essays in *Signs*, "Indirect Language and the Voices of Silence" and "On the Phenomenology of Language" (both originally from *Les Temps modernes* in 1952), it is developed most fully in the posthumously published study (from those same years), *The Prose of the World*.[3]

In "Indirect Language and the Voices of Silence," Merleau-Ponty writes: "if we rid our minds of the idea that our language is the translation or cipher of an original text, we shall see that the idea of *complete* expression is nonsensical, and that all language is indirect or allusive — that is, if you wish, silence."[4] And further: "If we want to understand language as an originating operation, we must pretend to have never spoken, submit language to a reduction without which it would once more escape us by referring us to what it signifies for us, *look* at it as deaf people look at those who are speaking, compare the art of language to other arts of expression, and try to see it as one of these mute arts" (*Signs*, p. 46). And from *The Prose of the World*: "We may say that there are two languages. First there is language after the fact, or language as an institution, which effaces itself in order to yield the meaning which it conveys. Second, there is the language which creates itself in its expressive acts, which sweeps one on from the signs toward meaning — sedimented language (*langage parlé*) and speech (*langage parlant*)" (*Prose* 10).

Merleau-Ponty is claiming here that there are effectively two types of language.[5] One (*le langage parlé*) is "sedimented" and "spoken" once it is already established — something like an already motivated relation between the signifier and the signified — even though, in the Saussurian understanding, the relation is purely arbitrary. It is as though this one type of language were a transformation and limitation placed on language by language itself. The other type (*le langage parlant*) makes itself in its practice. It is not bounded by the established, sedimented elements of an already constituted language — one in which there is a "stock of accepted relations between signs and familiar significations" (*Prose* 13). In this second type of language, the set "arrangement of already available signs and significations alters and then transfigures each of them, so that in the end a new signification is created" (*Prose* 13).

In other words, this second type of language is not bounded by laws, conventions, and established understanding. It corresponds to Kristeva's *semiotic* that is not limited, circumscribed, and constrained by the *symbolic* paternal law, by the set of semantic prescriptions that are carried in language.

For Merleau-Ponty, the two types of language — the "sedimented" language and the creative, revolutionary, and indirect language operate in opposition to one another. The tendency of sedimented language (*le langage parlé*) is to consolidate, to formalize, and to regulate established meaning whereas speech (*le langage parlant*) or speaking language actively breaks out of these controlled, limiting circumstances. Merleau-Ponty asks: "How are we to understand this fruitful moment of language in which an accident is transformed into reason and there suddenly arises, from a mode of speech that is becoming extinct, a new, more effective and expressive mode — in the way the ebb of the sea after a wave excites and enlarges the next wave?" (*Prose* 34). His point is that novelty and creativity in language has no place in sedimented language, in the already established, formed, and confirmed mode of speech. What breaks out from the bounded is another form of expressivity, another type of communication, an indirect language that has not yet become codified and solidified and that often appeals to alternative modes of expressivity. Often Merleau-Ponty appeals to painting as a paradigm. Although painting for Kristeva is to be read, she does not find in it quite as much the emerging sense of newness and revolutionary creativity that Merleau-Ponty discovers there. With Merleau-Ponty, painting demonstrates the powers of indirect language — a language that is expressive, that speaks without always turning into what Kristeva calls the symbolic. Yet for Merleau-Ponty, poetry — but more often literary language in general — is capable of enacting this indirect language, this language of silence, in which what speaks is not the established meaning but rather another order of sense and expression. For Kristeva, poetic language (as in Mallarmé and Lautréamont) exhibits features of the semiotic as they work in concert with and in dialectical opposition to the symbolic. What is relevant here is that both Merleau-Ponty and Kristeva understand indirect language or the semiotic, respectively, as a poetic or pictorial function, a function in which the positing, assertive, formal, or systematic features of a language are not determinative.

In Merleau-Ponty there is the worry that the specter of a pure language will predominate in some important way, that the algorithm will take over and stifle all possibility of expressivity and fullness of sense. By contrast, in choosing the term *semiotic* to characterize the undifferentiated, revolutionary, unbounded mode of language, Kristeva is indicating that the use of sign systems does not negate these special conditions for language. Yet Merleau-Ponty's sympathetic reading of Saussure's account of signs and signifiers in the mid-1940s is hardly reducible to what he is calling a 'pure language.' He deplores only the scientifizing of language as a metalanguage devoid of accident, flexibility and ambiguity.

Merleau-Ponty's "inventions of style" carry as much weight as Kristeva's notion of "significance"; namely, the unlimited and unbounded process of meaning production. Yet, although Merleau-Ponty is committed to dialectic, especially throughout the 1950s, he places little weight on a dialectic between indirect language and pure language. By contrast, in opposing the two and in stressing the difference between spoken language and speaking language, he is implicitly proposing that they are in a dialectical — and even creatively dialectical — relation. For Kristeva, however, the dialectic between the symbolic and the semiotic is active and crucial. Indeed, her whole notion of the signifying process depends upon it.

2. THE SIGNIFYING PROCESS AND
THE TEXT OF THE SPEAKING SUBJECT

The semiotic and the symbolic are two modalities of the same signifying process. For Kristeva, they are in dialectical relation. *Significance* is this unlimited and unbounded generating, heterogeneous process. It is both a bringing together of the divergent orientations and a separating of them at the same time. As Kristeva puts it: "This heterogeneous process, neither anarchic, fragmented foundation, nor schizophrenic blockage, is a structuring and de-structuring *practice*, a passage to the outer *boundaries* of the subject and society. Then — and only then — can it be *jouissance* and revolution" (*RPL* 14).

This radical and yet also consolidative reading of language allows for the multiple dimensions of the signifying process. What remains to be explored is the role of the speaking subject in this process.

The signifying process, for Kristeva, involves three elements: the semiotic, the symbolic, and significance. The differentiated unity of these three elements is the process of the subject. The symbolic is able to posit the subject — but as absent — whereas the semiotic offers drives — as demonstrated through psychoanalysis — of the subject in process–on trial (*en procès*). The *thetic* element of signification occurs during the signifying process in such a way that the subject is constituted without being reduced to the process — for the subject is "the threshold of language." In this area, the subject is neither reduced to a phenomenological foundational ego — which would function as center and source of all knowing acts — nor denied the thetic phase by which signification comes about. Hence, in Kristeva, neither is the subject a posited entity, a centered self, nor is it devoid of significance. The self-decentering effected here makes it possible to posit the subject, but always as an aspect of the signifying process itself. As we have learned from a long itinerary (which includes not only Sartre's transcendence of the ego, Derrida's self-decentering deconstruction, and Foucault's archaeology of the absent subject, but also Merleau-Ponty's embodied subject), the subject cannot have a centered existence, the subject cannot posit itself as positing itself or anything else. To posit the subject is to posit an object that is discrete and identifiable. And the subject in identifying itself as an object — the mother as phallus, the father as phallus, the self as phallus — opens up regions of desire (in language) that are specifiable.

For instance, and most notably, for Kristeva, the text is a signifying practice. It is distinguishable from the "drifting-into-non-sense" that characterizes neurotic discourse. As a signifying practice, the text incorporates the subject, but as distributed throughout the text semiotically or as posited at relevant places symbolically (*RPL* 51). The sociohistorical function of the signifying practice is to insert itself into everyday discourse such that it will irrupt at relevant places out of the maternal *chora* and as a posited symbolic formation.

For Kristeva, the speaking subject is itself a text. It is inscribed within the signifying process — not as a posited entity but as the semiotic, symbolic, and signifiable features of the signifying process. Yet the speaking subject is also not simply identical with the signifying process. It is rather the absent element in the syntax of what is spoken, what is said, what is articulated. When the subject reemerges as object, it is symbolically constituted as speaking, as holding a position, as being an object. The reemergence of the subject involves a disturbance in the syntactical relation as well. Hence Kristeva allows for various ways in which the passage from one sign system to another (*transposition*) and the specific articulation of the semiotic and the thetic for a sign system (*representability*) can account for some of these disturbances in the relation between the semiotic and the symbolic. What is especially important here is that the motility of the speaking subject is at once the flexibility of the signifying process.

For Kristeva, a speaking subject is already dispersed into an intersubjective world. This world is understood in terms of an intertextuality in which the text of the speaking subject inscribes itself with significance both semiotically and symbolically. For Merleau-Ponty, the speaking subject is set off against the thinking subject. Merleau-Ponty's earlier move to the 'tacit *cogito*' is transformed into an account of indirect language. And the transformation is a shift from an account of the speaking subject as that which is experienced, that with which one communicates, and that which speaks gesturally and through the body, to an expressivity in which signification is the essential ingredient. What is crucial here is that, in speaking, the subject is *not* speaking, acting, or being *from a standpoint*, but rather as an *embodied, historical,* and *social* being. As such, it is the incorporation, insertion, and inscription of the self in the intersubjective world.

Between Merleau-Ponty and Kristeva, where the semiotic is informed by the symbolic and where speaking speech and spoken speech delimit an embodied experience, the speaking subject speaks but at the same time places pure, scientific, controlled, strong language in question. At the margins of this symbolic–pure language is a semiotic–indirect language, one that displaces the self in its centered being, one that marginalizes language itself into the expression of either 'poetic language' or the language of the 'neurotic' (filled with melancholy or depression).[6] Even when the speaking subject is not fulfilling the ideals of the culture (inaugurated by the Greeks, codified by the Romans, and carried on in the Western tradition), it provides a place for these ideals by marginalizing them, by delimiting them, by controlling spaces of expression — either indirectly or semiotically. This is not the romantic creation of a 'natural,' individual, pastoral idyll. Rather it is a delimitation, weakening, dissemination of the self's identity into an undifferentiated, yet not inarticulate space of self-textualization. The text of the speaking subject is both its direct, symbolic modality and its edges, its borders, its margins in the indirect, semiotic dimensions of language. This alternative space of language is a revolutionary, abnormal, nondominant form of expression in which the speaking takes place but where the subject is already a displaced self, a marginalized mode of expression — as in that of women, poets, neurotics — and unconventional philosophers...

NOTES

1. Response to a question concerning the role of Merleau-Ponty in Kristeva's account of the speaking subject that I raised during her seminar and again in a private conversation while she was Visiting Distinguished Professor at SUNY–Stony Brook during Fall Semester 1988.

2. Julia Kristeva, *Revolution in Poetic Language*, trans. Margaret Waller (New York: Columbia University Press, 1984), p. 29; henceforth cited as *RPL*.

3. Maurice Merleau-Ponty, *Prose of the World*, ed. Claude Lefort, trans. John O'Neill (Evanston, Ill.: Northwestern University Press, 1973); henceforth cited as *Prose*.

4. Maurice Merleau-Ponty, *Signs*, trans. Richard C. McCleary (Evanston, Ill.: Northwestern University Press, 1964), p. 43; henceforth cited as *Signs*.

5. For a further and more detailed discussion of Merleau-Ponty's

theory of language, see Hugh J. Silverman, *Inscriptions: Between Phenomenology and Structuralism* (London and New York: Routledge, 1987), esp. Chapters 6 and 9.

6. The issues of depression and melancholy are the focus of Kristeva's more recent writings, especially her book *Black Sun* (New York: Columbia University Press, 1989). Because it is outside the focus of this discussion, I invoke this new direction in her work and its place in the present consideration of the semiotic only to suggest an avenue for further investigation. I am grateful to Piero Palmero for raising the question during a lecture presentation of this essay at the University of Torino (Italy) in December 1989. And my special thanks to M. C. Dillon for his perspicuous and helpful comments on an earlier version of this paper.

8

The Thinker and the Painter

Jacques Taminiaux
Translated by Michael Gendre

The title of my presentation, "The Thinker and the Painter," is intended to suggest that in Merleau-Ponty's eyes there was a link between the activity to which, as a philosopher, he had devoted his life and the activity to which painters devote theirs.

Such a proximity calls for a clarification and an explanation. It needs to be both clarified and explained because it does not go without saying. I need only to recall that for the founder of the Western philosophical tradition those two activities are antithetical. Plato, one recalls, strongly maintains in the *Republic* that to paint amounts to refuse to think and that the activity of thinking requires a sort of detachment from perception and the perceived, which is the very element to which the painter is attached. To paint is to refuse to think because for Plato the painter is par excellence the one who takes sides with appearances, which are labeled adverse to Being. He copies appearances without ever taking into consideration the essence (or he deals with copies without ever being concerned with their models). He celebrates the shadowy lights — the *clair obscur* — of the sensible realm as well as the equivocities that surface throughout it, and he fails to recognize that, beyond this confused area, it is possible for the eyes of the mind to have access to the clear and peaceful ordering of intelligible Ideas provided that the mind be detached from the sensible realm. This access to Being beyond Appearance, or more precisely this access to appearances devoid of the ambiguities of the sensible, is reserved for the thinker. It allows him to understand with total clarity that what the painter prides himself on is worthy only of disdain: the work to which he devotes so much effort is in vain as, at the time when the painter believes he captures what truly is, he lets something that is nonbeing lead him astray. Although he wants to raise sensible things to the glory of a pictorial radiance, he achieves only the

195

flimsy fabrication of nonreal copies of entities that are themselves devoid of being and truth because the sensible realm is not the medium within which the true aspect (*eidos*) of things is apprehended. The sensible aspects of things are nothing but the distorted reflection of their true physiognomies. Fascinated by the sensible appearances of things, the painter therefore produces only reflections of reflections.

Now is not the time to question the transformations undergone by the Platonic conceptions throughout the history of philosophy, nor even to evoke their persistence, under different forms, in the writings of philosophers of painting.

Those writings are relatively scarce, because only at the beginning of the nineteenth century, with Hegel and Schopenhauer, does one find philosophers of the first rank producing elaborate analyses of pictorial works.

Let me restrict myself to mentioning that, even when those analyses grant considerable attention to painting and seem to bestow upon it the privileged status of a form of thought, they continue to function within the space of those bimillennial oppositions elaborated by Plato: the thing itself and its copy, the real and the imaginary, the sensible diversity and the intelligible unity, the body and the mind. In other words, what those analyses seem to give to painting with one hand, they take back with the other. Thus Hegel, in contrast to Plato, entertains the notion that Art is the manifestation of the Idea. But he immediately adds, in perfect accord with the Platonic distinction between the sensible and the intelligible, that the element within which art produces its works, the sensible, is not adequate for a genuine manifestation of the Idea.

Likewise Schopenhauer, also in contrast to Plato, maintains that the Idea is manifested by Art, which does not mean that Art manifests the rational character of the Idea as Hegel thinks, but instead manifests the profoundly absurd character of the thing-in-itself, the insatiable Will. Yet there is also a profound agreement between Schopenhauer and Plato. This agreement emerges when Schopenhauer specifies his general thesis with the claim that Art — even though it is an eminent form of thought because it exhibits the truth of reality; that is, the truth that reality is absurd — still is not adequate to think what it attempts to grasp. The reason for this inadequacy is simple: Art continues to entangle us in sensible phenomena (and therefore in the emanations of the will to live) at the very moment when it shows the absurdity of these emanations.

Schopenhauer, in spite of the abyss that separates him from Hegel, agrees with the latter, and finds himself in profound agreement with Plato when he says that the flaw of Art is that it rivets us to the sensible. And both continue to maintain with Plato that, in the final analysis, thinking and being attached to the sensible are antithetical attitudes and terms.

Such an antimony is precisely what Merleau-Ponty, from the beginning until the end of his work, never stopped denouncing. To think, for Merleau-Ponty, does not mean to turn away from the perceived; rather it means to grant it the status of a first ground, to dwell within its boundaries, to listen to its echoes, to interrogate it, to always go back to it. Now it is precisely because thinking for him was fundamentally attracted to the perceived that thought, in the sense he gave to it in his own work, has to free itself from the dichotomies in which the philosophical tradition was trapped.

1. PERCEPTION

To what degree does the perceived invite thought to rid itself of these dichotomies if thought takes the perceived as its privileged theme of meditation? Exactly to the degree that the dualistic oppositions that originated in Plato are not applied to the perceived. Already the Husserlian descriptions, whose importance and innovative character Merleau-Ponty had been quick to acknowledge, stood for him in contrast to the Platonic heritage carried along and transformed by Descartes to fashion the scientific project of the modern *mathesis*; those Husserlian descriptions were able to show that the phenomenal character specific to the perceived brings about a constant overlapping of those terms deemed antithetical and heterogeneous in the tradition. The tradition of modern philosophy, whether it be rationalistic, empiricist, or Kantian, finally relegated the perceived to the realm of pure multiplicity and diversity. Such a tradition maintained that the perceived as such is recalcitrant to unity and identity.

It is against this notion that Husserl reacts. He shows that it is not beyond the diversity of its aspects — the famous Husserlian profiles — or above them, that the perceived thing acquires its unity and its identity. These two features do not occur to the thing from the exterior and after the fact by virtue of a synthetic act of the understanding or an associating repetition. It is at the very core of the diversity of those profiles that, from the outset, the unity of the perceived thing emerges. In the perceived realm, the unity is not heterogeneous to multiplicity, rather it is folded within the multiplicity of the thing and is even required by it. Likewise the identity of the thing is not the antithesis of a difference. The perceived entity would lose its perceptual density, its incarnated existence, and would cease to be perceived if the aspects that are presented by it did not announce other aspects, which are not yet offered to sight. These latent sides form the horizon hidden by the first ones. A thing perceived from all sides would not be a perceived thing. In a rather similar manner, the realm of perceived entities does not fall prey to the classical antinomy between the particular and the general.

The perceived never presents itself as some strictly individual feature, some singular form, some incomparable color. At the outset, as the Gestalt psychologists discovered at the beginning of the century, perception generalizes: we do not see this particular white as strictly particular but as an example of whiteness. At the outset, too, perception stylizes: we see at the same time this singular tree as singular and as a token of the type "tree;" together with its singular form, we apprehend the type that connects it to all other trees.

In addition to an overlapping of the particular and the general, the perceived attests to a surprising overlapping of our fellow beings and the "I," a pluralistic interweaving of subjects. From the start, I am aware that the profiles of a thing — which remain latent for me so long as I remain within a given vantage point — are manifest to others who see the thing from another point of view. And even the aspects given to me do not present themselves as private images that occur within the solipsistic theater of my states of consciousness, but as aspects of the thing that bear witness to the thing's constitution and that cannot be denied by the person next to me. On this point, the descriptions given by Merleau-Ponty can claim as theirs Husserl's motto: "We see and we understand not simply as an individual among other individuals, but as individuals along with others (*miteinander*)."

To those various overlappings that allow the perceived to overcome the classical dichotomies, one should also add analogous overlappings on the side of the perceiving subject and in the very relation which this subject maintains with the perceived.

According to a traditional and established way of looking at things, vision and movement are heterogeneous: it is one thing to see, it is another thing to be in motion. As a consequence, the perceiving subject is more or less spontaneously interpreted as a spectator who, in addition to the capacity for seeing, has the unrelated capacity to move around. But such a distinction is shattered by phenomenology. Phenomenology requires that one recognize in the one who sees — qua seeing, and not by virtue of some extrinsic accident — "an intertwining of vision and movement,"[1] such that to see is, at the outset, to be able to come within proximity of what is seen, to hold it at arm's length and to come within closer range. As Merleau-Ponty says so well, "the map of the visible overlaps that of my intended motions" and "this extraordinary overlapping...makes it impossible to consider vision as an operation of the mind that erects in front of it a representation of the world" (OE 17; EM 162). But this overlapping of vision and motion, which blurs the traditional opposition of contemplation and action, goes hand in hand with another "intertwining," the one between vision and visibility. What such an intertwining of vision and visibility calls in question is another traditional distinction that has always been taken for granted: the distinction of activity and passivity, more precisely of spontaneity and receptivity. The point is that the being who enjoys both vision and movement is an integral part of the visible: while seeing the visible, the perceiving being is at the same time visible and in the act of seeing. Moreover, that being's moving body, which is itself part of the visible, is at the same time moved and self-moving, in the same manner as it touches things and is touched by them. By virtue of that fact, the body is at the same time decentered and centralizing. It is paradoxically the same thing to say that, "as visible and self-moving, my body is to be counted among things, is one of them" and, in apparent conflict, also to say, "Since [the body] can see itself and move itself around, things are maintained in a circle around it, are encrusted within its flesh as part of its full-fledged definition, and the world is made of the very stuff from which the body is made" (OE 19; EM 163). Those intertwinings, those over-lappings, have the effect of dismantling a great many traditional oppositions; furthermore, they move as a barrage against the classi-cal notion of reflection as *cogito me cogitare*, as the presence to itself of the *cogitatio* within its *cogitatum*. The teaching of the phenomeno-logical analysis of perception is that, in contrast to the classical notion, a reflective capacity exists at the very core of perception, but this reflection does not allow us to see perception as a "thought of seeing" in the sense that Descartes used to give to the expression. Because it is linked to "the impossibility of dividing the being who sees from the seen entity," the reflexivity that arises at the very core of perception is one of a flesh caught by fleshly ramifications at the very same time it becomes a self.

In all this, there is an interiority that, as Merleau-Ponty says, "does not precede the material arrangement of the human body" (OE 20; EM 163) because the interiority occurs thanks to that arrangement, yet does not result from assembling various parts for the sake of an intended sum total. To say that the interiority precedes the arrangement of the body would make it as enigmatic as a spirit descending into some automaton and would be equiva-lent to saying that "the body itself is without inside or 'self.'" To say that the interiority results from the arrangement of the body is to conceive that this interiority is the aftereffect of the disposition of the parts of the body. It would be necessary therefore to conceive this arrangement as *partes extra partes* without granting to the body itself — taken as parts, whole, and interaction of parts and whole — the possibility of reflecting upon itself. It is true that,

> if our eyes were made so that not one part of our body could fall within our purview, or if some tricky arrangement made it impossible for us to touch our own bodies without affecting how we move about things — or simply if we had lateral eyes that do not produce an overlapping of the visual fields as some animals do — such a body, unable to reflect upon itself, would then be incapable of feeling itself; such a body almost as rigid as stone, which would not quite be flesh,

could not be the body of a man, and would be devoid of humanity. (OE 20; EM 163)

But this does not mean that corporeal reflexivity is produced by the spatial disposition of organs in which each has a strictly determined function, because that disposition as such, precisely because it would be *partes extra partes*, would also be without overlappings, without intertwinings, without the interwoven reality of fleshly existence. One must therefore grant that it is an interweaving, an intertwining which must count as the basic datum for which no mechanical theory of the body will ever give a proper account.

2. THOUGHT

The phenomenal features specific to the perceived and to perception cast a light on the activity of thinking, inasmuch as the account of thinking that seeks to give them full justice and follow them closely is very different from the account of thinking that emerged from the Platonic tradition or the tradition of modern classical philosophy. This contrast is highlighted in the preface to *Signs*,[2] which dates back to the same period as the essay on *Eye and Mind*.

According to the Cartesian tradition, thought is a pure activity that penetrates with light anything that appears to it and that is revealed to itself free of any shadows in the mode of a pure presence to itself. Such a notion is rejected by a thought that takes the primacy of perception so seriously as to define itself in terms of the phenomenal features already present in perception. "The philosophy of the overview," Merleau-Ponty says in memorable words, "was an episode, and it is now over" (*Signes* 20; *Signs* 14). To the question 'what is thinking?' one who has turned the world of perception into his dwelling place cannot answer in the manner of Descartes or Plato. Valéry somewhere in his work uses the expression "flesh of the spirit."[3] Two themes allow Merleau-Ponty to stress the appropriateness of this remark: time and language. It is the intrinsic link between thought and both time and language that compels thought to be defined, as perception was defined, in terms of intertwinings and overlappings. To think, in the Cartesian sense, means to intuit a clear and distinct idea at the present time: thought is performed exclusively in the present. And as that thought is pure intuition, language is not essential to it; it is nothing more than an instrumental means destined to preserve some former intuitions that, as such, transcend language.

In contrast to the Cartesian perspective, Merleau-Ponty stresses the intrinsic link, not between thought and the present, but between thought and the nonpresent, the nonactual. If thought is alive, he says, it is "by virtue of the sliding motion which pushes it outside of the present into the non-actual" (*Signes* 21; *Signs* 14). Thinking indeed always means to rest on some previously acquired thought that by definition is always a past, but that, instead of being just obsolete, opens "a future for thinking, a cycle, a field" (*Signes* 21; *Signs* 14). In the activity of thinking thus understood, what is successive and what is simultaneous are not contradictory terms as they would be for Descartes. They overlap. Thus Merleau-Ponty writes: "If I think, it is not because I step outside of time into an intelligible world, nor is it because I recreate meaning out of nothing, but rather it is because the arrow of time pulls everything else along with it and causes my successive thoughts to emerge, in a sense, as simultaneous or at least as legitimately overlapping each other" (*Signes* 21; *Signs* 14). On a closer inspection, what takes place here is a double overlapping: that of the successive over the simultaneous and also that of the past (the acquired) over the future (the field of thought that calls for an exploration). And on even closer inspection, to those two overlappings several others are linked. The time to which the activity of thinking is linked is not constituted by the thinker who would rule over it: the thinker is affected by the push, the onrush of time; the thinker receives it, is receptive and sensible to it. To say that "my thought is nothing but the other side of my time (*l'envers de mon temps*)" amounts therefore to saying that it is "the other side of my passive and sensible being" (*Signes* 22; *Signs* 15). But to acknowledge that is also to acknowledge that I cannot think without remaining assigned, affixed to the sensible at the very time I distance myself from it to reflect on it. It is to acknowledge also that the solipsism of the *ego cogito* is nothing but an abstraction. It is true that one must isolate oneself to think, but within that very isolation others remain included. There is therefore both an overlapping of the sensible on thinking and of the others on the one who thinks. Merleau-Ponty condenses these overlappings in a superb formula: "But if it is true that my thought is nothing but the reverse of my time, of my passive and sensible being, then whenever I try to understand myself, the whole fabric of the perceptible world comes too, and with it come the others who are caught in it" (*Signes* 22, *Signs* 15).

Thinking does not require that one leave the sensible to move to the intellectual, it requires that the individual reflect and retrieve the intertwining structures that are the very ones at work in the sensible. Just as to see is already to have seen and yet to remain open to what remains to be seen, likewise to think is always already to have thought and to be open to what remains to be thought. In both cases the same connection with time comes into play. Spontaneously we have the tendency to believe that perception is nothing but a spatial relationship of a "here" that is perceiving to a "there" that is perceived. But time is secretly involved in that relationship. The thing that I perceive, I see as being already there, before my eyes set down upon it, and in that sense it is past. But at the same time, it offers itself as belonging to the future, as a "hoped-for thing" ("*la chose espérée*" in Merleau-Ponty's expression); that is, as arousing the power I have of exploring it, of investigating it from all sides. My perception is therefore the overlapping of two dimensions: the present and actual with the nonpresent and nonactual, or in other words, *the visible and the invisible*. Other individuals are involved in such an overlapping, because what is invisible for me is from the outset apprehended by me as visible to those who face the perceived things from another side. To appear perceptually is at the outset to appear, not only to one single being, but to several beings. And just as the most insignificant perception bears witness to the plurality of human beings, the most unpretentious thought bears witness to the presence of other thinking individuals. Indeed, what is it to think but to be in a dialogue with oneself? In such a dialogue we are carried along by words of which we are not the authors and that others have transmitted to us.

The connecting bond of time, the bond weaving thought to language, confirms the appropriateness of Valéry's phrase of "the flesh of the spirit." Similarly, the fact that one cannot think without talking to oneself, albeit silently, the fact that words give rise to thoughts, constitutes an overlapping that makes us suspicious of the appropriateness of the Cartesian idea of thought that in its own solitude gains and retains the position of a universal legislator.

This overlapping is something quite different from a parallelism between two levels of reality, both of which are construed as complete and comprehensive, the level of Ideas and Meanings and the level of the code that expresses them. On this subject, Merleau-Ponty writes: "The weakness of every brand of parallelism is that it takes for granted correspondences between the two levels and masks from us those operations which produced them in their overlapping" (*Signes* 26; *Signs* 18). Just as my vision of the object at a distance finds in my body a correspondence in my ability to acquire a closer vision of it, in the same way it is my being immersed within the existing body of concrete words — upon which I depend when I speak and that I received from a tradition of speakers of the same language — that connects me with the art of thinking what still remains to be thought. But in these conditions, the position of the thinker has nothing in common with the regal condescension of Plato's philosopher or with the solitude of the Cartesian *cogito*. Just as to perceive is first and foremost to be caught by the visible, that is, to be included in it, in the same way, to think is first and foremost to be caught "by a Speech and a Thought which we do not own, but which own us" (*Signes* 27; *Signs* 19). Whereas the thought of the overview "held the world subdued at its feet" (*Signes* 31; *Signs* 22), in contrast the thought that takes root in the various overlappings just recalled is capable of accounting for what Merleau-Ponty calls the "verticality" of the world.

3. PAINTING

I trust that I have provided enough context that we may now turn our attention to painting.

But before doing so, because the notion of overlapping has played a major role in my exposition, I would like to be allowed a few words to illustrate that notion with an example familiar to everybody which will clearly indicate the deficiency of the classical alternatives. What I have in mind is the intersection of two gazes.

When two gazes, two pairs of eyes, intersect and meet, there is an overlapping of the one who looks and the one who is seen. The philosophy of reflection — which first posited the "I think" as a principle — cannot take this into account, as it moves within the asserted duality of the same and the other, of the *cogito* and extension, or, as Sartre, a Cartesian, puts it, of Nothingness and Being. For the philosophy of reflection, what is at stake here is a juxtaposition such that either one of the two conscious beings relegates the other to the status of being an object, or is so relegated by the other, in such a way that there is "only one *cogito* at any given time" (*Signes* 24; *Signs* 17). The alternative postulated by reflection is simple: either I cast my gaze on the other individual and then I am the subject and the other is the object; or else it is the other's gaze that is cast on me and then I am the object and the other person the subject. What this reflection fails to understand is that the crossing of the two gazes surmounts that antinomy: what happens is that there is indeed an adjustment of one individual to the other, or as Merleau-Ponty says, "two gazes, one inside the other (*deux regards l'un dans l'autre*)."

The idea central to Merleau-Ponty's meditation on painting, in particular in the essay on *The Indirect Language and the Voices of Silence*[4] and in *The Eye and Mind*, is that all the problems of painting concern the overlappings that, as I have suggested, led Merleau-Ponty to define thought itself in terms of overlappings.

Painters, for example Dürer, have often said that the outline of their paintings had been derived by them from an inspection of the things in nature, out there; but no less frequently they would say conversely that this outline had been found within themselves. Thus I may invoke Cezanne, who used to say that "nature is inside,"[5] but I could also mention the classical advice of a Chinese painter who used to say that to paint a bamboo, one must first be able to grow it inside oneself. Taken together, these suggestions indicate that the painter paints not only what is visible, but the intertwining of the visible with the seeing. I proposed the view that the dimensions of the visible are inseparable from the seeing individual, from the echos that they provoke in our bodies inasmuch as it is our bodies that gather those dimensions. Such echos are what each painting makes noticeable. In this regard, Merleau-Ponty asks: "That internal equivalent, the carnal formula for their presence which things spark in me, why in turn wouldn't they give rise to an outline, still in the visible realm, inside of which any other seeing eyes will uncover the motifs which sustain their own inspection of the world?"[6] And then he answers: "Thus emerges something visible to the second degree, the carnal essence or the icon of the first" (OE 22; EM 164). There is an aphorism of Paul Valéry's that Merleau-Ponty used to like: "The painter brings in his own body." This seems a trivial point: one cannot conceive of an individual as capable of seeing a motif, of mixing colors, of handling a brush, unless that individual had a body. But the aphorism ceases to be trivial if it is taken to mean that the painter is the one who expresses on his canvas the schema of one of the manifold relationships of overlapping that the sensible realm weaves with our body.

If this analysis gives us a faithful description of the phenomenon of painting, a picture is never a *trompe l'oeil*, a fake of a thing, or a double, or a copy; painting is never a system of elements, or fragments, or "visual data" borrowed from the world, the so-called real world, to envisage reality in its absence, as Plato used to think in Antiquity or Descartes and Pascal at the beginning of Modernity.

The picture is not an unreal double of reality; it manifests to our gaze the unmistakable schema of the life of things within our bodies. Even Giacometti, one of those artists whose works might seem at first to be only remotely related to common perception, can write: "What I am interested in when I look at any painting is the resemblance." And he adds as if to emphasize that this resemblance has nothing to do with the phenomenon of *trompe l'oeil*: "that is to say what for me is resemblance: what allows me to discover a little bit of the external world" (OE 24; EM 165).

Under these conditions, the work of the painter comes to disrupt the standard distinction between the real and the imaginary (the latter being conceived as unreal or fictional). What the artist's work brings under our gaze is not the unreal double, the fictional copy of the real, but what Merleau-Ponty calls without contradiction "the imaginary texture of the real." Hence the overlapping of the visible world and the seeing individual must now be associated with a second overlapping: the one between the real and the imaginary. This overlapping is often expressed by the creators who apparently are most prone to giving free rein to fantasy. The words of Max Ernst, for example, might well stand as a manifesto for all surrealists: "The role of the painter," he said, "is to project what is visible and seen within himself" (OE 30–31; EM 168). Color also attests to this overlapping, if it is true that, already in the everyday visual field and to a greater extent in painting, each color is inseparable from the symbolic or cultural significance invested in it and is never ultimately a pure "sensorial datum," except in the laboratory of the psychologist.

It might be objected that this schema which things evoke in the body of the painter belongs strictly speaking to him or her alone, that it is the artist's private world and therefore has no reality. But the paradox is precisely that this supposedly private world, as soon as it is expressed, becomes constitutive of a common world. Thus the schema that became a picture and a painting elicits echos in different individuals and imposes upon each one a specific way of looking at the world. In his novel, *Remembrance of Things Past*, Marcel Proust notices that shortly after the time when Renoir's paintings of women were the targets of sarcasm and reprobation because of their supposed failure to look like real women, people began to look at women in light of Renoir. One could say almost the same thing concerning Modigliani's paintings or the drawings and cutouts of Matisse. Strange though they were when they were first released, those works were quickly seen as awakening echos in all of us and eliciting carnal recollections, thus allowing us to recognize a collective schema of femininity.

Thus the intertwining of the visible and seeing blends the overlapping between real and imaginary together with the intertwining of the private and the shared. It is as if painting attested to a generalized overlapping function. But let us return to the intertwining of the visible and the one who sees. It works indeed in two directions: the visible, as we just said, elicits in the seeing individual a carnal schema of what the visible realm is; but in addition, the seeing individual is part of the visible realm, too. This notion was expressed by a variety of painters who, as Merleau-Ponty observed with regard to Paul Klee, liked to say that they felt "looked at by things" (OE 31; EM 167). This is also what, as early as the classical period, painters expressed in an iconographic manner either by

depicting themselves in the process of painting (Matisse does this
in some drawings) or, as in many Flemish and Dutch interiors, by
installing some sort of onlooker in the form of a mirror in which
the entire scene is reflected. The mirror, as Merleau-Ponty says,
functions "as a pre-human gaze that is the symbol of the gaze of
the painter." And he adds: "The mirror appears because I am
seeing-visible, because there is a reflexivity of the sensible; the mirror translates this reflexivity and redoubles it". And further on:
"...It is the instrument of a universal magic which transforms
things into spectacles, spectacles into things, myself into someone else and someone else into myself" (OE 33–34, EM 168). If
Merleau-Ponty speaks here of magic, it is not of course because of
some exotic taste for the irrational, but instead because he wants to
highlight the contrast between the actual vision and its reconstruction by analytical thinking in a philosopher of reflection such as
Descartes, for example. Such a reflection in principle refuses the
promiscuous contact of the seeing individual and of the visible to
such an extent that "a Cartesian does not see *himself* in the mirror:
he sees a mannequin, the 'outside' of a being" which for him is not
the carnal appearance of his flesh, rather it is a simple "image" —
upon which his thought makes the judgment that it is the mechanical reflection of his own body, a reflection to which his thought in
a second move grants, in the same way as to an effect, some resemblance to its cause (OE 38–39; EM 170).

   These intertwinings are far from being the only ones expressed
by painting. Indeed, what painting expresses most forcefully is the
reciprocal overlapping of all the dimensions of the sensible — light,
shadows, colors, reflections, lines. For a thought of the Cartesian
type, it goes without saying that line and color are distinct just as
much as form and content are different: the line determines the
contour of a thing, or its envelope, which color then fills up. But a
distinction of that kind, which is not problematic for the understanding, is precisely what painting brings into question. A few
lines, and only lines, are sufficient for the prehistorical painters of
the cave of Teruel in Spain to make us see a group of hunters.
Merleau-Ponty recalls that Leonardo da Vinci in the *Treatise of
Painting* proposed as a task for each painter to discover within each
object "the unique and specific curve woven in it which permeates

throughout its extension as its generating axis" (OE 72; EM 183). To take a more contemporary example, Paul Klee is a painter for whom one single line is enough to set up in front of us the character of a "Timid Brute" and more generally to make visible a kind of genesis of things. This shows that, instead of being a limit, a line can express the entire thing and paradoxically function as a "total part." What is true of line is also true of color: it, too, functions as a total part capable by itself, without any lines, of presenting the object in its specific form and voluminous character as in Cezanne who used to say, "When color is at a perfection, form is at its fullest."

No less indicative of the overlappings that I am talking about is the fact that often good painters — I am thinking of Degas, Picasso, and Matisse — also turn into good sculptors, in spite of the fact that the manipulations and processes required to be a sculptor are very different from those required by painting. In this, Merleau-Ponty sees "the proof that there is a system of equivalences, a *Logos* of the lines, of lights, of reliefs, of masses, a presentation without any concept of universal Being" (OE 71; EM 182). Painting shows, he says somewhere else, "a polymorphism of Being."

It is again the notion of overlapping that guides Merleau-Ponty's meditation on style in his essay on Andre Malraux's book on Art, *The Voices of Silence*.

One meaning of style is the structural cohesion achieved by an individual work, a cohesion with which the spectator quickly becomes familiar and that allows him or her to recognize as works of painter X or Y paintings he or she has never seen before. On this topic, Malraux mentions a "coherent deformation" and he talks as if the shaping into a form effected by the artist was purely arbitrary with regard to the visible in the sense that style creates its own system. More precisely, he speaks as though styles were imposed from the top by the artist, without any prior anticipation in the visible. "The plastic arts," he writes, "are never born out of a way of looking at the world, but of shaping it." It is this voluntarist stand, this idea of a sovereignty, this acosmic attitude, to which Merleau-Ponty objects. And what he objects to in those notions is the fact that they are based on the previous dichotomies and dualities. In sum, Malraux confronts us with a choice between the visible world and the spiritual world of the creator; and as the artistic world has no antecedent in the visible one, the victory of a style seems to imply the abdication of the many who live in the visible in favor of the sovereign genius of the creator. There is no abdication, Merleau-Ponty objects, but only recognition. Recognition here is based on the fact that a style imposes itself simply because it adheres to the visible and somehow or other finds in the sensible its own antecedents; precisely because of this, a style is accessible to others, it is interindividual and does not emerge *ex nihilo* from the stormy solitude of the genius (*Signes* 67–68, 72–73; *Signs* 53–55, 57–59). From the perspective of others, the painter can sometimes appear as the creator of a counterworld, but for the painter at work there is but one world, and this world is what beckons him or her to work in a call to which the work will never stop responding.

One last mode of intertwining remains to be investigated. Not only do painters respond to what the visible world elicits in them, rather than merely continuing the task instituted by their own beginnings, they also inscribe themselves within a tradition of painting that overlaps on their work, just as their work is intertwined within the tradition. Here again the debate with Malraux is instructive. Malraux insists that painting forms a unique temporal adventure such that there is an affiliation among past and present painters, some kinship of present and past in the pictorial problems and solutions, in short, a sort of unity of painting as such. But that unity is expressed by him in such terms that it appears to be only retrospective, that is, made present and visible, and constituted after the fact, only by virtue of the modern phenomenon of the museum. In this view, the unity of painting seems to be transhistorical, and in the actual history Malraux sees nothing but scattered disunity, the struggle of each painter against others, forgetfulness, failure to be acknowledged.[7] It is to such a duality — the unity created by the museum on the one hand, and historical dispersion on the other — that Merleau-Ponty objects. To say that the unity of painting is retrospective amounts to failing to recognize that, just as to see is always to see more than one sees (for it provides access to a fringe of invisible features that have no place within the totality of strictly visual data), in the same way to paint is always to paint more than one paints. As soon as there was painting, it was in excess of itself.

At the same time as it offers a field of visibility that goes beyond the given picture, the perceptual power of the painter is doubled with a prospective power. So, rather than oppose the nontemporal unity of the museum to the scattered character of actual history, the point is to understand actual history in terms of temporal over-lappings. By virtue of these overlappings, neither the acquired nor the new can be regarded as entirely acquired or entirely new, and "the idea...of a totalization of painting...is meaningless" (OE 90; EM 189).[8]

If it is true that such overlappings constitute the roots and the resourcefulness of thought, and if it is true on the other hand that painting itself has its roots and its resourcefulness in analogous overlappings, then one understands why Merleau-Ponty could speak of a "mute thought of painting" (OE 91; EM 189).

But by the same token it is evident that Merleau-Ponty stands oceans apart from the philosophers who, ever since Plato, have been proclaiming in one guise or another that there must be an overcoming of painting — whether this be in the name of Platonic or Cartesian ideas, in the name of the History of the Spirit, in the name of material Praxis, in the name of the absurdity of the Will, or in the name of the History of Being. The reason for this notion of an end of art is that the attention of those philosophers, when they happen to be concerned with things pictorial, never dwells on the specificity of the visible. If one grants the visible realm its own full rights, then — against the pronouncements made by those grand narratives which, starting with the Myth of the Cave, proclaimed the death of art — one should be able to maintain: "Should the world still last millions of years, for painters, if some are still left, that world would still remain to be painted and will end before being completely captured" (OE 90; EM 189).

NOTES

1. Maurice Merleau-Ponty, *L'Oeil et l'esprit* (Paris: Gallimard, 1964), p. 16; henceforth cited as OE. "Eye and Mind," trans. Carleton Dallery, in *The Primacy of Perception*, ed. James M. Edie (Evanston, Ill.: North-western University Press, 1964), p. 162; henceforth cited as EM.

2. Maurice Merleau-Ponty, *Signes* (Paris: Gallimard, 1960). *Signs*,

trans. Richard C. McCleary (Evanston, Ill.: Northwestern University Press, 1964).

3. *"corps de l'esprit"*

4. In *Signes*, pp. 49–104; *Signs*, pp. 39–83.

5. Quoted by Merleau-Ponty (OE 22; EM 164).

6. *"Cet équivalent interne, cette formule charnelle de leur présence que les choses suscitent en moi, pourquoi à leur tour ne susciteraient-ils pas un tracé, visible encore, où tout autre regard retrouvera les motifs qui soutiennent son inspection du monde?"*

7. *Par le fait même l'unité de la peinture semble être, pour Malraux, trans-historique et dans l'histoire effective il ne voit guère que morcellement, lutte de chaque peintre contre tous les autres, oubli, méconnaissance.*

8. *Empiétements tels que ni l'acquis ni le nouveau ne le sont jamais tout à fait et que "l'idée... d'une totalisation de la peinture... est dépourvue de sens."*

Notes on Contributors

M. C. Dillon is professor of philosophy at the State University of New York at Binghamton. He is author of *Merleau-Ponty's Ontology* and several articles related to Merleau-Ponty's thought.

Edward S. Casey is professor of philosophy at the State University of New York at Stony Brook. He teaches in the areas of philosophical psychology, aesthetics, phenomenology, and contemporary poststructuralism. He has translated Mikel Dufrenne's *The Notion of the A Priori* and is the cotranslator of Dufrenne's *The Phenomenology of Aesthetic Experience*. In addition to many articles, he has written *Imagining* and *Remembering*. At the present moment, he is finishing a book entitled *Getting Back into Place*.

Duane H. Davis is a doctoral candidate in the department of philosophy at The Pennsylvania State University, where he is presently completing work on his dissertation, "Merleau-Ponty: The Development of Subjectivity and the Communion of Language." Davis is author of "Completing the Recovery of Language as an Existential Project," recently published in the *Journal of the British Society for Phenomenology*. His philosophical interests include the study of language in the continental philosophical tradition, phenomenology, existentialism, hermeneutics, and ethics.

David Michael Levin is professor of philosophy at Northwestern University. He has written numerous studies in phenomenological aesthetics and phenomenological psychology and is the author of *Reason and Evidence in Husserl's Phenomenology, The Body's Recollection of Being, The Opening of Vision: Nihilism and the Postmodern Situation, The Listening Self: Personal Growth, Social Change, and the Closure of Metaphysics*. He is also editor of *Pathologies of the Modern Self: Postmodern Studies on Narcissism, Schizophrenia, and Depression*. Dr. Levin currently is at work on a book of essays in ethics and critical social theory and is editing an anthology of papers on *Modernity and the Hegemony of Vision*. His current research is primarily concerned with the work of the Frankfurt School, Foucault, and Habermas and centers on the notion that the "self" is a formation of experiential and discursive practices.

Alphonso Lingis is professor of philosophy at The Pennsylvania State University. He is author of *Excesses: Eros and Culture, Libido: The French Existential Theories, Phenomenological Explanations,* and *Deathbound Subjectivity.* Lingis has also translated Merleau-Ponty's *The Visible and the Invisible,* and written numerous articles on philosophical and psychological themes in contemporary continental thought.

Gary Brent Madison is professor of philosophy at McMaster University and also occupies the position of professor of philosophy in the graduate faculty of the University of Toronto. Madison is author of *La phénoménologie de Merleau-Ponty, une recerche des limites de la conscience, Understanding: A Phenomenological-Pragmatic Analysis, The Logic of Liberty,* and *The Hermeneutics of Postmodernity: Figures and Themes.* In addition to numerous journal articles on contemporary continental philosophy, Madison's interest in the hermeneutics of the social sciences has also led him to write in the areas of political and economic theory.

Joseph Margolis is professor of philosophy at Temple University. He has recently completed a trilogy titled *The Persistence of Reality.* Vol. 1. *Pragmatism without Foundations: Reconciling Realism and Relativism;* Vol. 2. *Science without Unity: Reconciling the Natural and Human Sciences;* Vol. 3. *Texts without Referents: Reconciling Science and Narrative.* The trilogy will expand to a quartet with the forthcoming appearance of Vol. 4. *Life without Principles: Reconciling Theory and Practice.* He has also recently completed a short volume, *The Truth about Relativism,* and is at work on a systematic account of metaphysics.

Hugh J. Silverman is professor of philosophy and comparative literature at the State University of New York at Stony Brook. He is author of *Inscriptions: Between Phenomenology and Structuralism* and more than fifty articles on continental philosophy, philosophical psychology, aesthetics, and literary theory. Silverman is editor or coeditor of eleven collections on recent continental thought and postmodernism. He is also editor of the Routledge Continental Philosophy series.

Jacques Taminiaux is professor of philosophy at the Université de Louvain-la-neuve and Boston College. Among his books are *La nostalgie de la Grèce à l'aube de l'idéalisme allemand, Le regard et l'excédent, Recoupements, Lecture de l'ontologie fondamentale*. He has also translated major texts by Hegel and Heidegger.

Name Index

217

Subject Index

Reality, Real World, 4, 55, 56, 58,
61, 82n3, 91–96, 99–101, 103, 104,
107, 117–119, 124–126, 128, 132,
137–139, 143n20, 144n25, n27,
171, 187, 196, 207, 208
Reason, Rationality, xxiii, xxviii, xxxi
n13, 38–41, 72–74, 77, 78, 80,
83n11, 95–98, 118, 134–136,
143n23, n24, 145n26, 147n40,
151n63, 158, 189, 211; as
communicative, 47, 53–55, 61,
83n9; as critical, 133, 134; as
embodied, 47, 61, 64, 65, 76,
83n9, n11; as instrumental, 139,
140; as subject-centered, 47, 55,
61, 77
Reciprocity, Reciprocity of Being, 32,
39, 49, 50, 52, 54, 61–63, 65,
70–72, 75, 77–81, 81n2, 82n4, 124
Referentialist, 133, 148n46
Reflection, x–xii, xvii, xix, xxx n7, 9,
49, 50, 54, 55, 58–60, 63–72, 74,
76, 77, 81, 92, 113, 130, 131,
143n23, 158, 159, 161, 196, 200,
201, 203, 205, 208
Re(-)presentation, Representationalism,
xxii, xxv, xxvi, xxxii n21, 1, 2, 4,
6, 8, 16, 18, 34, 91, 94–112, 119,
133, 148n46, 156, 157, 199
Response-ability, Responsibility,
Responsibility of Ideality, 31, 32,
34, 37, 39–41, 42n1, 71
Reversibility, Lived Reversibility, xvi,
xix, xxiii, 21, 31–41, 45n36, 49,
50, 53, 62, 66, 70–81, 83n9
Rhetoric, 134, 135, 149n51

Science, Cognitive Science, Objective
Science, xii, 91, 95, 100–113, 118,
119, 125, 131–133, 136–139, 142n15,
144n26, 147n41, 148n46, 152n66,
157–162, 167, 169, 172, 175, 177,
190, 192, 197
Semiological Reductionism, xxv, xxxi
n12

Semiotic, Symbolic, 166, 169, 183–193
Sensation, Sense, Sensibility, 1–4, 7,
18, 21, 23n9, n11, 28n64, 91–95,
97–102, 107, 108, 110–115, 125,
126, 142n15, 148n48, 152n65, 155,
157, 159, 167, 173, 174, 176, 177,
189, 190, 195–197, 202, 206, 208,
210
Sign, Significance, Signifier, x–xiv,
xxi, xxiii–xxix, xxix n2, xxxiii n21,
xxxiv n36, xxxv n37, 117, 125,
128, 130, 136–138, 146n32, n34,
147n40, 150n58, 151n62, 152n65
Sign and Sign System, Signifying
Process, 185–192
Social, Sociality, Socialization, 40,
48–80, 82n3, 157, 158, 172, 185,
187, 191, 192
Solipsism, 45n34, 56, 70, 156, 157,
166, 169, 172, 176, 198, 202
Space, Spatiality, xx, xxi, xxiii, xxiv,
xxix n1, xxx n8, xxxiii n19, 1–12,
15, 18, 23n4, n11, 25n26, n33,
n35, 29n71, 93, 95, 99, 101, 103,
105, 111–113, 203
Speech, 14, 31, 34–36, 40, 78, 130,
137, 149n29, n51, 152n65, 188,
189, 192, 204
Strabism, 169, 171, 172, 176, 178
Structure, x, xi, xiv, xvi, xxv, xxviii,
xxxii n17, xxxiv n36, 11, 22, 49,
52, 60, 73, 96–98, 103, 104, 107,
109, 110, 112, 115, 121, 133, 138,
142 n11, n12, 153, 154, 159,
161–165, 168, 172, 176, 178, 185,
186, 190, 203, 209
Style, 36
Subject, Subjectivity, xiv–xix, xxix n1,
xxxi n11, n13, xxxiv n36, 47–50,
53, 54, 59–69, 72–80, 82n4,
155–161, 166–172, 186, 198; bodily,
embodied, xvii, 20, 32, 65, 136,
138, 152n65, 192; perceiving, 4,
10, 37, 128, 199; reversible; 32,
36, 37, 39–41, 45n36; speaking,